TAKEDOWN

TAKEDOWN

Inside the Fight
to Shut Down Pornhub
for Child Abuse, Rape,
and Sex Trafficking

Laila Mickelwait

THESIS

Thesis
An imprint of Penguin Random House LLC
penguinrandomhouse.com

LIBRARY OF CONGRESS CATALOGING-IN-PUBLICATION DATA
Names: Mickelwait, Laila, author.
Title: Takedown: inside the fight to shut down pornhub for child abuse,
rape, and sex trafficking / Laila Mickelwait.
Description: [New York] : Thesis, [2024] | Includes bibliographical references and index.
Identifiers: LCCN 2023051215 (print) | LCCN 2023051216 (ebook) |
ISBN 9780593542019 (hardcover) | ISBN 9780593542026 (ebook)
Subjects: LCSH: Child pornography—Case studies. | Internet pornography—Case studies. |
Child sexual abuse—Prevention—Case studies. | Child trafficking—Prevention—Case studies.
Classification: LCC HQ471 .M624 2024 (print) | LCC HQ471 (ebook) |
DDC 362.76072/3—dc23/eng/20240124
LC record available at https://lccn.loc.gov/2023051215
LC ebook record available at https://lccn.loc.gov/2023051216

Printed in the United States of America
1st Printing

BOOK DESIGN BY CHRIS WELCH

Some names and identifying characteristics have been changed
to protect the privacy of the individuals involved.

This book is dedicated to every survivor of abuse on Pornhub.

And to my father.

Author's Note

Much of this story was written as it was happening. Knowing that meticulous documentation of evidence would be crucial to a successful civil trial and criminal prosecution, I was diligent to preserve and document the information presented, including conversations as they happened. Most of the dialogue included here is recounted nearly verbatim. Where dialogue was not documented, it is recalled to the best of my memory and ability.

Over the course of three and a half years, as this story was unfolding, I was contacted by numerous confirmed sources at MindGeek, including management and senior-level employees, as well as insiders personally close to MindGeek's CEO Feras Antoon. During dozens of hours of conversations, online, by phone, and in person, these sources revealed intimate details about Feras's life, his family, his businesses, and how he presided as CEO over MindGeek.

The story is primarily told chronologically, with a few exceptions. Some names, including those of victims, whistleblowers, and sources, have been changed to protect the privacy and preserve the anonymity of those involved.

Contents

Prologue: Wisam's Impact   1

Introducing the Pornhub Behemoth

1   The Discovery   9

2   #Traffickinghub   18

3   Pornhub's Censorship Tricks   24

4   Welcome New Bedfellows   32

5   Betting on Bowe   37

6   The Zuckerberg of Porn   45

7   A Family Man and Porn King   49

8   Blake the Fake   56

9   My Sicilian Side   59

10   Playboy Mansion to Prayer Room   67

11   When Snakes Are Cornered   73

12	Who Is @EyeDeco?	78
13	Pornhub's Admissions Unearthed	81
14	"Cleanest Porn Ever"	85
15	Betrayal from Within	88
16	Confronting the Credit Cards	91
17	The Deputy Doxer	96
18	The First Million Signatures	100
19	Meet the Moderator	103
20	How to Profit from a Black Box	110
21	Content Is King	115
22	The Ultimate Insider Reaches Out	120
23	The Secret Owner Revealed	124
24	A Meeting Worth Getting Dressed For	129
25	The Other Lilly	133
26	This Hellhole of Rape	136
27	Plausible Deniability: Priceless	141
28	Serena Steps Forward	148
29	The Attacks Turn Physical	153
30	Demonizing the Crazy American Woman	157
31	The Children of Pornhub	163
32	A Billionaire Activist Investor Gets Active	169
33	The Credit Cards Drop Pornhub	174
34	Feras Goes for Broke	176
35	Fucking Stupid	180

36   **Pornhub on Trial**   184

37   **Feras and David Take the Stand**   189

38   **My Turn to Testify**   199

39   **Fabian's Surprise Intervention**   206

40   **Feras's Mansion Ablaze**   210

41   **Locating Bernard, er, Bernd**   213

42   **Mike's "Novel"**   218

43   **Death at the Door**   222

44   **Before You Break**   225

45   **Now I'm the Defendant?**   231

46   **The Credit Cards Sneak Back**   236

47   **Meet "Filthy Ramirez"**   240

48   **Who Torched the Pornhub Palace?**   248

49   **Feras Dethroned**   254

50   **Big Plastic's Lip Service**   258

51   **Visa's Motion to Dismiss Is Denied**   262

52   **"One of the Biggest Stories in Business"**   267

53   **Finally, a Pariah**   271

54   **The Call I've Been Waiting For**   274

Epilogue   278

Letter to the Reader   281

Acknowledgments   285

Notes   287

Index   297

TAKEDOWN

WISAM'S IMPACT

Three nights after learning one of his daughters was being sexually abused, my father died of a heart attack in his sleep. The details of my sister's story will be spared here at her request, but the abuse she endured was a devastating shock to our whole family. My dad took it the hardest. He was crippled with guilt for not being able to see what was happening. His heart couldn't slow down, and his distressed mind raced, trying to figure out how he could solve this problem and erase her trauma. But he couldn't.

On that last night of his life, he was exhausted yet unable to rest. He was both a general and vascular surgeon, due to operate on a patient early the next morning. My mother recalls him checking his own blood pressure before they went to bed, and it being at an all-time high. Tears pooled in his eyes, something she had only seen a few times in their decades of marriage. Then he whispered in a tone of defeat: "I can't believe this happened to her."

My sister called me the next morning, earlier than she would ever normally call.

"Laila, are you sitting down?"

"Yes. What is it?"

There was a pause. "Daddy died last night."

The words didn't seem real.

"His heart stopped, and he didn't wake up," she said.

She forwarded a photo of him lying in bed with his head resting on the pillow and his eyes closed. He looked peaceful—like he was asleep. His hand was tucked under his chin as usual when he slept, but his fingers looked curled and stiff, and the color was gone from his face.

This is real. He is dead.

I melted onto the floor as I began to wail uncontrollably, pressing my face into the carpet.

My hero, my rock, my gravity . . . gone at the age of sixty. For two decades, he had managed his heart disease and high blood pressure with medication. I know this intense pain, regret, and guilt ultimately killed him. For every victim of abuse like my sister, there are an exponential number of secondary and tertiary victims, like our father and those he left behind: patients, friends, and family.

My father's name is Wisam, which in Arabic means "Medal of Honor," and that is what he was to me and his whole family. He was the one who delivered me in the hospital when I was born; it was in his arms that I entered the world. He gave me the Arabic name Laila, meaning "night," and pronounced like "Delilah." Following Arabic tradition, my middle name is his name. From birth he and I had a special bond.

He grew up amid tumultuous political upheaval and civil war in Amman, Jordan, and his recollections were images most Americans only see if they pay attention to news from the other side of the world. The story that I remember most vividly was of soldiers using the roof of his family's two-story house as a staging ground to fire at enemies below. A teenager at the time, a bullet missed my father by inches, but his cousin, Haifa, was shot in the head. The bloodstains from her splattered brains were left on the wall as a memorial, and our family buried her in their front yard.

My father left for boarding schools in India and England, and then fought his way to the top of his class in college and medical school in the United States. Even after he began practicing medicine in California and became a US citizen, he felt connected to the plight of oppressed groups around the world who were fighting for their rights and freedom. Having grown up as he did, my dad was forever sensitive to the universal human power struggle and the atrocities it produces.

He was always watching the History Channel, documentaries, and the BBC with me and my sisters, encouraging us to learn about what he called the "root causes" of wars and famine, genocide and slavery. He cautioned us about how important it was to understand these things. After the attacks of September 11, 2001, my father experienced heightened levels of discrimination because of his Arabic affects, and spoke against it. He also rejected Islamophobia, recalling how kind his Muslim neighbors in Jordan were to his Arab Christian family. He understood the tragedies that could result if prejudice was allowed to go unchallenged. "History repeats itself," and "if you don't learn from history, you are doomed to repeat it," he often told us in his thick Middle Eastern accent as he recalled humanity's darkest moments like the Holocaust and Rwanda genocide.

One night in 2005 my dad called me into the living room to watch a TV documentary with him. It was about child sex trafficking in Calcutta, India. It was shocking and had a profound impact on me. That moment was the catalyst that inspired me to research and ultimately engage in the fight against sex trafficking. Before that I didn't know there was such a thing as "modern slavery" or "trafficking" because hardly anyone was talking about it then. That would change as the internet, mobile devices, and social media evolved.

The very month my father died, the social media–savvy terrorist group ISIS abducted thousands of Yazidi girls and women into sexual slavery as the world watched in horror. That same year, Boko Haram kidnapped nearly three hundred high school girls in Nigeria. Cell phone photos and videos shot these images around the world, making their suffering real to those of us living in the West. By that time worldwide smartphone ownership had soared, and the ability to record, share, and monetize images of abuse had exploded.

Women, girls, and boys all over the world are coerced into sexually abusive situations—sometimes as an act of war or a desire for control, and often for financial profit. Sex trafficking has always existed, but now it is easier to see—even in the US—if you are willing to look. Because of my father's impact on me, I am looking.

My father died in 2014, just as I was in the thick of researching the porn industry's ties to sex trafficking, rape, and other harms. The day of his funeral, after everyone went home, I made my way back to the graveyard alone at night to say a last goodbye. As I stood over his grave, I made a promise to him and to my sister: I would never give up the fight to hold abusers accountable and bring justice to victims.

I've devoted the last twenty years of my life to studying and combating the crime of human trafficking. I earned a master's degree in public diplomacy from the University of Southern California's Annenberg School, which partnered with visiting scholars and diplomats from the US State Department. While at USC, I interned in Washington, D.C., with the United Nations' University Millennium Project, where I added the issue of human trafficking to their annual "State of the Future" report, endorsed by UN Secretary General Ban Ki-moon.

My anti–sex trafficking activism eventually led me to work for the organization Exodus Cry. I was drawn to its mission, which focused on fighting modern slavery and trafficking by using the model of historical abolitionist William Wilberforce, who ended slavery in the United Kingdom by raising awareness and changing laws. My role as director of abolition at Exodus Cry was based on the work of Wilberforce. At the end of 2020, I left Exodus Cry to launch my own nonprofit organization called the Justice Defense Fund, and I remain committed to abolishing sex trafficking and online sexual crime.

It's important to note that I desire to abolish *illegal* trafficking. I do not aim to abolish the legal pornography industry. What consenting adults do with each other is their business, not mine—as long as it is lawful and not harming another person. I myself have hardly lived the life of a prude or an enemy of the entertainment business. Growing up in Southern California, I spent New Year's Eve partying at a Playboy Mansion party with Bill Maher and Andy Dick, appeared with my ratty minivan on MTV's *Pimp My Ride*, and for a few hundred dollars bounced in a bikini on Jimmy Kimmel's famous late-night trampoline segment on *The Man Show*. As an accomplished young teen acrobat, I was even offered a role in Montreal's Cirque du Soleil. My father refused to let me join the circus, though.

The year 2020, when this story begins, was one of the most polarizing in modern times; yet liberals and conservatives and people who didn't even consider themselves political joined me in making the fight against Pornhub our common cause. In fact some of my most helpful allies were employed by the porn industry. Mobilizing a diverse movement was essential, and I welcomed everyone, from all backgrounds, into the fight. As the American abolitionist Frederick Douglass wrote, "I would unite with anybody to do right and with nobody to do wrong."

This is the story of how I discovered one of the biggest websites in the world was knowingly profiting from sex trafficking—including child rape—and the lengths the company went to in order to keep profiting after it was exposed.

In 2020, Pornhub was the tenth-most-visited website in the world.[1] It was also the largest and most popular porn site, with 130 million visits per day, 47 billion visits per year,[2] and enough videos uploaded every 12 months that it would take 169 years if you watched them back-to-back.[3] Pornhub was the world's YouTube of free user-generated porn with more site traffic than Amazon, Yahoo, and Netflix, and more daily visits than the entire populations of Canada, Australia, and France combined. Its 4.6 billion daily advertising impressions were helping the site rake in hundreds of millions of dollars each year for its parent company, MindGeek. In 2020, researchers named Pornhub the third most influential "tech" company on global society just behind Google and Facebook.[4] With billboards in Times Square, faux commercials on *Saturday Night Live,* and multimillion-dollar PR campaigns, Pornhub was a cultural icon.

It was also an unchallenged crime scene.

Pornhub was globally distributing and profiting from countless videos of real criminal sexual abuse, child rape, sex trafficking, and torture. Yet for reasons we will uncover in the following pages, these ubiquitous sex crimes remained hidden in plain sight for over a decade.

That changed at the start of 2020. After years of investigating the intersection between pornography and sex trafficking, I made a discovery that compelled me to launch the "Traffickinghub" movement to "shut down Pornhub and hold its executives accountable" for distributing and monetizing mass sexual crime. The mission statement was impossible considering all I had was a Twitter account with a few thousand followers, and MindGeek was a global behemoth that had obtained a monopoly on the global porn industry.

But, thanks to the help of many people, by the end of 2020, in what *Financial Times* called "probably the biggest takedown of content in internet history,"[5] Pornhub deleted 80 percent of its entire website by removing 10.6 million unverified videos[6] and over 30 million images.[7] Over the next two years they were financially crippled because Visa, Mastercard, and Discover suspended all business with the site[8]—leaving them with only cryptocurrency and bank wires as payment options. After more than a decade of being a cultural icon, Pornhub suddenly became a pariah, being shamed in thousands of media articles worldwide. Today, Pornhub is facing landmark individual and class-action lawsuits on behalf of hundreds of victims, totaling billions in potential damages.

All of this only happened after our sustained, grassroots movement attracted hundreds of organizations and millions of followers, including courageous victims who came forward, brave Pornhub and MindGeek whistleblowers, porn actors, producers, consumers, technology specialists, superlawyers, superjournalists, and regular people like me who, once they opened their eyes and looked, refused to turn away.

Pornhub and its owners have faced a reckoning, but the site is still online, its executives are still at large, and laws to prevent copycat websites are lacking. The fight against this abuse continues and is more important than ever before.

———

My father's genuine humility struck me on a medical relief trip we took together to Myanmar in 2012. Everyone from a small poverty-stricken village gathered in a hut with a dirt floor to hear him teach about medicine in the sweltering heat. He opened by saying "I don't have all the answers, I am here to learn from you too."

Now that I know all I know about Pornhub, I wonder: In this age of smartphones, user-generated content, big tech, and big porn profiteers, how can we protect sexually abused people—including children—from having their trauma monetized, globally distributed, and forever memorialized online? I, Laila Wisam, have answers, but I am here to learn from you too, because this movement needs all of us.

1

THE DISCOVERY

If the woman never, uh, really . . . cried . . . too much. . . ." The man halts as he collects his thoughts, and then continues in Greek-accented English. "Uh, it's a weird thing to say: We wouldn't consider it *rape* . . . At the end of the day we just had to guess if it was rape or not."

There was a lot of guessing in his former job as one of Pornhub's content moderators. For three years he had been employed by MindGeek, the company that owned Pornhub, to guess about consent in videos, and to guess about the ages of people whose most intimate—or traumatic—moments lived on their site. Was she eighteen or sixteen? A petite nineteen-year-old dressed as a fourteen-year-old, with pigtails and a teddy bear? "No one really likes to watch children suffering. We just had to review them, get past them, and finish the video and go to the next one. If we stopped to think about it, we wouldn't get anything else done."

Regretful of the work he had done, this moderator reached out in the summer of 2020 to tell me what it had been like to work for MindGeek and Pornhub. He had been one of only thirty moderators working ten at a time, on eight-hour shifts, tasked with viewing a thousand or more user-uploaded videos per shift. If they viewed fewer than seven hundred, they would be reprimanded by management.

"Our process of reviewing every video was to fast-forward through them with the audio shut off, so it was muted. . . . So that was a flaw in our system." Using that system, you can't hear genuine cries for mercy or see the terror and pain in a child's eyes.

And in cases when a content moderator couldn't tell how old someone was? "They wouldn't really care. They would just pass it and it would be okay. It's more money for the site anyway," he said.

"The lines of consensual to nonconsensual are often very blurry in porn," the moderator told me. "So, for us, it was very hard for us to make that distinction."

It's impossible when your employer doesn't want you asking too many questions.

Before my conversation with that moderator, a man in Alabama named Rocky Shay Franklin drugged, overpowered, and repeatedly raped a 12-year-old boy. Franklin filmed the assaults and uploaded twenty-three of the rape videos to Pornhub. The videos were monetized with advertisements and sold as pay-to-download content. Pornhub and Franklin split the profits from the sale of each video. Franklin was sentenced to forty years in prison for what he did.[1]

The court documents detailed how before Franklin was sentenced, police reached out to Pornhub multiple times to get the assault videos taken down but were ignored.[2] The videos were finally removed after seven months and multiple demands by police. By then the rapes had been viewed hundreds of thousands of times and downloaded, guaranteeing the child's trauma could live online forever.

When this story begins, I had yet to learn these details, but I did know about crying children. You could even say that my battle against Pornhub unexpectedly started because I was pulled out of bed one night by my own baby's tears.

———

In the dark hours before dawn on February 1, 2020, my baby's piercing scream startles me awake for the fourth time that night. I collect Jed from the bassinet beside my bed, wanting to comfort him but knowing any success will be fleeting. I feel powerless, battered, and drained—I'm afraid of how long this might go on. Three months ago Jed had an emergency birth complication called shoulder dystocia. He survived without permanent damage, but he hasn't stopped crying for more than a few hours at a time since birth and I'm at the end of my rope.

In a different season of my life I would have prayed for God to heal Jed's pain, but since my dad's sudden death I stopped believing that God cares about human affairs or even hears when we call for help.

I am disillusioned, not only with my faith but also with my anti-trafficking work.

I have spent thirteen years trying to make a difference, with no real progress. I fought for seven years to pass a sex trafficking prevention bill in the US Congress that could have an impact on trafficking worldwide, but it faced endless roadblocks and ultimately failed. I traveled country to country screening a documentary about sex trafficking to audiences of thousands around the world. Each time I would watch them weep as victims told their stories, but most wiped their eyes when it was over and never thought much about it again. I don't fault them; people feel compassion for victims but don't know what they can do to help in a meaningful way. Honestly, at this point neither do I.

Year after year, I'd witnessed sex trafficking getting worse despite everyone's best efforts to stop it. Among activists and their allies, there is a collective discouragement about the possibility of holding perpetrators accountable at scale, bringing justice to victims, and preventing abuse in the future. Even though I'm discouraged, I can't bring myself to quit. My advocacy work is the only thing keeping me sane. It's my distraction from the repeat cycle of crying and chaos. So I continue.

My informal maternity leave has ended, and I am working from home part-time, on an hourly basis for the anti-trafficking organization Exodus Cry. I know how fortunate I am to have this arrangement. And how fortunate I am that we don't need my income; my husband, Joel, and I have been married for twelve years and he provides for me, Jed, and our three-year-old daughter, Lily Rose. Though round-the-clock nursing practically immobilizes me, at least I can still research and post online while I hold my phone in one hand and keep Jed supported in my other arm.

Tonight, as I rock Jed in the darkness of my bedroom, I turn once again to thinking about this work. I remember a story I read nine days after he was born—a story I keep coming back to. A fifteen-year-old girl from Broward County, Florida, was missing for a year. She was finally found when her distraught mother was tipped off by a Pornhub user that he recognized her daughter on the site. The mother found fifty-eight videos of her child being raped on Pornhub that were uploaded by an account named "Daddy's_Slut."

Her daughter's filmed assaults were being monetized with advertisements and offered as pay-to-download content to 130 million daily site visitors. This meant users could download, possess, and reupload the videos again and again across the internet for the rest of the girl's life.

The girl's mother notified the police, who matched the perpetrator in the videos with surveillance footage from a 7-Eleven convenience store and identified him as thirty-year-old Christopher Johnson. When the police rescued the girl from his apartment, she told them he filmed the videos inside the apartment and also impregnated her.

It's hard for me to believe Johnson was only charged with lewd and lascivious battery and Pornhub is facing no consequences. I'm frustrated by the fact that there is nothing I can do about it besides share the news article on social media.[3]

Each time I think about the story it strikes me that this young teen's abuse videos would have been side by side with a sea of similar-looking content on Pornhub. I know from my advocacy work and Pornhub's own press statements that one of the most-searched terms on Pornhub is "teen."[4] A quick search for the word "teen" turns up titles such as "Young Girl Tricked," "Innocent Brace Faced Tiny Teen Fucked," "Tiny Petite Thai Teen," "Teen Little Girl First Time," and on and on ad infinitum. Many of their videos feature girls who look thirteen years old at best—girls with braces, pigtails, flat chests, no makeup, and young faces, holding teddy bears and licking lollipops, all while being penetrated. Pornhub claims[5] such videos are "legal" and "consensual" content made to satisfy "various user fantasies."[6] They are saying these are merely adult actresses made to look like underage teens and everyone seems to believe them.

And it isn't just this victim's story that has been bothering me lately.

I have been heartbroken by a criminal case in the news about a mother of two small children, like me. Her name is Nicole Addimando and she is being sentenced to life in prison in New York for killing the man who repeatedly sexually tortured her, filmed it, and uploaded the abuse to Pornhub.[7]

Then there is the GirlsDoPorn sex trafficking operation out of San Diego, California, that has been getting headlines. The trafficking ring tricked, coerced, and forced over one hundred women into sex videos that were uploaded to one of Pornhub's most popular "partner channels" and viewed over 600 million times on the site.[8] Twenty-two of the victims won a civil trial against GirlsDoPorn, which led to criminal convictions.[9] The ringleader fled the country and is on the FBI's 10 Most Wanted List.[10] Pornhub is somehow escaping any consequences for what happened.

It isn't only underage teens and adult victims on Pornhub that have recently ended up in the news. A few weeks ago I read an investigation in the London *Sunday Times*, "Unilever and Heinz Pay for Ads on Pornhub, the World's Biggest Porn Site," which revealed that dozens of illegal videos were found on the site within minutes, some of children as young as three years old.[11]

Shortly after, Pornhub's spokesman repeated his company's same canned line about how horrific child abuse is, followed by their standard deflection: "Oftentimes videos described as 'hidden camera footage' or 'young teen' are in fact legal, consensual videos that are produced to cater to various user fantasies. They are in fact protected by various freedom of speech laws."[12]

I noticed his choice of the word "oftentimes."

Pornhub has been claiming they don't tolerate criminal material on their site, and these are actors and actresses pretending. But do they *really* check the millions of videos and images on their site to make sure they're of consenting adults? With 6.8 million videos uploaded each year, how could they?

The idea that Pornhub properly vets these videos for the age and consent of their subjects is an assumption I'm making along with hundreds of millions of other people. Perhaps it's because Pornhub has done an effective job of presenting themselves to the world as a mainstream brand. People wear their apparel proudly in public and Pornhub even has a philanthropic arm called "Pornhub Cares." With massively marketed PR campaigns to save the oceans, save the giant pandas, save the bees, plant trees, and even donate to breast cancer research, Pornhub sends the message that they care about health and safety. Besides this, millions of people each year go through the process of uploading content to Pornhub and no one has sounded any noticeable alarms about the process. Everyone, myself included, has assumed it's fine.

Jed has finally settled down and as I hold him in my arms pondering all this, a phrase my father used to say comes to mind.

"Assumption is the mother of all screwups."

His wise words resonate. If the assumption is wrong, it would certainly be the mother of all screwups for advocates like me who would have let it go unnoticed.

Suddenly I have an idea. I am going to upload content to the site myself to see what it takes and how the videos are screened.

I'm going to test Pornhub.

———

I lay a sleeping Jed in the center of the bed and sink back into the recliner with my laptop and phone. I get my wallet ready in case I need my driver's license as ID, and I begin typing in my browser's navigation bar: *Pornhub.com.*

On the left side of the dark page, its categories are listed: "Amateur," "Anal," "Arab," "Asian," "Babe," "Babysitter" . . . going down further: "Old/Young," "Party," "Pissing," "Public" . . . "Rough Sex," "School," "Small Tits." Then, the category with the most sex trafficking implications: "Teen."

I click the "Sign up" button and enter an email address. They want a username and password. Next, I'm directed to confirm my email address by clicking a link. Done. I wait for the site to verify my identity.

Nothing.

That was too easy.

If I'm a child abuser or sex trafficker, what are the checks on uploading videos and images of my victims?

I find the "Upload" button, click, and just like that I'm instructed to choose a file.

I take a video of the rug in the dark room and my computer keyboard. I go to upload the video and they prompt me to click a box with fine-print legal jargon that I don't bother to read, and neither does anyone else. The file is accepted. I glance at my wallet sitting on the desk beside me. The next step must be entering some kind of ID. Maybe there is a consent form?

Nope. There is no other prompt for anything else.

I'm not asked for an ID to prove that I'm over eighteen, or that the subject of the video I've uploaded is not a child. Neither am I asked for any documentation of consent pertaining to the people in the video, to ensure they are not victims of rape, trafficking, assault, or revenge porn.

No form. No check.

Moments later, an email notification pops up. It's a message from Pornhub.

"Congratulations! Your video is now live!"

The email has a URL linking to the file I uploaded minutes earlier, which is now available to the five million visitors on Pornhub in that hour alone. Congratulations? What if the video was of a fourteen-year-old being raped? It would be live on the site right now for anyone to download for free and recirculate.

I look at the Pornhub search bar to see the number of videos on the site today: 10,758,054.

Almost eleven million videos are available this day along with forty million images,[13] presumably acquired through the same nonprocess I just went through. And that is just what is on the site *today*. Pornhub has a vast library of content amassed on their servers since its creation in 2007.

If Pornhub isn't verifying age or consent, how many of these eleven million videos are of real sexual assaults? How many are of children? I realize Pornhub's servers are potentially the largest collection of child sex trafficking and rape in North America, if not the world.

The world's largest porn site is likely *infested* with *real* sexual crime.

The site is set up to enable abuse. Does anyone besides me realize this? How come none of the millions of other Pornhub uploaders have said anything about it? How could I have not thought of testing the upload process sooner?

Most important, what do I do with this information now?

In this moment, I forget that quitting ever crossed my mind. Pornhub has been hiding its dirty secret in plain sight for over a decade and now I know I must find a way to expose it. But how?

2

#TRAFFICKINGHUB

With each click, I descend the dark rabbit hole of Pornhub. More videos show young women so drunk they can hardly move or speak a coherent word, their bodies limp and compliant and their minds unaware of what is going on.

"Abuse," "manipulated," and "coerced" are words easily searchable that bring up a never-ending number of videos. I search the words "drunk" and "drugged"—thousands of videos come up. I see the title "Teen to Drunk After Party Real Home Made!!" The girl is so drunk she's incapacitated. Pornhub's algorithm directs me to "Misadventures of a drunk girl," which has been on the site for months with over 50,000 views.

114   71   Add To   Share   Download

Misadventures of a drunk girl

55,350 VIEWS 👍 62%

It's a poor-quality homemade video of a naked young woman on the floor of a messy bedroom. She is crawling on the floor on all fours, so drunk she can hardly keep her eyes open. "I have to pee," she says in slurred words as she presses the side of her face on the carpet and begins to heave as if she is going to vomit. "I'll never drink this much again," she laments. The man holding the camera mocks her as he points out a large red gash on her back he says is from her falling. The camera focuses on her nude body as she slowly claws her way to the bathroom and grabs the toilet. Commenters mock her, saying, "I would take advantage of her all night" and "So hot. Love how drunk she is."

This is not a porn performer. She is not pretending. I might have been willing to believe Pornhub's line before I put my kids to sleep, but after testing the upload process, my perspective has shifted. Any homemade video on the site is a potential crime.

I'm not sure what to do with what I have discovered. As I ponder the options, I realize that the only thing I *can* do is post about it online to the few thousand followers I have amassed on Twitter from years of advocacy work. I know I will likely be shouting into the wind, but I can't keep quiet about this. I post to Twitter:

> "PORNHUB IS A TRAFFICKER'S DREAM COME TRUE. The site just let me upload content in 8 clicks—all that's needed is an email address. NO ID, NO 'CONSENT' form—nothing. Stop with the 'all women on Pornhub are consenting adults.' IT'S A LIE . . ."

I understand that Pornhub is an enormous target. A few angry activists on Twitter will mean nothing to them. I need to get someone in a position of power and influence to understand. I start tagging senators, celebrities, the FBI, members of Congress, even the prime minister of Canada and the president. While we're staying with Joel's parents north of Seattle, I'm on

Pacific time. My early morning tweets are read by followers on the East Coast who are already on their way to lunch.

I've tweeted about victims on Pornhub before, but this time unleashes an outpouring of outrage like I've never seen. Followers are stunned by the news that Pornhub doesn't verify age or consent, and share my posts. Then more people begin to notice and share what I'm saying. I remind my followers that sex trafficking is legally defined as any commercial sex act involving a minor *or* any commercial sex act induced by force, fraud, or coercion.[1] *Every* sex act on Pornhub is commercial—the videos exist to make money for the site. This means that every child on Pornhub and every nonconsensual sex act *is* an act of sex trafficking. It is illegal to engage in, or knowingly profit from, sex trafficking in the United States, and MindGeek has offices, servers, business partners, and users across the country.

A new Twitter follower tells me that anybody in the world can also become an officially "verified" Pornhub user with a special blue check by their name, implying they are a vetted adult porn actor—but no ID or consent verification is required. I go to the site and confirm it for myself. All it takes to become "verified" on Pornhub is to send in a photo of yourself holding a piece of paper with your *username* and the phrase "on Pornhub." That's it. No ID or even real name is required. I tweet what I've confirmed about Pornhub's nonverification process, and people respond with disbelief and outrage.

Another person who saw one of my posts tells me that Pornhub created a mirror site on the dark web of encrypted networks designed for anonymity. "You are right about underage girls and child porn on Pornhub," he confirms. Then referring to a software project noted for its onion-like layers of protection and nicknamed "Tor" for "the onion router," this person tells me, "Pornhub even has an onion link that can be used via the Tor browser to watch Pornhub on the dark web while remaining anonymous. Child porn is the #1 issue facing the Tor community." A quick Google search confirms it's true.[2] Pornhub even put out a press release about it. They went through the trouble to launch a dark web mirror site, yet they couldn't be bothered to implement even the most basic safety measures for those who are in the videos?

With each passing hour, another wave of information damning Pornhub comes across my Twitter account. "The 15-year-old missing girl from Florida was verified by Pornhub as one of their amateur models. Pornhub admitted it on Twitter but then quickly deleted the confession," another random person tells me. They send screenshots, links, and archived online caches to confirm Pornhub's admission.[3]

It's true. Pornhub admitted to verifying the missing child. As I digest what I am learning, a disturbing reality hits me.

Pornhub is not a porn site, it's a crime scene.

In a burst of inspiration, I share the hashtag #Traffickinghub for the first time. A new follower designs the hashtag into the form of the world-famous Pornhub logo. Pornhub has spent millions on advertising over the years to make the Pornhub logo instantly recognizable. Now we are flipping the script, using their own marketing dollars to hijack the brand and expose them. "Pornhub is a #Traffickinghub" becomes my mantra, and I am excited to see the hashtag catching on across social media.

I realize I must get what I am learning out to a bigger audience than my Twitter following. So, without consulting Exodus Cry or anyone else, I stay up till dawn writing an essay between Jed's nursing sessions. As I am writing I begin to get clarity on what must happen now. We can't allow the owners of Pornhub to hide behind a corporate veil. They can't merely be given a slap on the wrist and then go on with business as usual after they have allowed the global distribution and monetization of countless victim's trauma for over a decade. Pornhub must be shut down, its executives must be criminally prosecuted and its victims compensated. Anything less will not deter future abusers—anything less is not real justice.

On February 9, nine days after I tested the upload system, the *Washington Examiner* publishes the essay[4] detailing my findings that I offered to several news outlets. The *Examiner*'s editor titles it "Time to Shut Pornhub Down," drawing from my closing sentence: "It's time to shut down super-predator site Pornhub and hold the executive megapimps behind it accountable."

The moment my piece goes live, it flies far and wide. People begin flooding me with messages of support and expressing their desire to help. Serendipitously, the day after my article is released, my credibility is bolstered when the BBC publishes a bombshell in forty-one languages titled, "I Was Raped at 14 and the Video Ended up on a Porn Site."[5] The porn site is Pornhub. The BBC describes the abduction at knifepoint of a fourteen-year-old Ohio girl named Rose, who was then raped and assaulted for twelve hours. Her torture was recorded and uploaded to Pornhub. "The titles of the videos were 'teen crying and getting slapped around,' 'teen getting destroyed,' 'passed out teen.' One had over 400,000 views," Rose told the BBC.

I am moved to google Rose and send her a direct message of admiration for her courage. She responds and tells me the BBC has been working on her story for a year. I am in awe of the timing—that how, completely unplanned, the BBC published her story the day after my article, and together they are a powerful one-two punch.

When I see an email from the *Washington Examiner* editor, I immediately open it and am shocked:

Hi Laila,

Just wanted to close the loop on this piece and say thank you
for sending it to us. It's still getting a good deal of traffic . . .
FYI, I grudgingly added a minor correction that says MindGeek
is technically based in Luxembourg (for tax purposes).
The fact that they saw the piece and complaining about
that technicality was all they had to say speaks volumes.

We'll be glad to run more pieces from you in the future.

This is quite a development. I made damning accusations, any of which they could have sued me for immediately if they could prove they were untrue. At the very least, they could have demanded a retraction if they could prove I was lying. But they have done no such thing. Yes, their silence speaks volumes.

I change my Twitter bio to my favorite quote, attributed to St. Augustine: "The truth is like a lion . . . Let it loose; it will defend itself."

| 3 |

PORNHUB'S
CENSORSHIP TRICKS

Hello, I just saw a video on Pornhub of an Indian girl being raped."

As my essay continues to be shared and the #Traffickinghub hashtag is spreading, Pornhub users around the world start sending me content from the site that they suspect is illegal.

This particular link takes me to a shaky, grainy, homemade video of a young woman in India who is in visible distress, crying and shielding her face from the camera as she is raped by multiple men in the back of a car. The video has thousands of views and a download button. A comment on the video says, "this is fucking r**e!!!!!! bastards!!!!!"

It strikes me as odd that the word "fucking" appears next to a censored word—"rape." I screenshot the comment and the woman's covered face

and post them to Twitter. The video has been on Pornhub for years, flagged by commenters as rape. Yet MindGeek finally removes it just hours after I tweet it.

Why are users uploading these videos? I know they aren't afraid of getting caught since they can be totally anonymous, but over 80 percent[1] of the videos on Pornhub are free and don't earn money for users. So what is their motivation? I realize users do it for social currency—views, likes, clicks, and comments. In most cases the only profiteers are the owners and executives of Pornhub, who are monetizing all of this free porn by selling 4.6 billion ad impressions on the content every single day.[2]

An Indonesian sender points out a video title in his native language that he claims uses the actual word "rape." Google Translate tells me it's true. Like a tour of the worst that the world has to offer, I am directed by Pornhub's algorithm toward videos from Pornhub's special "partner channels" called "Exploited Teen Asia" and "Asian Street Meat."

I am especially disturbed by a video on the Exploited Teen Asia[3] channel that shows a young Asian girl with pigtails in a room that has children's
toys strewn all over the ground. She is face down, squeezing a small toy in
her hand as she is crying out in pain while being raped by an old man. The
comments on the homemade video describe what is taking place:

> "we really know sex trafficking when we see it!! This is a real victim."

> "I can't believe 9k liked the image of an old perv humping a helpless
> GIRL! Flag the fuck out of this. My heart breaks for her."

> "She was crying 'kurushii' meaning 'painful' and was begging him
> to stop!"

> "Post nut clarity hit and now I'm crying for the girl I just got off to."

> "She looks unde***e af."

I note that the word "underage" has been censored.

I report the video to the National Center for Missing and Exploited
Children (NCMEC), which is the clearinghouse in the United States for
child sexual abuse material. They work with agencies and law enforcement
around the world to take down child abuse from the internet and, when
possible, help apprehend abusers. Next, I screenshot the comments from
the video and post them to my Twitter account. I am careful not to post
the video title because I don't want to direct anyone to the video.

But Pornhub is obviously watching my Twitter account now, because
when I go back to the video of the girl with pigtails and toys, it has been
swapped out for a studio-produced video of a grown Asian woman. Also
gone are all of the comments about trafficking and child abuse. But what
remains is the same exact URL connected to the video, the same title, tags,
view count, and even the same exact date and time of upload. There is my

proof: no user has the capability to do such a thing to the site; only Porn-hub does. They see me watching and are trying to hide the evidence I called out. But I documented what they did with the screenshots I took.

On a video called "Very Young Teen" with over a million views, I again notice the censoring of specific words in the comments and take screen-shots.

"SHE LOOKS WAY UNDE***E SMH"

"disgusting she looks like a c***d. remove that shit"

"She looks unde***e the nawty little slut"

"It's c***d porn."

"If this video is not taken down I'll report this to all c***d pornography policing channels"

Someone else writes, "Looking for something younger?" with a Hot-mail email address listed where people can make a deal for child abuse videos.

Now I have seen the words "child," "underage," and "rape" on Pornhub dozens of times and *every single time* they are censored in the exact same way. MindGeek is censoring the comments to obscure the words that flag crime.[3] They have intentionally set up their system to detect the words so they can hide them, but they leave the crime scenes untouched on the site. This means MindGeek has the capability to easily find and take down each flagged video, but they are *choosing* not to, and the trauma of these victims remains on the site for weeks, months, and years earning advertis-ing revenue.

The intelligence of Pornhub's algorithm ensures that since I witnessed one criminal abuse video, I will see more and more and more. I see a

Ukrainian girl being coerced into giving oral sex to an older man in a forest. The video was uploaded by an account named "UASex" that seems to stand for "under age sex." The tags on the video say "CP," standing for "child pornography" and "not18." In the comments a user says he knows the girl in the video and that she is fifteen years old. Under the video I notice it's listed as a "featured" video, meaning Pornhub *chose* the video to be *featured* on the homepage in order to get more clicks and views.

Advertising child sexual abuse is a felony crime.

"If you truly want to take down the hub, then the answer has been hiding in plain sight."

The anonymous email from someone following me on Twitter continues: "If you surf around Pornhub you will quickly notice that many of the videos are marked with 'unknown' or uploader unknown. This is because Pornhub received a takedown notice for an upload from that user. Pornhub takes down just the one upload but none of the other infringing videos from the uploader. They then strip away and delete the uploader's information from their system, leaving illegal videos from 'unknown' uploaders all over the site."

Next, he tells me that users, including pedophiles, leverage Pornhub's private video feature to upload illegal content. Since the videos are private, only the uploader and those granted viewing access can see them. He says there's a "community" of users who upload child abuse.

"Pornhub is also allowing underage teens to upload nude videos of themselves and some of these underage accounts have thousands of friends."

I verify his claims about the private sharing feature. He's correct. Pornhub users can upload privately where only "friends" can see the content behind the blurry thumbnails.

believeincake uploaded 1 new video!
2 years ago

PRIVATE

changing diapers

This is obviously a low-risk way for pedo-criminals to share child abuse. One man with the username "DaddyLuvsTinyPussy" is using this private sharing feature. His bio admits, "I'm an avid admirer of girls and all their beauty, but since that includes girls under 18, I'm labeled a pervert among other things."

As I continue investigating, I come across a homemade video of a woman's rape in a dingy motel room that looks like it was originally filmed by a camcorder in the 1990s. Her mouth is duct-taped so she can't scream, and her hands and feet are tied with rope. Her eyes are wide with terror. An overweight, middle-aged man with thick glasses stands above her as she squirms. As he throws her onto the bed, I notice a huge black-and-blue bruise that takes up most of her right thigh. He pulls out a small knife and holds it to her throat, then he proceeds to sexually assault her while she cries. Without question, this girl is not acting.

The video was uploaded three years ago, and the uploader is "unknown."

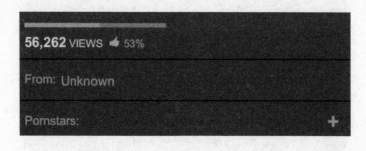

The day after my *Examiner* article is published I get a message from a woman who is moved by what she read, and she asks me to start a petition to shut down Pornhub. She says if I don't do it quickly, she will start one herself. I feel a responsibility to guide this swelling outrage, so I quickly create a Change.org account and copy and paste my op-ed into the body of the petition. The title comes naturally.

"Shut Down Pornhub and Hold Its Executives Accountable for Aiding Trafficking."

I post about the petition on social media and many people start to share it. I watch as the live feed counter on the petition is updated in real time. It feels like I am winning a slot machine jackpot, but it doesn't stop pouring out the winnings. In 24 hours, the petition gains 17,000 signatures. In 48 hours, it has 41,000 signatures. By the end of day four, it's almost to 100,000 and shows no signs of slowing down.

Messages of encouragement flood in.

"If this petition will succeed, this will be one of the biggest historical milestones of the women's rights movement," one new follower says.

"This is an awakening and a paradigm shift that many have been waiting for," another stranger states.

Another follower writes, "You are disrupting the space and shaking the entire system. You are not alone; we stand with you."

I also get messages that are so deranged, they leave me utterly bewildered as I read them.

Dear Laila, I am a 44-year-old porn addict and I saw on Twitter that you are posting about underage girls on Pornhub, I agree with you Pornhub sometimes shows underage girls in porn and that is wrong but for us chronic masturbators Pornhub is a nice website that helps us masturbate many times every day for free so please don't close it down ok? Thank you very much in advance.

On second thought, the message is encouraging. At least he thinks we can actually shut down Pornhub.

4

WELCOME NEW BEDFELLOWS

I n order to fully understand the Pornhub Network, follow the money trail," an undercover journalist who saw my petition soon tells me. This journalist has been investigating MindGeek for the last ten years and sends me a two-hundred-page file containing years of the company's financial statements, formation and registration documents, merger documents, and much more from Luxembourg, Cyprus, and Canada. He explains how Pornhub unlawfully collects and stores the user data of people who visit without their consent and then monetizes the data for their advertisers through a service they own called TrafficJunky.

"When you click on Pornhub or its sister sites like Redtube or YouPorn, you automatically agree to their 'privacy policy' and these documents state that they will collect your data and deploy web beacons and other special tracking technology to your device to harvest your data."

The privacy policy states that they can collect, use, store, and transfer different kinds of personal data about you and that includes your IP address, country, city, neighborhood, zip code, payment details, what browser you use, what language you speak, your income, email addresses, and login data. They even assign your sex and sexual preferences based on the videos you watch. All this data is being harvested for forty-seven billion visits to Pornhub alone per year, not to mention the billions of visits to Mind-Geek's other major free porn tube sites. "All that massive big data is what they sell to advertisers to make money," he explains. Going against various laws implemented around the world, they don't ask for permission or allow users to opt out. In fact he says privacy activists in Italy are preparing to sue Pornhub for violating Europe's General Data Protection Regulation (GDPR).[1] This news doesn't surprise me. Pornhub's disregard for consent clearly isn't limited to those in the videos.

I thank the journalist and tell him I want to organize a meeting with him soon.

"Good," he replies. "I will give you all the help I can."

I am amazed at what I am learning from this incoming flood of messages, emails, and calls. I don't take all information at face value, but instead take time to discern who is credible based on if the information can be confirmed or corroborated. One particular subject line grabs my attention: "Material of Interest." It's from an anonymous MindGeek insider who says he has a damning buried video of Pornhub's official brand ambassador, Asa Akira, admitting to wanting to molest a thirteen-year-old child. He explains that Asa and MindGeek have been monitoring the internet so they can take down the video anytime it pops up, but he has a copy.

He sends a download link and I watch with disgust as Asa speaks about her sexual attraction to a particular child. When asked point-blank by someone else in the room if she would "have sex" with the child, she confesses that given the chance, she would. She goes on to justify her desire for the boy. "No one would consider that rape . . . except maybe his mom . . . And that's only if she's, like, a total bitch." Another person cuts in, "and the law." She retorts, "Yeah, and the law. *Whatever.*" She then turns to the guy next to her and asks how he would feel about her if she had "sex" with the thirteen-year-old.

"I would feel bad for you because you're going to the pokey," he replies.

"Why would I, why would I go!? Who's gonna tell? No snitching . . . snitches get stitches," Asa protests.

The guy with a conscience says, "Hmm, well, we have the *law* . . ." to which Asa replies, "Yeah, let's put that to the side." He then says to her, "You would be fucked, because you'd go to prison, and you—"

Asa interrupts him. "We're not talking about the law right now! Jesus!"

It's hard to believe what I am hearing and seeing.

"Fuck the law! Snitch! What are you, a fucking do-gooder or something . . . What are you, the protector of thirteen-year-olds or something?"

"I think somebody has to," he replies.

"What a nerd," Asa says condescendingly. She then goes on about how she thinks there is nothing wrong with grown adults having sex with minors and even expresses her disdain for laws against statutory rape.

It's mind-boggling that MindGeek appointed Asa to be their longtime, official brand ambassador while knowing what she believes about abusing minors. I share the tapes with a journalist at *The Sun* who later exposes the video. The headline reads, "Pornhub ambassador says she would rape 13-year-old boy and blasts 'f**k the law' in sickening unearthed video."[2] But even after the story is published, Pornhub keeps Asa as their global brand representative.

———

I am building the case against Pornhub publicly online, hour by hour. One story I come back to is the investigation[3] done a few months ago by London's *Sunday Times* that found "dozens" of illegal videos on the site "within minutes," some of children as young as three. Something strikes me that I hadn't noticed before. The article says 118 cases of child abuse were confirmed on Pornhub by the Internet Watch Foundation (IWF). "Almost half the content was classified as falling into category A, the worst kinds of abuse," it reads.

Category A isn't photos of kids playing naked in a bathtub, as bad as that would be on a porn site. Category A–level child sexual abuse images involve painful penetration, sexual abuse involving an animal, or other sadistic acts of abuse meant to induce pain and terror.

I call the author, who confirms the report, but when I speak with the spokesperson at IWF, she is surprisingly short with me. When pressed, she confirms the cases of child abuse on Pornhub but says that they don't focus on or investigate mainstream porn sites and weren't looking for them. She then says something that disturbs me in both content and tone.

"There are worse sites out there than Pornhub, you know that, right?"

How do you know? I think to myself. *You just told me you don't investigate the site.*

But now I have another substantial piece of evidence to use against Pornhub—over a hundred confirmed cases of child abuse that they monetized with advertisements and globally distributed with a download button to more than five million users per hour. Still, I am upset and surprised by IWF's dismissive attitude. I would have expected the Internet Watch Foundation to care more.

And yet, the people who do care surprise me in the best possible way. Hundreds of porn producers and performers are signing and sharing the petition. There aren't many issues in which people are universally united, but *everyone* agrees that no one should be raped for profit on the world's largest porn site. They are outraged like everyone else by the news that Pornhub is infested with child abuse and rape, though they also have other reasons to hate MindGeek and Pornhub. The company built its empire on profiting from stolen and pirated professional porn content.

Jenna Jameson, named the "Queen of Porn" and the "most famous porn star of all time," shares it with inciting comments.

"Pornhub is a rathole of child pornography, they need to be crushed and held accountable for pushing child trafficking and abuse of minors . . . Take a stand against these monsters at MindGeek . . . Shut it DOWN," Jenna writes.

"Shut them the fuck down," another independent porn producer tells me as we talk on the phone. She says she's sick of spending two hours per day scouring MindGeek's porn tube sites looking for her stolen videos and issuing takedown demands. Another porn performer tells me that while searching Pornhub for her stolen content, she regularly finds obvious child abuse and other sex crimes. She begins to send me the links whenever she comes across illegal videos.

Joining together is such a wide range of people from all backgrounds. Over three hundred anti-trafficking, child protection, and women's rights organizations are now participating in what has become the "Traffickinghub movement," and there are half a million signatures on the petition from people across the globe. I see support and action from those who are pro-porn, anti-porn, conservative, liberal, Republican, Libertarian, Democrat, old, young, atheist, Christian, Jewish, and Muslim.

With the petition continuing to gain viral traction, I am being contacted at all hours of the day and night by journalists from around the world and the headlines are piling up. I notice some that paint a David vs. Goliath picture, pitting me alone against Pornhub, and it makes me uneasy. This *must* be much bigger than me. Pornhub can handle me alone exposing them to my few thousand followers, but what they *can't* handle is a growing movement of people coming together for the singular purpose of shutting them down.

I tell my colleagues in the anti-trafficking field who are helping the cause that Traffickinghub cannot be owned by any one person or organization. I am adamant that it has to continue as a decentralized global effort in order to be effective. "This *must be* a *movement* where everyone feels invited to take ownership of advancing the cause." I am unwavering on this principle, because I know that the only way we will make a dent in this behemoth of criminal abuse is to empower *everyone* to collectively attack it.

5

BETTING ON BOWE

Bradley Myles is the former CEO and founder of Polaris Project, one of the US' largest and most respected anti-trafficking organizations. In 2017 he won the Skoll Award, which is like winning the Academy Awards of social change work. As an all-star in the anti-trafficking movement, Brad has frequently been called as an expert witness for televised congressional hearings. I had long admired his work and we eventually got acquainted as our professional paths crossed. Over time Brad has become a priceless friend, resource, and ally.

One morning in February 2020, I update Brad on everything that's happened in the last few weeks: about the undercover journalist, the media coverage, the petition's viral traction, and all of the organizations that have joined the effort. I also tell him about the victims that have been reaching out to me daily, many of whom ask for help in taking down their abuse videos and pursuing lawsuits.

What these victims want resonates with my longtime conviction that civil lawsuits are the most effective tool to rein in the sex trafficking industry. Trafficking is a transactional crime, done primarily for money. Megapimps like MindGeek have one consideration—what will make them the most profit. Lawsuits would hit them where it hurts, their bank account, and bring much-needed relief to victims. For a long time, I have considered starting an organization to support victims in their pursuit of justice in court, but it never felt like the right time. Now might be.

As Brad and I are talking about this, he has an idea.

"There is a Wall Street attorney I'm in touch with that has thirty years of experience and is looking for a significant trafficking case he can help with. His skills may be perfect for taking on a corporation this big. I'll give him a call and fill him in and see if he would like to talk to you. His name is Michael Bowe—pronounced like the singer David Bowie. You should look him up; he has done some impressive cases."

Mike Bowe, I soon learn, was the son of a firefighter and a risk-taker by nature. A blue-collar Irish Catholic brawler, only his nearsightedness kept him from becoming a firefighter himself. After graduating from Fordham University, a full scholarship to New York Law School opened a different door. He did so well, he was hired by the elite, white-shoe law firm Sullivan and Cromwell, where he stood out from his fellow associates— mostly WASPy Ivy Leaguers. Despite his irreverent personality, Mike comfortably represented powerful clients including Microsoft, Bank of America, Elon Musk, and Goldman Sachs. He litigated high-stakes, multibillion-dollar cases at Sullivan and Cromwell, then top Wall Street litigation firm Kasowitz Benson Torres, and later Brown Rudnick.

A few years into his position at Kasowitz, Mike took a hedge fund in- sider trading case that other top firms deemed impossible. The guy who brought it to him was one of the most secretive traders on Wall Street and some thought he was crazy. After a year of investigating, Mike dropped a stunning 150-page complaint with a big story on *60 Minutes* and a piece in *The New York Times*. Shortly after, he brought an insider trading case against hedge fund titan Steve Cohen and SAC Capital that he litigated on behalf of Fairfax Financial. He worked closely with the FBI and Depart- ment of Justice to help produce a criminal indictment against Steve Cohen and SAC Capital that resulted in the company shutting down, jail time for company traders and managers, and a $2 billion fine.

It has been named the biggest Wall Street insider trading case in history, and it was an exceptionally creative application of the statute known as RICO—the "racketeer influenced and corrupt organizations" act. RICO cases frequently target the Mafia, but Mike's life experience helped him detect gangster-style criminality in places where no one else would think to look.

Mike had been reading news reports about human trafficking for a while and was deeply moved for the victims. He remembered the work he was most proud of weren't cases on behalf of billionaires, but pro bono work he did for marginalized gay men who were in the hospital dying of HIV/AIDS and needed legal advice. He hungered for more meaningful work that could benefit from his expertise.

He knew of several anti-trafficking organizations in Washington, DC, so while there on business, he reached out to Bradley Myles of Polaris Project. Over lunch Mike explained his background and his desire to use the latter part of his career to make a dent in the human trafficking industry. He asked Brad to alert him if ever a case fit his profile.

Pornhub gave Brad every reason to pick up the phone to Mike's New York office, located in 7 Times Square Tower, with a 180-degree, all-glass view looking down on Manhattan. Plopped in the center of his sleek, modern workspace is an old, round, and beat-up oak restaurant table from the bar Mike and his team used as a war room during the drawn-out SAC Capital hedge fund insider trading case. Scrawled across the top with a thick red sharpie is Mike's motto, "DON'T FUCK IT UP."

———————

Brad sets up a three-way call for me to meet Mike Bowe. When the phone rings, I hand off Jed to my mother-in-law and rush out to the cold garage where it's quiet, without any distractions. Staying with Joel's parents has enabled me to keep my advocacy work going day and night with small children, while Joel is in the midst of a major life change. He is a dentist who discovered—having done countless hours of relief work in Haiti and other vulnerable places around the world, both pulling rotten teeth and building homes—that he much prefers using a drill on two-by-fours than on people's heads. As he transitions out of dentistry and into real estate, he is traveling back and forth to build us a home in the Colorado mountains that he loves so much. In addition to being a pilot, and an instructor at that—a skill that could be useful in his volunteer work—he is also a skilled mountaineer. After he climbed every fourteen-thousand-foot peak in Colorado, he knew that was where he wanted to live.

Brad tees up the call with Mike by introducing me, then hands it off to me to explain the situation. I start from the beginning, even though I know Bowe has been doing his own research.

"Pornhub is the largest and most popular porn site in the world and it's full of rape, sex trafficking, and child abuse . . ."

Bowe is matter-of-fact. In his unmistakable New York accent, he says, "Look—this is clearly a bad actor operating in a rogue, unregulated industry that needs to be reined in. I am not interested in a one-off case, the kind that's just the cost of doing business for these guys. My interest is in doing something that can produce industry-wide transformation, a case that can pose a big enough threat that MindGeek is forced to change or shut down—existential-threat-level litigation, and not just against Mind-Geek. There must be pressure put on their financial partners and the corporations that enable their existence. Visa, Mastercard, Discover, PayPal, Google, the servers, the advertisers—all of them have to feel the heat in order for this situation to permanently change."

My ears buzz as Mike speaks. Brad and I had already been talking about the importance of putting pressure on the credit card companies and here is Mike confirming the strategy.

Credit card companies essentially deliver the envelopes of cash from advertisers and porn consumers to Pornhub's executives, keeping Pornhub in business and taking a cut from each illegal transaction. American Express avoids "adult digital content," so they aren't involved with Pornhub. But Visa, Mastercard, and Discover need to be confronted with the difference between the legal pornography they claim to support and the sex trafficking enterprise they're participating in.

Mike talks about suing the individual owners and executives *personally*, along with MindGeek, and using RICO, child pornography, and sex trafficking laws that produce "treble damages" for victims—meaning jury awards will be tripled. Then he notes the importance of an accompanying media blitz. "With the filing of the cases and with each major decision there must be a media shitstorm to keep the spotlight and pressure on these companies." Mike's words are inciting and exciting. I find myself pacing circles in the garage and nodding as he speaks.

"The case has to have more than one or two plaintiffs," Mike continues. "It needs many victims filing individual lawsuits at the same time, not a class action. Class-action cases sound impressive to the public, but they're better for defendants since they deal with the problem in one settlement for pennies on the dollar. They're better for lawyers because they get paid a lot, for less work, but they are worse for victims. I am not interested in a class action." Several lawyers had brought up class-action lawsuits they wanted to pursue, and I completely support them. But Mike's legal vision seems more strategic and comprehensive than anything I've heard.

Mike says big cases like the one he is envisioning aren't cheap; it takes multiple millions to go toe-to-toe with corporations like MindGeek and Visa, and win, so his partners will have to buy in. But he is interested.

I like Bowe's ideas, I like his attitude, and I like his energy and strategy. I have a feeling that he can do something significant, and that he has the heart, experience, and grit to take this on in a big way. I make the decision then and there.

I am betting on Bowe.

———

After meeting Mike, I decide it's time to launch the nonprofit organization I've dreamt about for the last decade. Mike's vision is a high-stakes, high-risk, massive case, using legal theories against the credit card companies that have never been tried before. His firm is qualified to go toe-to-toe with these big corporations, but getting them into the ring with MindGeek and the credit card giants will be challenging without them first understanding the full nature and potential of the cases. To help Mike get liftoff, he needs funds to hire a skilled team of investigators to research the company and the claims of numerous victims coming forward. Victims will also need therapy and advocacy support to go through the intense process of litigation. I want lawsuits to be an empowering and healing experience for survivors.

My longtime colleague in the anti-trafficking fight and good friend Morgan Perry has shared the vision for years, so I ask if she will launch the organization with me. Morgan agrees without hesitation. I file with the IRS, and we name it the Justice Defense Fund. Morgan reaches out to a longtime mentor, and anti-trafficking supporter, to ask for help. Within the hour he agrees to provide whatever financial support is needed to help Mike get the case to the point of filing. And just like that, Mike is off to the races.

My first chance to connect Mike to a victim comes quickly. A twenty-year-old woman sends me an email and tells me to share it to expose Pornhub. She says from the age of nine to seventeen, she was "raped, beaten and videotaped by hundreds of men, women and even married couples." She describes in horrific detail how she was tortured as a young child. "I was forced to drink ammonia until I passed out and was raped for hours after that even though my mouth and throat were burning so bad."

Now, years later, she still suffers from nightmares and extreme PTSD. Fortunately, she was rescued from her abusers and is with a safe new family that helps her through the flashbacks. She implores people to act on behalf of victims like her: "It's not fair that my life is so hard now because I was forced into a life of sex and pornography as a child. I had to get police involved on multiple occasions to try and get videos removed from Pornhub of me being raped AS A MINOR. I don't understand why it's so difficult. Please, stop allowing people to make money off the torture and coercion of children."

Responding to her, I arrange a call for us to speak. On the phone she has a kind, soft voice, and even if I didn't know she was twenty I would be able to tell she is young by her tone and inflection. But her words make it clear that she has a depth beyond her years. She explains that her abusers are responsible for raping her, but that Pornhub turned her abuse into a perpetual nightmare by allowing her assaults to be downloaded, monetized, and globally distributed. She can hardly leave the house on some days because she's terrified she will meet someone who has seen her torture. This brave survivor makes it clear she has one goal: to stop Pornhub from causing other victims to live out her nightmare. But she wonders out loud if it's even possible.

"Do you want to talk to a lawyer?" I ask her.

"Yes."

I set up a conference call with Mike and feel proud of him as he speaks with her. I know he isn't used to this kind of interaction. His clients are high-powered executives with deep pockets, and he doesn't need to be sensitive with them. This is different. Mike listens well. He makes sure she knows there is no pressure to have a second conversation, but if she wants to talk about her options to pursue justice, he is ready to talk further. I can tell Mike is moved by her story, and from the sound of his voice, I know there is no way he is going to turn back from this fight.

A few days later, I am going over the conversation with Mike again. Money is the bottom line for MindGeek—every decision is driven by profit.

Follow the money.

And *how* do they make their money? Through billions of daily ad impressions, paid downloads, and premium memberships . . . all of which are processed by Visa, Mastercard, and Discover. I decide it is time to use our momentum to start pressuring the credit card companies to cut ties with Pornhub.

When I begin speaking publicly about the idea, I find I'm not the only one with an interest in chasing credit card companies. Some of the most influential anti-trafficking organizations have already been on Visa's case for processing trafficking transactions. A few take immediate interest in going after them for doing business with Pornhub. We devise a plan to send a joint letter signed by thousands of advocates to the CEOs of Visa, Mastercard, and Discover, demanding they cut ties with Pornhub. We agree to execute the plan within a couple weeks.

It's easy to identify the leaders of the credit card companies, so we know who to contact. MindGeek, however, is a different story. I find myself spending a significant amount of time trying to unravel and understand the complicated MindGeek corporate structure and ownership. An experienced forensic accountant from Ireland lends me his help poring over all of the documents and financial statements the undercover journalist sent me. It soon becomes clear that MindGeek is obscured in secrecy. And until we can figure out how it functions and who owns it, we won't be able to hold the company accountable.

6

THE ZUCKERBERG OF PORN

So, who actually owns MindGeek? Publicly available information suggests that two men named Feras Antoon and David Tassillo are the only owners, but they are two high-level holdover VPs who were with the company from the beginning. It's impossible that they had the money on their own to purchase MindGeek. Feras and David had remained with the company when it was first acquired by a German entrepreneur named Fabian Thylmann, who has been dubbed in the press the "Zuckerberg of Porn."

Starting as a self-proclaimed computer "geek," Fabian grew into a shrewd and powerful businessman with an ambition to crush competitors at any cost and dominate the global porn industry. Fabian came of age during the era of big computers and the high-pitched screeches of dial-up modems. After installing the Linux operating system and the new Netscape Navigator on his computer, one of the first things he did was to go to Playboy.com. He was impressed.

As an adult he became the owner of Playboy's digital assets.

Fabian found his way to the forums on CompuServe, where he chatted with strangers and found ways to access free porn by acquiring and sharing porn site links and passwords. Back then the only way to access porn was to pay for it, and he was too young to own a credit card. The seed was planted in his mind at that time—Fabian would someday find a way for the whole world to access free porn.[1] His vision for global free porn would one day come with a steep human cost.

When he was fifteen years old, he got paid to build a website for a neighbor. By the time Fabian was seventeen he had created a statistics service for tracking and harvesting online user data using bits of code and he needed access to high-traffic websites in order to use it. Incidentally, or not, the sites with the most traffic were porn sites. As he began meeting people online, he eventually met some who owned porn companies themselves.

With the advent of YouTube in 2005, the first of the free user-generated porn "tube sites" had begun to pop up, and Fabian took notice. Suddenly porn creation was no longer reserved for studios and porn professionals; anyone with a camera could make porn and upload it online. As Fabian observed the business trends in porn, he began to notice that the paywalled professional porn sites were taking a steep dive in traffic and revenue, as the free porn tube sites began to grow.

He noticed that many owners of porn subscription sites wanted to sell while there were still profits to be made. At the same time, free porn sites that were being poorly run were also being sold at a discount. An opportunist, Fabian saw this new disruption in the porn industry as his big chance.

His plan was to buy up both the free and pay sites together. The big idea was that if he owned them both, he could use the free websites to advertise his subscription sites. He figured out that if one company could dominate both types at the same time, it could create a profitable ecosystem by driving traffic and revenue for one another.

Fabian's big search for acquisitions eventually brought him to Montreal, where he seized the opportunity to scoop up a troubled porn company named Mansef. He bought the company for $130 million dollars, merged it with his own sites, and renamed it—retaining Feras Antoon and David Tassillo as VPs at his new Montreal company. Feras quickly became Fabian's right-hand man.

Fabian achieved his biggest coup when he acquired a $362 million, high-interest loan from Colbeck Capital and 125 secret investors who were later outed as including Cornell University and J.P. Morgan Chase.[2] With the new capital, Fabian went on a buying frenzy and rolled up the porn industry by purchasing most of the world's porn companies, including studios, tube sites, webcam sites, and brands. He was now the proud owner of Pornhub, Playboy online, Playboy TV, Brazzers, YouPorn, Tube8, Gaytube, PornMD, Peeperz, Mofos, Twistys, Digital Playground, Thumbzilla, Men.com, PornIQ, SexTube, Wicked Pictures, BigTitsWork, SexProAdventures, Lesbea, Spankwire, Webcams.com, SeanCody, Extremetube, Reality Kings, and countless others. Reality Kings alone had forty-four separate porn sites.

Within three years, Fabian's porn empire grew from two-hundred-plus employees to a staff of twelve hundred, with corporate offices expanding to Ireland, Cyprus, and the British Virgin Islands. Fabian had seized a monopoly on the global porn industry and was bringing in forty million dollars per month from sixty-five million visitors to his sites per day. Fabian had personally become so rich that the enormous fish tank in his lavish home required a diver to clean it once a week.[3]

But on December 4, 2012, at 7 a.m., one hundred Belgian police officers and German tax investigators drove through the private entrance of his luxurious estate in the exclusive suburb of Brussels called Tervuren. The brigade of law enforcement walked past his large collection of expensive sports cars, knocked on his door, and presented Fabian with an arrest warrant for tax evasion.

They raided and searched his house as well as his Hamburg offices, and investigators collected multiple terabytes of data. Suddenly Fabian's porn empire was on the verge of disaster. He needed to transfer ownership quickly.

While being held in a Belgian jail cell, he began planning his speedy exit from the company. According to public records, he sold most of the company to his VP Feras Antoon, who had been part of the evolving porn behemoth from its genesis. The rest he sold to VP David Tassillo. Feras became the new CEO and David became the COO. They renamed the company once again and this time they called it MindGeek.

The undercover journalist who sent me hundreds of pages of intel on the company tells me that based on his investigation, the "sale" to Antoon and Tassillo was just a show. He says Feras and David own only a small part of the company, but no one knows the identity of the person, or people, who own most of it. Fabian might still be a secret shareholder. Or he might not. *Someone* is the secret majority owner.

The real owners clearly don't want to be known.

Then the journalist gives me my first stern warning about what I am getting into. He tells me that Feras, particularly, is "brilliant, shady, and ruthless."

"Secure all your communications. Do not just open links anyone sends to you. Have two computers. One with your personal stuff and one for this case, but keep all important info on separate drives. Their tech is so advanced they could easily be spying on you. Change passwords often. This is who you are fighting."

He sends me two links to two online photos of "Feras Antoon."

"One of these is a fake photo and one of these is real," he says. "They hire search engine optimization companies to scrub their information from the internet and create fake profiles with fake pictures to throw people off."[4]

7

A FAMILY MAN AND PORN KING

Feras Antoon was born in Syria to George Antoon and Lailah Bouze, both of whom were engineers. People close to the Antoons told me that after they married, Lailah and George moved to Dubai to pursue their engineering careers, but women at that time were not allowed to both work and have babies. So when Lailah became pregnant with Feras, she went back to Syria to give birth to him and left him there with her mother for two years until they were reunited in Dubai. The family later emigrated to Montreal, Canada, and that is where a teenage Feras met classmate Nicole Manos and they fell in love.

After high school graduation, Feras and Nicole ended up at Concordia University in Montreal and continued their love affair. Nicole's brother, Stephan Manos, also a student at Concordia, and his classmates Ouissam Youssef and Matt Keezer were up to something secret and exciting. They were getting into the business of online porn, and it was doing surprisingly well. Manos soon invited Feras Antoon into the fold. In addition to being his sister's love interest, Feras was a genius with numbers. Feras and the other three launched the successful porn company Brazzers together in 2005.

The name Brazzers was a tribute to how they and their Middle Eastern friends pronounced the word "brothers."

Pornhub entered the picture when Keezer bought the domain name Pornhub.com at a Playboy Mansion party for $2,750. The site was launched by the four men in 2007, the same year Netflix began streaming videos. Their companies Brazzers, Pornhub, Sexpro, KeezMovies, Racks&Blacks, Tube8, and Extremetube all consolidated under the name Mansef (a combination of Manos and Youssef); and the company thrived while their owners kept low profiles.

The guys slept in their offices and worked weekends while hiring friends and fellow classmates, one of them another Concordia University student named David Tassillo. David was good at business, so he was able to help find financing and clients for the porn business and became part of the team. Mansef continued to grow, nearly doubling in size each year and going from 80 employees in 2007 to 250 in 2009.

But their good fortune suddenly ran out. In October 2009, the Organized Fraud Task Force of the US Secret Service seized $6.4 million from Mansef. Court records say Mansef created Premium Services, LLC, and opened a bank account with an initial deposit of fifty dollars. According to the criminal court documents, there was never any cash or checks deposited or withdrawn from the account, but in under two months they did sixty-seven wire transfers. The incoming wires totaled $9,460,105.07 and were from sources labeled by law enforcement as being high risk for money laundering.[1] Mansef was in deep trouble.

That is when Fabian showed up, bought the troubled porn company, and turned things around. But it wasn't long until Fabian himself was in legal trouble and had to "sell" the company to Feras. And although Feras publicly inherited Fabian's crown as the new King of Porn, he is still beholden to someone. It is known at the highest levels of the company that Feras has to report revenues on a monthly basis to a figure behind the scenes, a hidden partner who has an empty office in Montreal next to his, with no name written on the door.

––––––––––

When Feras moved into the executive suite on the sixth floor, he laid down a $20,000 imported rug and bought a red Ferrari and a yellow Lamborghini with vanity license plates that read "YALLA" (meaning "let's go" in Arabic) and "MRCEO." Feras got to work, but not as much for MindGeek as for himself and his kin. He had personal ambitions that extended beyond his porn conglomerate. Insiders close to Feras, with documented evidence and intimate knowledge of his professional life, personal life, and family life, educated me about this secretive man. They informed me that he oversees more than forty personal business ventures. Employees report that he comes to work just a few hours a day when he isn't off on expensive seven-week international luxury vacations with his extended family, paid for by MindGeek. Even though the company hasn't been getting the management attention that it needs from Feras, MindGeek is still a lucrative ATM for Feras and his family.

Family means everything to Feras. He is fiercely dedicated and loyal to them. He and his mother, Lailah, are so close that they try to have breakfast together multiple times per week. She knows all of his affairs and offers him constant advice. She has always supported his decision to get into the porn business. Her rationale has been, "If Feras doesn't make money from it, somebody else is going to, so it might as well be him." His father is a dedicated Catholic and didn't want his son to become a pornographer.

Feras has been married to Nicole for over a decade and he cherishes his three children. In step with Middle Eastern tradition, he has taken his role as eldest son of the family seriously and works to ensure his family is always provided for. His brother gets to be a VP at MindGeek, his sister buys and sells all of his real estate, and his brother-in-law is paid $15,000 per month by MindGeek to manage the "cafeteria." The MindGeek cafeteria is essentially a restaurant with a built-in customer base of over 1,000 employees daily. There is a free continental breakfast each morning for employees that includes Middle Eastern favorites such as za'atar bread, but I'm told lunch and everything else rakes in cash for the Antoon family.

Thanks to MindGeek Feras lives like a king. MindGeek pays for Feras's personal assistants, who do everything for him, including purchasing his underwear. They also pay for his personal rental property manager, who oversees his forty-seven high-end condominiums and luxury chalets in Quebec, for building supplies and expensive furniture for his new mansion, for his chauffeurs, and even for people to fill up his gas tank so he doesn't have to.

With a love for real estate investing, Feras went into business with a construction company called Broccolini to purchase new luxury condos in Montreal and also works long hours managing the design and construction of his own dream castle. He paid two million dollars to purchase land for his new home in one of Montreal's most exclusive neighborhoods nicknamed "Mafia Row" because its extravagant homes served as the hub of Montreal's Cosa Nostra, including the notorious Rizzuto crime family. His wealthy Italian neighbors with questionable pasts were livid when Feras cut down trees in the neighborhood's nature preserve to make way for his mansion. The house is nearing completion and he and Nicole are getting excited about moving in soon. The sprawling luxury residence has twenty-one rooms, nine garages, seven bathrooms, and four powder rooms, along with an infinity pool, a sports complex, and more. The kitchen alone is worth $700,000.

All of this extravagance has bled into a company culture where the VPs of MindGeek are known to their employees as "The Divas." The parking garage under the office building looks like a high-end car show, and the executives are obsessed with how much they can flaunt their wealth. Feras is known to be generous with his VPs, offering big raises and large bonuses, and giving out expensive presents. Yet he is only selectively generous to a handful of men who are loyal to him, who will look the other way when things seem legally suspect, and who take risks for him so he can do things with what he calls "plausible deniability." Feras and these men manage the sprawling, complicated MindGeek international structure of over two hundred related corporations in a way that is questionable by any legal standard. The group of top executives and Divas who preside over MindGeek with Feras has become known internally as the "Bro Club."

While Feras is extravagantly generous with those closest and most loyal to him, he is cheap with the rest of his foot soldiers. Even though he throws big holiday parties, the salaries for lower-level employees at Mind-Geek are notoriously low. His live-in nanny from the Philippines is reported by family insiders to work from 6 a.m. to 10 p.m. every day instead of a normal eight-hour shift. Although she is hired to take care of the children, he also demands that she cook, clean, and do laundry, all for $450 per week. When he goes on his extended vacations, he doesn't allow her the time off; instead he ships her to one of his relatives' homes so she can work for them while he is gone.

David Tassillo, the COO, was given the office nickname "Santana," and David and the employees in turn have their own nicknames for Feras. Some employees call Feras "Shrek" behind his back. The often-frustrated Chinese accountant Hongjun shared with his closest coworkers that he nicknamed Feras a "criminal." Feras and David have a contentious relationship. They mutually dislike each other, but David has reluctantly conceded that Feras is the one with the power. When there is a dispute on a decision, it's always Feras who gets the final word.

David and Feras are opposites in many ways. David mows his own lawn and often comes to work looking unkempt, in jeans and distressed T-shirts. Feras, on the other hand, arrives at the office with what little he has of his hair perfectly in place, his face devoid of wrinkles thanks to his regular

Botox injections, and dressed in thousands of dollars' worth of designer clothing. This includes a pink Valentino jacket his employees mock him for behind his back. David's vices include sexual escapades—which apparently everyone knows about, including his wife—drugs, and cars. His Porsche, three Lamborghinis, and seven Ferraris are brought to him by a special elevator from his mansion's lower level. While both men love porn for obvious reasons, Feras doesn't drink or do drugs. Some call him the "respectable one" of the pair.

If there is one thing to be said about Feras, it's that he is arrogant and entitled to an extreme degree. His power is something he doesn't take lightly. When an employee performs well, he doesn't *ask* them if they *want* to renew their contracts. He *tells* them they are *going* to renew their contracts. If employees so much as express any level of disagreement with him, he has been known to stand up at his desk, put his fists down, lean forward, look them in the eye, and say, "Do you know who I am? I am the CEO. No one crosses me, not even my VPs. You will do as I say."

I am told by sources close to Feras that I had better be careful. "He is paying a lot of money to private investigators, hackers, and IT professionals to go after you," they say. Not long after my article and petition went viral, Feras took notice and began following me on Twitter himself. At first I laughed when I saw the notice "Feras Antoon and 33 others followed you." Out of curiosity I clicked on the account with the handle "Feras-CEO." It had no profile image and only followed me along with a handful of Montreal-based accounts. At first, I thought it was a joke, but when the account suddenly changed its name to "Firras Anron" and its location to France, it seemed suspicious. To try to confirm who it was I did a log-in attempt with the username and clicked to reset the password. The email that showed up associated to the account was ce*@m*******.com. I stared at the address for a moment and quickly realized the email was ceo@mindgeek.com. No one but Feras would own that address tied to the MindGeek domain.

My Twitter became the go-to source for MindGeek employees to find out what is going on with "the scandal." MindGeek's lawyers advised Feras and David to be tight-lipped because anything they said could be used against them. Employees aren't getting updates or explanations, so they go to my Twitter account for the truth about what is happening. Feras wanted to know what they were reading about his company.

But Feras isn't the only MindGeek figure trying to hide his identity.

8

BLAKE THE FAKE

A new MindGeek whistleblower who calls himself "Rene" reaches out to me with information about the company, for which I'm grateful. He tells me that the executives and VPs of MindGeek in Montreal have been very careful to hide their identities and positions from the public. He then sends me the names of all VPs and executives in Montreal.

What Rene reveals next is disturbing. He tells me that the men who are named hundreds, if not thousands, of times in news articles as the official spokesmen for Pornhub are not real.

"What do you mean, they aren't real?" I ask.

He explains that Corey Urman, the VP of Pornhub whom he calls "the main boss of Pornhub," uses fake personas in order to hide his real identity from journalists and the public. Some of the names he uses include "Corey Price" and "Blake White." I instantly recognize those names, having seen them quoted in news stories. I contemplate the irony: the executives of Pornhub on the sixth floor of their shiny aquamarine Montreal tower hide their identities like cowards and criminals while filling their bank accounts with profits made from exposing the naked bodies of unwilling victims.

When I message Rene using an encrypted messaging app, he says he's happy to answer any questions but wants to remain anonymous since

Montreal is a "small town" and he doesn't want to put his family or friends in danger. Rene tells me that people running MindGeek are "rich men in the shadows financing it due to no competition." One piece of information he shares is especially significant.

"Read 2257 laws. If people had to adhere to 2257 when uploading, it would ruin Pornhub. 2257 scares them the most since it means legitimate ID on anyone that uploads," Rene says.

United States Law 18 USC 2257[1] is a federal law that was passed in 1988 requiring those who produce, transfer, and sell porn to obtain identification and age verification documents for each individual depicted in the videos. The law carries criminal penalties for violations, including up to five years in prison. The law was passed because without mandatory age verification, the porn industry would be awash with videos of underage victims. Anyone with half a brain understands this. But verifying the identification and age of those on Pornhub would cause more friction when uploading content, which means less content would be uploaded and less profit made. MindGeek claims they don't have to abide by USC 2257 because it's the site users who film and upload the videos.

I continue to chat for a couple weeks with this insider and by mid-March he is hearing that MindGeek management isn't happy with all the negative press generated by my petition, which is gaining thousands of signatures per day. "They're telling the employees that you are lying, and this will all go away soon." Then he adds a final stomach-turning fact, pertaining to the worldwide COVID lockdowns that have begun to shut people inside, causing them to feel isolated, anxious, bored, and needing distraction.

"Pornhub's profits are better than ever because of the virus."

———

Finally, after weeks of ignoring journalists, Pornhub starts responding to Traffickinghub in the media. I see the fake "Blake White," aka Pornhub's

VP Corey Urman, try to defend Pornhub against my statements in an article where I explain how anybody can get verified without showing proof of ID, age, or consent.

"Verified users are confirmed human uploaders, and content that violates the website's terms of service is removed as soon as we are made aware of it,"[2] the fake "Blake White" says.

Confirmed humans? What a relief. I'm so glad Pornhub is making sure that verified users aren't bots, aliens, or animals.

Mocking the ridiculousness of his defense, I pounce on Twitter with a screenshot of his "confirmed human" statement. Then referring to the rest of his absurd defense, I quote his "as soon as we are made aware of it" disclaimer. Victims spend weeks, months, and years begging MindGeek to take down their rape and child abuse videos, sometimes the videos are never removed, and he knows it. MindGeek shouldn't be allowing this content on the site to begin with.

Next, Corey tells *Daily News* in Australia that cases of confirmed child abuse on Pornhub "only amounts to less than one percent of its content."[3]

In response, I publish a screenshot of his words, adding:

"Here is Pornhub admitting they have children being raped & trafficked on their site. So 1% of videos featuring children being raped is the cost of doing business? Pornhub has 6.8 million uploads yearly, so as long as they stay under 68,000 child rape videos per year, no problem for them?"

Dozens of journalists are now following my Twitter account and my post spurs another news article. It feels good to see the media taking my cues and piling on.

But my amusement ends when I see a message from an anonymous account.

"If you get Pornhub shut down you're going missing too."

9

MY SICILIAN SIDE

For the past week, every time I type in a website or go to Google, my browser redirects to strange URLs I've never seen before. At the same time, Joel keeps getting notices that his various accounts have unusual log-in attempts or password changes. I shut down all my personal social media accounts and ask Joel and both our moms as well as immediate family members to do the same. This is inconvenient but not a huge loss. What hurts is taking down the memorial website we made for my dad. I never use my Twitter account for anything except anti-trafficking advocacy, so I keep it intact.

A tech friend connects me with a high-level data and security expert named James. When we talk, I am surprised at how much he knows about MindGeek. He says he's been researching them ahead of our call and suspects Eastern European organized crime is behind MindGeek. He also lets me know that they can easily hire a hacker to find out everything there is to know about me. "I guarantee they've already done it," James says, explaining that it is likely they already hired someone to look into my whole family.

I soon find out from a company insider that MindGeek has its own highly paid, unscrupulous French hacker and technology genius. "He is paid more than you can imagine, and is very good at his job," the insider tells me. "You need to be extremely careful."

James offers to hack me to show me my online vulnerabilities and I gratefully agree. A couple days later, he calls to tell me what he found that was compromising my online security and offers some useful tips.

"If you continue to draw attention to the crimes on their site and threaten their revenue, they will retaliate," James says. He tells me to be extra careful about protecting Joel and my devices. "If this traction continues, at some point they will accuse you or Joel of uploading child pornography yourselves. I won't be surprised if they try and hack you or Joel to plant it on your computers."

A couple days later James sees more headlines about me and Traffickinghub in the news, and he sends me another message.

"You are likely aware, but next thing they are going to do is try and discredit you," he tells me in a text. "Intimidation is always first. If you haven't gotten threats today, even with the coverage, you will soon. If it hasn't happened already, there are gonna be private investigators posing as allies or victims and asking questions.

"They will try and pry into your history or make one up. Your friends and family need to know two words: 'No comment.' They may try and claim you are in trouble or in danger. They may say that they already have dirt. They will really say anything to provoke a reaction, so nothing is best."

Another disturbing warning comes from a seasoned attorney who's been going after the notorious sex trafficking operation GirlsDoPorn that runs a popular partner channel on Pornhub. "We've had moles from the opposition posing as victims in order to get intel on what we are doing. Be very cautious about who you let in and what you reveal."

Two other security professionals I'm put in touch with agree with James. One of them is ex-CIA and the other has done security for the Bill and Melinda Gates Foundation, Christine Blasey Ford during the Judge Brett Kavanaugh Supreme Court hearings, and other high-profile clients. They both separately say that MindGeek certainly looks to them like organized crime is behind it. There is the complex corporate structure of nearly two hundred "brass plate" subsidiaries and related corporations around the world that are merely PO boxes and bank accounts. Then there is the registration in Luxembourg, the banking from Cyprus, a long history of financial crime, completely unknown owners, secretive executives using fake identities, and incredible amounts of money pouring in through a complex international web of sister companies.

"If it walks like a duck . . ." one of them says to me.

All of this starts to get to me. I want to fade into the background and stop pressing their buttons publicly.

I reach out to a child protection advocate who has been studying Mind-Geek for years to ask her opinion about what I'm hearing.

"Do you have a safe room?" she asks me in all seriousness. "If not, get one."

The next day Joel and I are asked to get on a call together with a friend who is a veteran attorney. He has spent decades managing crisis and criminal cases in Southeast Asia, Latin America, Russia, Turkey, and the Middle East related to organized crime. He has been looking into MindGeek since the petition started going viral and says he has some advice for us.

"I don't want to scare you, this isn't about fear, okay, this is about wisdom, not fear—I want you to be wise, okay, not scared." He then explains how he has dealt with these types of people and organizations for a long time. "I have a degree of confidence in telling you that organized crime is behind MindGeek."

I don't know how to respond. He is now the fifth experienced person I have spoken with who has said the same thing. "So what should I do?"

He doesn't answer, but instead asks another question. "Do you use a VPN on your devices when you go on Pornhub?"

"No."

I have heard of VPNs that people use to mask their location and IP addresses, but I have never used one.

"That means MindGeek knows where you are located, okay. No question. Download a VPN right away on all your devices. Don't text or call anymore directly on your phone, use an encrypted service like Signal or Threema. I also think you need to get a new phone and computer and get a secure modem to protect your internet signal. The modems I am talking about are a few thousand dollars so I will send you one for free. Since they already know where you are, I suggest that you and Joel and the kids leave your in-laws' house as quick as possible."

After we hang up, Joel and I look around in silence for a moment, thinking about what he just said. It feels to me like these advisors are over-reacting, but are they? Why would they? None of them are getting paid to help me. I don't have the money it would take to pay for the level of security services they provide, and they know that. They are helping because they care about the cause. There is no incentive for them to exaggerate any of this. But it still seems too crazy.

I trust Joel's judgment more than anyone. Not only is he skilled in the practical—he is a dentist, pilot, and builder—but he is also wise, thoughtful, and usually right about most things.

"What if what they are saying is true?" I ask him. "Should I just shut the petition down and stop all of this?"

In his usual levelheaded, matter-of-fact way, he gives an honest answer. "No way. Don't stop. You are meant to do this."

———————

I send screenshots of James's warning messages to my mom and sisters in a group text, which turns out to be a mistake.

My mom immediately calls, and I silence the ring. But as usual when she has something she thinks is important to tell me, even if it is just to remind me to call my grandma to say hi, she calls again . . . and again—until I answer. I ignore her second call, but she is unrelenting. I finally answer because I know she isn't going to stop.

"Hi, Mama. I love you. What?"

I'm slightly annoyed but not mad. We are close, and I know she loves me "more than her own life"—something she tells me frequently.

"You better stop this right now. You are putting yourself in danger! It's not worth it, you have done enough already! Shut down the petition and stop this!"

Like the passionate Sicilian mother she is, she curses a bit and offers a threat to emphasize her point.

"If you don't stop, I am going to call all of your coworkers and tell them you are in danger and they are responsible for making you stop this."

She doesn't have their phone numbers, I think with a smile, completely aware it's an empty threat.

"Mama, it's *fine*. Don't worry! You are *way* overreacting!"

"That's it, I am not taking this. You better call all this off *right now*," my mom says, and then hangs up on me.

My sister chimes in over our group text and doesn't help my case.

"Laila, you are being so irresponsible. Why would you put your kids and family in danger by continuing this? Focus on your own kids, they are what is important. My advice is stop now before you regret it."

Am I being irresponsible toward my own family? Am I making my children sacrifice for a cause they never signed up for? These are the questions that disturb me the most.

Even some of my anti-trafficking colleagues start saying maybe now is a good time to begin flying under the radar.

A few hours later I see a new message from an anonymous sender.

"I don't think you really want to do this. If you get Pornhub shut down, I'll come after you."

———————

Maybe it's my mom's Sicilian blood in me, but I've never been afraid of a just fight.

In first grade the class troublemaker harassed the girls, always finding ways to kiss them against their will as they squirmed in disgust. I warned him to stop but he wouldn't listen. One day as I bent my head down to drink from the water fountain at recess, he swooped in, put his lips on mine, and laughed. So, as he got ready to go down one of the steepest slides on the playground, I rushed in from behind and pushed him with all my force, sending him crashing down the slide. He cried, and I felt a sense of accomplishment.

When I was twenty-one, Bank of America cashed a fraudulent check I was given as payment for a violin I sold online for my older sister. I had no idea I was being scammed, but after I was held accountable for $2,000 I didn't have, the bank manager told me it happens all the time—especially to the elderly. I sued Bank of America for not having a strict policy in place to verify the watermarks on cashier's checks before cashing them to protect unsuspecting customers. I represented myself in court and was disappointed when I lost. My dad paid my debt and told me he was proud that I tried to face off with one of the biggest banks in the world.

When Joel started to build and remodel houses, he ended up hiring a plumber who ran off with $7,000 and delivered no work. I tried to get the money back, but he refused.

I found other victims online complaining that the same thing had happened to them, and I couldn't let it go. I had to go after him. I organized and brought together all his victims from the surrounding counties, compiled all the evidence of his patterns of fraud, and then tracked him and his family down. A disgruntled ex-girlfriend of his became my best informant. I turned the information in to the police and gave them the exact location, time, and flight number for his planned escape to Hawaii. The police arrested him before he got away. He was convicted of felony theft, given prison time, and forced to pay the money back plus interest. I told him by text before all of it began to make it right with his victims and return their money or he would regret it. I don't think he imagined I was serious.

In another memorable incident, my younger sister, a singer, spent half a year and all her savings organizing a music tour around the country. She proudly bought a Honda van from a local used car dealer thinking it would be the reliable choice of transportation, but as soon as she drove off the lot the "check engine" light came on. Come to find out it didn't have a Honda engine at all. It had a broken junkyard engine and failing transmission. She was tricked and sold a lemon. She begged the owner of the dealership to give her money back, but he smugly refused.

It just wasn't right. I couldn't let this unethical car salesman get away with defrauding my sister. The same day, I walked into the city permit office and got a protest permit. I parked the van in front of the dealership plastered with neon signs that said "Junkyard Engine" and "Failing Transmission" and stood next to it waving huge pieces of posterboard that said, "They Sold Us a Lemon." I stood there calling out the dealer all day, every day, in the freezing rain as cars passed honking in support. Some people brought hot chocolate to help raise morale. The dealer thought I would eventually give up, but I told him I wouldn't stop until he gave back every penny and I wasn't lying.

He soon turned to gun threats and calling the police to get me to leave, but since I was on a public street with a permit, engaging in a peaceful protest, he couldn't get rid of me.

The dealership lost every customer each day (because I warned each one as they drove up) and his partner eventually quit in anger and shame. As a divine exclamation point, lightning struck the huge tree above his trailer office and the tree fell straight through the roof. The next day I finally got all the money back for my sister.

For as long as I can remember, I've had a soft spot for the underdog, long shot, and bully's victim. A desire to go after abusers must be part of my DNA. Whenever my friends or family needed someone to confront an unjust situation, they called on me to do it for them. Now looking back, experiences like those feel like they were preparation for what I am getting into right now.

10

PLAYBOY MANSION
TO PRAYER ROOM

To be sure, I haven't always been motivated by the cause of others. I have had my share of completely selfish ambitions.

In my early twenties, my big dream was to sport a BMW convertible and drive from Malibu to Hollywood every day on the Pacific Coast Highway, make boatloads of money as an entertainment attorney, and live a glamorous, star-studded life.

Why Hollywood? After years of training, my father held me back from joining Montreal's Cirque du Soleil, so I settled for performing in a local acrobatics show in Southern California where I befriended a young exotic dancer. She was incredible at pole dancing, a talent that made her good at the ribbon, trampoline, and everything acrobatic. She recruited me to join her as a "trampoline girl" on Jimmy Kimmel's *The Man Show* and I thought it sounded fun. After a few stints doing flips on a big trampoline in a bikini for a few hundred dollars, I met more and more people in the entertainment industry.

I dated producers, actors, and directors who made famous films, and was frequently being invited to premieres and parties where I mixed with industry professionals and celebrities—even at the Playboy Mansion.

But slowly the sparkle and glamour began to fade. One night at a party in Beverly Hills I was groped by a celebrity plastic surgeon. I felt disgusted and angry with myself for not stopping his unwanted advance. My tipping point came when I woke up one morning after a party and found myself on a dirty carpet that reeked of vomit, after a night of blacking out drunk and on drugs. I had no idea what had transpired the night before and the thought terrified me.

During that time, I also suffered a bad car accident and a devastating romantic heartbreak. I spun into a season of deep depression, feeling totally lost, empty, and not knowing what direction to go in life. I started taking narcotic pain medicine to numb myself and could only sleep by taking sleeping pills or crying until I was too exhausted to stay awake.

One particularly hard night I drew a picture of how I felt. I drew a flower at the bottom of a deep pit—I was the flower. Rain poured down, flooding the ground and filling up the pit, the deep water threatening to drown the fragile flower. As I sat on the edge of my bed, staring at the picture with tears dripping onto the page, I had the impulse to grab my childhood Bible from the nightstand drawer. I randomly opened it and read the first thing I saw on the page.

> Let not the flood water overwhelm me,
> nor the deep waters swallow me up,
> nor the pit shut its mouth over me.

It was a description of my picture. Spooked, I dropped the Bible, then started crying harder. "Someone is watching me," I thought. As I wept, fright transitioned into gratitude that maybe I wasn't alone. There was something beyond me, present with me in my darkest moments. After that incident, I started reading more. My favorite spiritual teacher became a man named Dr. Wayne Dyer, who wrote one of the most influential books on my life called *Inspiration*. His words resonated deeply:

Stop acting as if life is a rehearsal. Live this day as if it were your last. The past is over and gone. The future is not guaranteed . . . When you are able to shift your inner awareness to how you can serve others, and when you make this the central focus of your life, you will then be in a position to know true miracles . . . God's message is to love all people, without exception, so we can be in harmony with him . . . People need to learn how to respond to each other's hatreds with love—which is what Jesus taught us . . . don't be Christian, be Christ-like.

I had always been put off by the rigidity of organized religion and the hypocrisy of many churches and their leaders. But I was intrigued and inspired by Jesus and began to study his every word. He seemed like a counterculture rebel who flipped tables when he was angry, who despised and antagonized overly religious people, unconditionally loved social outcasts and the poor, and defended who the self-righteous liked to judge. I loved this wild, passionate, and irreverent man and started to take his words seriously.

One day I was inspired to go sit with the homeless community in my city and couldn't resist going back to spend more and more time with them. I didn't have anything to prove; they were so humble and made me feel comfortable being myself. We had fun joking, laughing, and talking about meaningful subjects. As I got to know them on a personal level, I soon came to love them.

After listening to their desires, I found little ways to empower them. I would let them use my address to get mail and access government assistance checks, help them fill out job applications, get them gas or drive them to appointments, vouch for them to landlords, and things like that. Over time, one by one, each of my friends got sober and off the street.

These friends gave me much more than I ever gave them. At a time of confusion and uncertainty about the direction of my life, they helped me understand where to find real happiness and fulfillment. I decided to focus my energy and studies in the direction of human rights and justice for oppressed groups like my dad always hoped I would.

Right after Joel and I married, I accepted an internship at the United Nations in Geneva, Switzerland. I was excited because the Geneva internship could open the door to a full-time position. My Big Dream shifted from Hollywood success to a job at the United Nations combating human trafficking. But soon I became disillusioned with the bureaucracy of the UN and met one too many jaded career diplomats who seemed to care more about titles and rank than the injustices they were there to fight. I left Geneva, unsure of what could be next.

I felt lost again. I spent years learning and training, up through my master's degree in public diplomacy at USC, focusing on the issue of human trafficking. I formed my own small nonprofit organization to provide necessities to those suffering from extreme poverty in some of the poorest countries in the world. I knew alleviating vulnerabilities by meeting basic needs was important upstream anti-trafficking work, but I felt a strong desire to do more.

Desperate for guidance, I committed forty days to meditation, prayer, and fasting to seek direction. Near the end of this time, I began to have recurring dreams about going to Kansas City, Missouri. This was unusual, as I had only passed through Kansas City or Missouri on the way elsewhere. In fact, I used to make fun of my childhood best friend from California who ended up there. "You live in misery, not Missouri," I would tease.

My curiosity was piqued, so I searched online for anti-trafficking organizations in Kansas City and came across a movie trailer for a new anti-trafficking documentary called *Nefarious: Merchant of Souls*. Produced by a small organization in Kansas City called Exodus Cry, it was one of the most compelling things I had ever seen. Their approach focused on fighting modern slavery and trafficking by modeling tactics of the historical abolitionist William Wilberforce, who ended slavery in the United Kingdom by raising awareness and changing laws. I loved it. With my background in political science, international relations, and diplomacy, it felt like a perfect fit, maybe even an inspired one.

I found the CEO of Exodus Cry, named Benjamin Nolot ("Benji"), on Facebook, sent him a friend request with a writing sample and résumé, and he quickly hired me. Joel agreed it was the right thing to do, so we took a chance and moved from the West Coast to Kansas City.

I quickly learned that Exodus Cry was born out of a weekly anti-trafficking prayer meeting at a place called the Global Prayer Room of the International House of Prayer, located near their office. This "prayer room" was a literal room that could hold a few hundred people when full, in an unassuming strip mall in a Kansas City suburb where people from around the globe were coming to meditate and pray—and it was open with music emanating from the room, twenty-four hours a day, seven days a week.

The people in the room were from all different denominations, different countries, different backgrounds, old and young. Protestants, Catholics, Messianic Jews, Episcopalians, Pentecostals, and more. It was a casual setting—some people were meditating, praying quietly, or reading. Students in hoodies were working on their laptops and others were singing to the music. Anyone could get on the microphone to pray.

Once a week there was a time of prayer focused on ending human trafficking. Benji, the leader of Exodus Cry, would pray not only for victims but for their traffickers as well. "God, please free them and free the hearts of their abusers," he would often pray with genuine tears of compassion.

I was rarely in the Exodus Cry office, spending most of my time traveling to different countries and speaking to government leaders, sharing the documentary, and advocating for laws that would prevent trafficking. It was energizing and exciting work, and I loved it. My coworkers knew I had a special interest in investigating the porn industry's ties to sex trafficking and they wanted to do a documentary on the subject. I was asked to help with the research and started spending more and more time looking into the connections between trafficking and porn.

When I wasn't traveling for my work, Joel and I spent much of our time with his family in Washington state. Joel filled in for local dentists when they needed help while getting his construction business running. I worked remotely for most of my time with Exodus Cry, but despite the distance, some of my colleagues were there for me more than anyone when my dad died. They were like a lifeline during those dark days, always encouraging me and constantly pulling me out of the abyss of depression and despair. They became real friends to me.

Then came an attack on them that I didn't see coming.

11

WHEN SNAKES ARE CORNERED

It's still the early days of COVID, and I am sitting on the floor of the play closet sporting a green pointy felt hat with a red feather, holding a cup of coffee in one hand and my cell phone in the other. I'm a lousy excuse for Peter Pan, but my daughter Lily Rose is splendid as Wendy. As always, I'm trying my best to put my heart into it and enjoy time with her, but my phone is suddenly demanding my attention. I feel Lily's tiny hand under my chin trying to pry my eyes off the phone and pleading with me to pay attention to our game, but I am too engrossed in what I'm reading. She starts to cry but I can't wrench myself away. It's too urgent—everything feels too urgent these days.

"You definitely have Pornhub's attention. They're watching you."

The warning comes from a Global News journalist in Canada. He says that MindGeek is keeping a close eye on exactly how many signatures the petition has and are watching my Twitter account closely. He wants to write a story about Pornhub, but they are trying to intimidate him.

"We have a platform of four million people, and this story needs to be told," he tells me. "But they are attempting to shut down media companies, which is why I have to be careful. They will pursue legal action, that is what they told me . . ."

I recently learned that MindGeek employed a high-powered New York public relations firm specializing in crisis management called 5wPR. The company describes itself as "a street fighter, an agency 'in the know' with the ability to turn stories around." They claim that "there is no more aggressive PR crisis agency in the United States." Specifically, MindGeek hired 5wPR's CEO and owner, who is noted for being "callous" and "ruthless in taking down his enemies."

"'Genteel' is not often used to describe me," he once told *Ad Age* with pride.[1] Because this man created a fake PR industry news site to bolster his own company and disparage his rivals, the Public Relations Society of America's New York Chapter unanimously voted to condemn him, calling his tactics "cowardly" and a "stain on our profession."[2]

Pornhub's VP Corey Urman may have fumbled his previous media statements, but now 5wPR is coaching Urman and he unleashes a vicious media attack. A Swiss journalist doing a story about Pornhub's victims warns me about what Pornhub is saying about me and Traffickinghub. She forwards me the emails she's exchanging with Pornhub's spokesman, likely Corey Urman in disguise again using a pseudonym. He claims my "accusations are simply categorically false" and that she doesn't have "the full story."

"The petition is factually wrong and intentionally misleading," he says. "The group behind it has constantly spewed hate speech against women's rights groups, anti-abortion, the LGBTQ community, minorities, Jewish people, and more. These guys have been getting a lot of publicity the last few weeks, but they are literally just a religious fundamentalist organization masquerading as a women's rights group in order to push their agenda under the guise of righteousness."

As "proof" he tells her I am connected to Exodus Cry and that the organization engages in prayer at the International House of Prayer. He then sends her screenshots of seven-year-old tweets from Benji, the founder of

Exodus Cry's personal account, where he denounces abortion and the legalization of same-sex marriage. Considering that Exodus Cry is an anti-trafficking organization that doesn't address abortion or same-sex marriage, this is an obvious redirection tactic. Besides that, although Exodus Cry supports Traffickinghub, the movement was neither started by nor is run by Exodus Cry. As I maintained from the beginning, Traffickinghub is a movement of many people and organizations from all backgrounds and no single organization owns it.

I know now that Corey is sending those lies to every journalist that reaches out to him regarding their "scandal." In the emails to the journalist, Corey kept promising to provide her with a statement she could publish, but not until he was done smearing Traffickinghub.

"Just get me your statement, please," she asked in exasperation.

Corey pressed her. "I'll get you the statement but is what I am saying impacting the premise of your piece at all? I think it is highly critical information that discredits every single thing this group is saying and doing."

"I am a journalist. I did my research."

Corey was relentless. "I'll get you a statement addressing your piece as soon as I understand what it is about. Is it about how an anti-porn fundamentalist organization is scamming people into signing a petition pretending they are a women's rights organization?"

"Please just send me your statement," she said.

"I don't want to see this story run before I speak with your editor," he replied condescendingly.

I soon see the first media statement since Pornhub's new attack strategy began. It quotes the *fake* Blake White again. He claims that Pornhub has a "steadfast commitment" to fighting all illegal content and boasts of supposed "state-of-the-art" actions they're "working to put in place." He finishes with his false attack: "The petition is not only factually wrong and intentionally misleading, but it was created and is promoted by a radical right-wing fundamentalist group in the United States . . . who've vilified and attacked

LGBTQ communities and women's rights groups, aligned themselves with hate groups, and espoused extremist and despicable language."

I am confused and exasperated—unsure of how to respond. These accusations aren't true, but people reading these statements in the news won't know that. They don't know me. They'll believe what they read, and the thought infuriates me. Corey is merely *projecting* everything that is on *their own* website at this very moment. I find fleeting consolation by telling myself Pornhub will regret their lies when their hypocrisy is exposed.

I pull out my laptop and painfully document a trove of actual anti-LGBTQ content on "Pornhub Gay" that uses derogatory words like "tranny," "faggot," and "shemale." Heartrending homemade videos abound, denigrating and abusing young-looking boys with titles like "Young Twink Gets Slapped and Spit On" and "Daddy Came Home Frustrated and Abused Boy to Crying." There is also a horrifying abundance of extreme racism, *actual* hateful and "despicable language" throughout Pornhub. They are even promoting a video of one of their own Pornhub "models" where the woman is wearing a "White Lives Matter" shirt, referring to African Americans as "monkeys." Even writing the words down is hard, but I'm compelled to show the world the disgusting reality. I post about it on social media and submit an article[3] to *The New York Post* exposing Pornhub's extreme racism as a counterpunch:

> A for-profit partner channel on Pornhub called Black Patrol sexualizes police brutality against African-Americans with titles such as "White Cops Track Down and Fuck Black Deadbeat Dad." Countless other titles on Pornhub feature variations on the N-word and "white master." "Exploited black teens" and "black slave" are suggested search terms deliberately promoted by Pornhub to its users. If the titles repulse you, imagine what the videos do to the ever-younger eyes and minds that daily encounter this hardcore, racist porn.
>
> African-Americans aren't the only community denigrated for

pleasure and profit on Pornhub. There are also loads of anti-Semitic content on the site. Pornhub had approved and monetized with ads videos with titles such as "Nazi Rick & Morty Have Sex at Auschwitz" and "Nazi Fuck Camp" (involving "Jewish corpses"). Wildly anti-Semitic videos such as these are uploaded by Pornhub verified users, accounts with usernames like "OvenBakedJew" and "Hitler the Jew-Slayer." Many of these videos have remained on the site for months and years and Pornhub places monetized ads all over these videos . . .

In addition to striking back at Pornhub myself, I suggest that Exodus Cry immediately post an official response statement online to get ahead of the attacks.

MindGeek *cannot* get the upper hand in the fight to control the media narrative.

Exasperated, I call Joel, who is currently in Colorado for the week working on our house building project. He listens quietly while I unload everything that's happening. When I finish, a long silence hangs in the air.

"Hello? Are you still there?" I ask in frustration.

Finally, he responds.

"Laila, the petition is growing by thousands every day, victims are coming forward. This is spreading all over the world in the news. These guys are scared of what could happen and that's why they're attacking. Snakes are the most dangerous when they're cornered."

Joel is a man of few words, but when he does speak his words carry weight.

After he hangs up, I take a deep breath.

Joel is right. The Traffickinghub movement is a growing nightmare for MindGeek. They aren't addressing the *facts* because they *can't fight this on the merits*. They have no choice but to attack with lies, and assaults on character and credibility to slow the truth about them from spreading.

One thing is clear: MindGeek plays dirty, and this is going to be a messy fight.

12

WHO IS @EYEDECO?

Inspired by the Traffickinghub petition, protestors are gathering on International Women's Day in front of the MindGeek headquarters in Montreal. Helping to lead the protest will be an Independent senator for Quebec named Julie Milville-Dechêne. A few days before the protest I post on Twitter about Senator Deschene attending, unaware of the consequences my simple announcement will bring.

Some account on Twitter named "@EyeDeco" attacks the senator and seems invested in fighting the protest. They are tweeting at her over and over, saying the same things that MindGeek has been saying to journalists—that Traffickinghub is a far-right, racist, evangelical, anti-LGBT hate group and that she should not associate herself with the protest. The senator calls to ask me about the attacks and I explain how they are lies. She understands that I'm telling the truth and sticks with the plan.

We're in the process of collecting hundreds of thousands of signatures on the petition to shut down Pornhub from almost every country in the world. Grassroots protests are being held weekly in front of MindGeek offices in Montreal and Los Angeles,[1] and articles exposing Pornhub are being published nonstop. Momentum is building, but resistance is building too.

In the last few weeks I have had prostitution escort ads made in my name, my face superimposed onto pornographic images being circulated online, and more threats. MindGeek has hired "journalists" to write hit pieces against me and the cause, sending them around to news outlets wanting to report on my work in an effort to smear and discredit the growing movement. Mike Bowe's investigators uncovered one such "journalist," a woman in the porn industry using the pseudonym "Justine Halley" who is being paid by MindGeek to carry out these kinds of attacks.[2]

The fight becomes even more personal when I learn that the Twitter account @EyeDeco has just doxed me and my family online. I'm alerted to this from a member of the Traffickinghub "digital street team," a small and dedicated group of Traffickinghub activists that has taken it upon themselves to look out for me and the movement online by flagging threats. The @EyeDeco account is posting our home addresses and other sensitive information, such as the address of a home that my mother owns, suggesting it is a brothel available for prostitution being rented by the hour. I report the posts in a panic trying to get them taken down, but they remain online. I call my mom and sisters to warn them about what is going on.

"There are people exposing our family online in order to intimidate me, so you have to be careful," I warn them. "Make sure you are securing your online accounts and changing your passwords."

I quickly take it into my own hands to fully disable my mother's social media accounts entirely, along with changing her iCloud password and all her bank account usernames and passwords. Soon I get a call from my sister, who speaks in a frantic voice.

"Laila—our bank accounts and credit card accounts were just hacked, and all the money was drained from each one. They hacked our iCloud too."

She proceeds to explain that a topless photo she had sent privately to her husband was taken from iCloud and sent to him over text from an anonymous number with a threatening message that it would be leaked further. These hackers also obtained family photos of their naked newborn along with photos of my sister giving birth. My sister is terrified this person is going to share these online. I can hardly believe what I am hearing.

As she talks, I remember the warning I received from a MindGeek employee about the highly paid MindGeek hacker and his team.

"Be careful, they are highly skilled, and they have no ethics. It's a dangerous combination."

I tried my best to secure my own accounts, but now I regret not trying harder for my family. They don't blame me for what is happening, but I have a sense of guilt thinking I could have prevented this had I stopped the fight when my mom and sisters told me to.

As I am trying to process what happened I see a Pornhub victim's number on my caller ID and pick up. It's Rose the victim featured in the BBC story published the day after my *Washington Examiner* piece.

"I am sorry to randomly call you, but I am so upset right now, my hands are shaking so badly and I can't text," she says.

13

PORNHUB'S ADMISSIONS UNEARTHED

Rose gathers her composure and goes on to tell me that Pornhub is publicly calling her a liar online and then sends me a link to a Reddit thread. I scroll through the comments and quickly spot what she's talking about. On Pornhub's official account, their senior community manager "Katie" is saying that Pornhub has access to every single video uploaded to their site since its inception and that they can't find the videos or titles Rose cited.[1]

I open Pornhub in another browser tab and type in the video titles referenced in the BBC article and videos with similar titles and tags are *easy* to find. I see "crying teen," "abused teen," "exploited teens," "extra young punished," and many more.

As I reread the response from Pornhub, something catches my eye that I didn't notice the first time. Pornhub's senior manager just openly admitted that they *store and possess* on their servers all of the videos and images they have ever had on Pornhub.

Katie said that they had access to *every* video in their vast library going all the way back to before 2009. This means they admitted to storing all of the *child* sexual abuse videos that have ever been on their site, which is a felony crime.

Pornhub just publicly confessed to a federal felony.

It is illegal for even a victim to possess their own child sexual abuse videos. I have to be meticulously careful when documenting evidence on Pornhub not to capture an explicit image of a child. If the subject of a video is a child, it is only legal to capture URLs, titles, tags, comments, advertisements, and only images of faces that don't show any nudity.

But here we have Pornhub openly admitting that they possess an untold number of these criminal images on their servers. I screenshot Katie's comments.

I wonder what else Pornhub's senior manager has openly posted about.

I spend hours combing through every comment that this person has made on Reddit and am amazed by what I am finding—a gold mine of incriminating comments from Pornhub's own mouth.

In one thread a distraught user says, "There is child porn all over Pornhub," and asks for advice on what to do. Katie from Pornhub jumps into the thread. "You don't need to report the URLs to an agency," she says, and directs the user to send Pornhub the links instead.[2]

A senior manager of Pornhub just told someone *not to report* child sexual abuse videos they found on the site to the authorities.

I screenshot it ten different ways. I suspect as soon as I expose this, they will start deleting things.

Soon I document her admitting that they don't verify age or ID because "It costs us money." She then admits they "would lose 50% of traffic" to the site if they were to age-verify to keep children off the site. "It would be a disaster," she admits.[3]

I keep going and find another admission. "Help I am underage and images of me as a child are on Pornhub!" a Reddit user posts in an obvious panic. Katie from Pornhub is tagged and there is no response. Then finally, well into the next day, she callously replies, "I was asleep."[4] No apology and no sign of any concern, empathy, or compassion for this desperate child. Katie tells the child to go to Pornhub to report her abuse and that was it.

I fume as I read the comment. Pornhub senior management just directed a *child* to their *porn site* to report *her own sexual abuse.*

Over the next few hours I find more and more evidence that Pornhub knew there was child abuse, rape, and nonconsensual content all over the site but didn't care. In one particularly disturbing post, someone begs Pornhub to take down videos of them being raped when they were a *toddler*. In response, "Katie" bristles, saying, "I see your three e-mails (*to Pornhub*) . . . the content was removed . . ." She adds that they supposedly reported the abuse videos to the National Center for Missing and Exploited Children.

Pornhub just publicly admitted that a toddler was being raped on their site.[5]

MindGeek may be big, but they are sloppy.

I email all the screenshots to Mike Bowe and start posting the evidence on social media.

As the global headlines keep piling up day after day, exposing more and more of the world to the fact that their website is a crime scene, Pornhub quickly moves deeper into defense mode, and in doing so they make a huge mistake. They post on their website and start adding to their public statements that "***Every*** *video and photo is reviewed manually before upload by a large and extensive team of human moderators.*"

Including videos of toddlers being raped.

Every video, Pornhub? Are you sure about that?

14

"CLEANEST PORN EVER"

By April 2020, reports of daily COVID death tolls have become the wallpaper of our lives and there is a palpable fear in the air. People are reaching what will soon be a breaking point if there is no relief, and tonight the world-famous *Saturday Night Live* comedy show offers millions of viewers much-needed laughter. The centerpiece of *SNL*'s show is a faux commercial.

As the "advertisement" begins to play, the city streets are empty while a piano plays somber and haunting notes. A weary woman stares out a window as a voice-over says, "We don't know how long this will last." Places look abandoned while people peer through bedroom blinds wondering what the future will look like. Everybody watching knows this is talking about the pandemic.

"But no matter what happens next, we'll be here for you because you've been there for us," the commercial says.

Various people are shown looking at their laptop, tablet, or phone until everything turns to white and the advertiser's name scrawls across the screen.

"Pornhub."

The famous logo is pictured while the soothing woman's voice continues her narration.

"Here for you, for however long it takes."

The fake commercial is comical—if you don't know the truth about Pornhub. But watching it makes my stomach turn. I wish I could pick up the phone and call the producers and share the reality of what they are making light of. So much pain and suffering, for so many victims. But to those who don't know, it's all just a big joke—a wink-wink to the cheeky and culturally relevant Pornhub, world famous for making everyone feel good.

Pornhub is loving it.

On top of this significant moment for Pornhub, the big New York crisis PR firm 5wPR is working overtime with MindGeek to clean up Pornhub's negative press and turn the story around. Pornhub has always done disingenuous PR stunts to prop up its public image; things like highly publicized campaigns to "save the whales," "save the oceans," and even to "save the boobs" by urging users to watch more porn to raise money for breast cancer research. Now they are taking it up a notch. They are rolling out a huge global campaign to capitalize on coronavirus. They changed the name and logo on Pornhub to "Stayhomehub" and announced to the press that they are donating fifty thousand masks to New York City first responders. The coup de grace of the PR blitz is MindGeek offering free Pornhub Premium to the *entire world* to help people "stay home" and "flatten the curve."

News outlets all over the world are churning out story after story about Pornhub's new PR stunt and their site traffic is exploding, hitting new all-time records. Headlines read:

PORNHUB TRAFFIC SURGES AS PREMIUM GOES FREE DURING CORONAVIRUS LOCKDOWN

MindGeek also creates a flashy new "safe for work" website for the PR campaign called Scrubhub. The *Forbes* headline reads, "Pornhub Says Wash Your Hands with Launch of Porn-Parody Site Scrubhub." The nauseating adulation of the *Forbes* journalist Curtis Silver lacks even an ounce of critical thinking as to why Pornhub would be doing these PR stunts. "Scrubhub is like Pornhub except with a lot more handwashing and a lot less porn . . . The videos serve the dual purpose of education through entertainment and sourcing donations for worthy charities."

A few days later, *Forbes*'s Silver is at it again, promoting the next installment of the media blitz: "Pornhub's 'Cleanest Porn Ever' Campaign Encourages Staying Clean While Thinking Dirty." He goes on: "If there is one industry that has been thriving through the novel coronavirus pandemic and its associated stay-at-home orders, it's the porn industry. Pornhub has fared especially well and continues to launch initiatives of an all-together altruistic nature. This week it's Pornhub's 'Cleanest Porn Ever' campaign . . . that educates the public on staying clean."

I feel ill as I read the nonstop global headlines praising Pornhub for their "clean porn" and "generous altruism." Because as the Queen of Porn, Jenna Jameson, said herself, Pornhub is a "rathole of child pornography."

15

BETRAYAL FROM WITHIN

At least Traffickinghub activists are not letting Pornhub off the hook that easy. On Twitter Pornhub posted a video bragging about the enormous jump in site "traffic" because of the coronavirus stunt, and to their surprise they were swarmed by hundreds of citizen activists, including victims, calling them out for being involved in the "traffic" of children. As I scroll the comments on the Pornhub post, I see hundreds of people posting screenshots of the news story of the fifteen-year-old from Florida who was raped in fifty-eight videos on the site. So many are using the hashtag #Traffickinghub, posting links to the petition and calling them out. It is like a swarm of killer bees has descended. Pornhub is blocking people, including actual victims of their site, left and right, but they can't stop the virtual attack. The relentless online activists start posting screenshots of being blocked by Pornhub as a badge of honor, tapping their followers to take their place as they get knocked out of the fight. They don't stop at this post. Now Pornhub can't post anything without being swarmed by activists calling them out. So what do they do? They shut off their comments to try to silence the onslaught of truth, and they don't turn them back on.

Unlike *Forbes*, Reuters at least makes a weak attempt to acknowledge illegal content on Pornhub as context for the new PR campaign. ". . . The offer by one of the world's biggest porn sites to stream its top service for free was condemned by critics as a move to exploit the coronavirus crisis and silence complaints that videos on its platform featured sex trafficking victims . . ."

The Reuters journalist asks me for a short response, and I point out that more traffic means more unvetted videos, resulting in increased criminal exploitation of victims. But the criticism is quickly shut down with a quote from the Internet Watch Foundation spokesperson I talked to a few weeks ago. She tells Reuters, "Everyday sites that you and I might use as social networks or other communications tools, they pose more of an issue of child sexual abuse material than Pornhub does."

Once again, I'm dumbfounded with her implied defense of Pornhub.

A huge "child protection" organization is publicly protecting Pornhub. Why?

I want to throw my phone as I am reading her words. I know Pornhub is going to milk that statement from IWF, and they immediately do as they start including it in nearly every defense statement in the media from that moment on. It just doesn't make any sense that IWF would do this, so I reach out to some of my friends at other organizations to get their opinions on why. One friend gives me a helpful answer.

"This kind of thing seems to always come down to funding. Have you checked out who their major supporters are?"

"No, but I should," I say. I've hardly had time to buy groceries and do the dishes with all of the incoming calls, texts, emails, meetings, interview requests, and comment deadlines from journalists.

That night after getting Jed and Lily Rose to bed, I start digging on Google. One of the things I search is the name of the CEO of IWF, Fred Langford. I find out he is also simultaneously the president of an organization that is a global coalition of nonprofits combating child sexual abuse videos online called the International Association of Internet Hotlines (INHOPE). Fred must be a busy man leading both IWF and INHOPE at the same time.

I keep plugging things in. "Fred Langford" and "MindGeek" . . . Nothing.

"IWF" and "MindGeek" yields no results. But when I type in "INHOPE" and "MindGeek," I gasp when I see what pops up:

MINDGEEK AND INHOPE JOIN FORCES TO PROTECT CHILDREN ONLINE

The headline of the June 2019 press release from MindGeek says it all.

> MindGeek, a global leader in online and mobile, high-quality entertainment, and the International Association of Internet Hotlines (INHOPE) today announced a formal partnership that will help further their mission of keeping children out of, and away, from age-restricted media. MindGeek will be donating to INHOPE to support the organization's efforts in this endeavor and will become an INHOPE corporate partner.[1]

For a moment I sit and stare at the screen.

It all makes sense now, but it burns. It is a betrayal, not just of myself but of the countless child victims MindGeek has made money exploiting. How could any child protection organization take funding from Mind-Geek? There couldn't be a more blatant conflict of interest.

Fred has some explaining to do. I call out Fred on Twitter by tagging him as I angrily post: "Fred as the CEO of the organization that confirmed 118 instances of child rape and abuse on Pornhub, why would you take money from them?"

He doesn't respond but instead goes dark and locks his Twitter account.

In anger and disbelief, I take the information to Martin Patriquin, a respected journalist in Montreal, and he starts digging. He finds out additional details and publishes a significant story exposing what amounts to a scandal. INHOPE returns the money to MindGeek, publicly condemns Pornhub, and apologizes for what they did.[2]

Then Fred resigns.

16

CONFRONTING
THE CREDIT CARDS

Joel and I take the kids to California to stay with my mom for a few weeks during the lockdown. Working from my father's old mahogany desk, I smile as I see my mom's brother Mario sitting in my dad's oversize recliner in the next room, shaking his head to a Beach Boys song playing through his old Walkman as he munches a Hershey bar in total bliss. Mario's physical and mental handicap has given him the mind, heart, and sweet innocence of a five-year-old child who will never grow a day older. My mother has been his caregiver ever since their own parents died before I was born, and Mario has always been more of a beloved brother than an uncle to me.

I am brought back to the present by my calendar notification chime. It's time to dial in to a meeting arranged by a national organization that fights sexual abuse called the National Center on Sexual Exploitation. They are giving me the opportunity to share what I have learned about Pornhub with their contact, Elizabeth Scofield, Visa's director of global brand protection. In the most diplomatic way I can, I make it clear to Elizabeth that Visa is profiting from sex trafficking, rape, and child abuse by allowing their card to be used to process Pornhub advertisements, premium memberships, and video sales.

She pushes back and questions some of what I tell her, but there is no getting around the facts as I continue to lay them out as clearly as possible. By the end of the call, she seems convinced. She says she genuinely wants to help and will take this information to the top of the chain at Visa to press for a decision. She follows up soon after the call, asking me to send her information that she can present to the other decision makers at Visa.

Is it going to be this easy? Will I get a call next week letting me know that the Visa executives reviewed the information and decided to cut off Pornhub? My dad's words of wise skepticism come to mind: "If it seems too good to be true, it probably is."

I send her a detailed presentation showing evidence of what I told her on the phone. I assure her it is safe to open because there are no explicit images, but it comes with a strong trigger warning. In addition to news headlines, I include screenshots of the faces of passed-out victims, women shielding their faces from the camera, and the horrific and haunting titles, tags, and comments I have documented. The presentation also gives examples of people put in prison for the abuse videos they put on Pornhub, with a thorough explanation of how Visa directly enables and profits from these crimes. Elizabeth writes back acknowledging that she received the presentation and thanking me for our phone call.

A few days later it is go-time again with the credit card companies. I, along with another large anti-trafficking organization, sign and send out letters to the CEOs of Visa, Mastercard, and Discover, using their personal email addresses to ensure they get them.

Ajaypal Singh Banga
Chief Executive Officer
Mastercard
May 1, 2020

Dear Ajaypal Singh Banga,

I am writing to you to express our deep concern about Pornhub's well-documented links to human trafficking and to urge Mastercard to terminate its partnership with Pornhub . . .

The Traffickinghub campaign launched earlier this year is calling for authorities to shut down Pornhub and hold its executives accountable for aiding trafficking—over 800,000 supporters have already signed the petition. We are alarmed at the lack of regulation in place on Pornhub's website that has allowed real footage of trafficking victims, including young children, to be consumed as monetized content.

The letter goes on to list examples of confirmed child abuse and trafficking cases on Pornhub.

But by terminating business with Pornhub, Mastercard can avoid being complicit in the trafficking of minors for profit . . .

Please do not hesitate to get in touch to discuss the campaign and your plans to terminate your relationship with Pornhub.

The same letter is sent to Alfred Kelley, the CEO of Visa, along with Roger C. Hochschild, CEO of Discover Card. I don't hear from Visa or Discover, but six days later I see an email from Mastercard in my inbox. It's Mastercard's general counsel Thibaut Gregoire. "Ajay Banga sent me your letter of May 1," he writes. "We really appreciate that you shared your concerns with us." Then he asks for a conference call.

I set up the meeting for a few days out.

When I join the call with Mastercard, I am pacing outside in the small decorative brick rose garden on the side of my parent's house that was one of my favorite places to smoke cigarettes as a teen when my dad wasn't watching. I glance at the clouds, wondering if he is watching now. On the line is Thibaut Gregoire, general counsel for Europe, John Verdeschi, senior vice president, Paul Paolucci, vice president of law and franchise integrity, and a couple other VPs.

I introduce myself and share how I've been combating the injustice of sex trafficking for almost fifteen years. I explain my discovery of Pornhub's upload system and how there is no ID required nor any consent form necessary to post videos.

"Because of this Pornhub is literally infested with filmed sexual crimes that are being mass distributed with a download button to millions of users per day. This is not a theory; it is a fact. People are already in prison for rape, trafficking, and child abuse that they filmed and uploaded to Pornhub."

I go on to list case after case that has already been proven in court. I don't allow them to respond yet, as I continue to make sure I get in what I have to say. I bring up the Trafficking Victims Protection Act, which makes it illegal for any entity to knowingly benefit from a trafficking venture.

"By definition any child under the age of eighteen used in a commercial sex act is defined as a victim of trafficking. Every video on Pornhub is commercial, therefore every child on Pornhub is a victim of sex trafficking.

"Mastercard is violating the law by knowingly profiting from illegal trafficking content on Pornhub. Do you know there is a download button on every single video that is uploaded to Pornhub? Sometimes you pay to download but most of the time it's free. It's not a download button like you might see on streaming sites where you just borrow the content to view when you are off the internet. This is an actual possession and ownership of that video. So, in that sense, Mastercard is involved in actually monetizing and distributing child pornography and trafficking."

A flustered and almost angry John Verdeschi quickly jumps in.

"Okay, hold on one minute, we want to have a productive dialogue . . . what you said was a very strong statement. Our cards are accepted by merchants across the spectrum of the universe. Our cards are accepted in two hundred and eleven countries around the world, we do not have the ability to monitor every single video that is uploaded or downloaded. So, look, we want to have a good, productive dialogue with you. There are hundreds of millions of transactions happening every day using Mastercard online. If someone decides to sell a product on Amazon that isn't legal to sell, we can't be responsible for monitoring all of those transactions . . ."

I cut him off.

"These aren't products that are being sold, John. They are people."

I try to calm the ruffled feathers, so I tell them I appreciate having this conversation and thank them for engaging with this issue. I say that Mastercard plays a big role in all of this, and I want them to be aware of what is going on.

"Well, we want you to know we take all of this very seriously," Verdeschi says. "That is why we reached out in response to your letter. We would like to stay in touch with you."

I tell him I will send them a presentation full of evidence, as well as links to illegal content live on the site and other important details. Thibaut is diplomatic by thanking me for this "productive" conversation.

As we hang up, I am struck by the realization that getting Mastercard to cut ties with Pornhub is going to be harder than I ever could have imagined. In fact, it may be impossible. But just because something seems impossible, doesn't mean you don't try. Now I have a direct line to the decision makers at Mastercard, and I'm going to use it.

| 17 |

THE DEPUTY DOXER

A victim named Sofia asks for help getting underage videos of her being forced to strip removed from Pornhub. I send the links to the National Center for Missing and Exploited Children in hopes that they can demand the removal of the videos, and potentially go after the abusers who uploaded them. I tell her I am connected with attorneys, therapists, and advocates who are helping victims like her and offer to connect her with those services.

"Are you comfortable sharing what happened and most important are you safe now?"

"I'm away from the people that did those things to me, but it was with a cost," she says. "My family promised we wouldn't intervene or even talk about what happened with anyone. They've left us alone and I don't want to risk it."

"I understand," I message back. "I am so sorry this happened to you. I am here if there is any way I can be of assistance."

Then suddenly Sofia decides to share more about her situation.

"I was trafficked by a family member at a young age. I was 9 years old when it started. I'm still a minor. I'm 16. My parents were in a lot of debt, and they let my aunt and uncle 'help' with the problem. I want to help hold Pornhub accountable if I can keep my identity a secret."

Sadly, what she says is not surprising. A significant amount of sex trafficking worldwide is perpetrated by family members.

She asks if many victims have had videos being uploaded to Pornhub.

"Yes, so many victims," I write to her. "Are you experiencing what
many others are in that these videos keep getting uploaded to Pornhub
again and again?"

"Yes, I've seen them a lot. This time it's not that bad, at least they didn't
reupload my assaults again."

Her words hit hard. "So sexual assaults of you as a child have also been
on Pornhub?" I ask her.

"Yeah, I've come to the point that I try to ignore it."

She next tells me that she lives in Guatemala. Her location exponentially complicates her situation. It's difficult enough to apprehend and prosecute traffickers in the United States, but even more so in a country with
little rule of law.

"Are you safe now? Are you still with your parents?"

"Yes, I live with my parents. When I turn eighteen, I'm getting out of
here. For now, I haven't had a customer in like six months."

A sixteen-year-old should never be saying something like this.

After our conversation I consult with colleagues in the anti-trafficking
movement and reach out to a skilled organization that has local offices in
Latin America to ask for advice on Sofia's difficult situation.

A few days later Sofia sends me a link to a stirring blog she decided to author anonymously.

> I am a survivor of child trafficking . . . My suffering did not end with
> those who had the power to use me, it continued but this time through
> a screen. Videos of my assaults and videos of me being forced to

dance and strip began popping up on the popular tube site Pornhub, in some of them I was as young as 9 in others I was 15. I didn't know what to do. I remember sitting in front of my phone and watching the view count go up. I used to spend hours reading the comments, people asking how much a night with me would cost.

I became so desensitized I stopped caring that videos continued to get uploaded, they would get deleted then a couple days later they would get reuploaded or new ones would pop up. Some of the titles of the videos that continued to be uploaded to Pornhub were "Young Girl Begging to Stop," "Screaming Teen Gets Pounded," "Barely Legal Getting Choked," "Sexy Brunette Forced to Strip." Some of the videos were reuploaded 6 times . . .

Immediately after hitting publish on her blog, Sofia creates an anonymous Twitter account where she shares the link to the blog. It starts getting instant traction but at the same time she is quickly attacked. The first online attack comes from the familiar account @EyeDeco, who has been consistently going after me online, along with politicians and other advocates speaking out against Pornhub. But whoever they are, they just crossed the line by attacking Sofia. It's one thing to attack an advocate, but it's another to attack a victim.

I message James, the data and online security expert, immediately with screenshots of what @EyeDeco is saying to Sofia—attacking her credibility, calling her a liar, and more. James isn't going to have any of it, and he gets to work right away to try to unmask this degenerate who thinks it is acceptable to attack a child online who is speaking out about her abuse. I'm amazed at how quickly he gets back to me. "We were able to identify who is behind the @EyeDeco account attacking Sofia," James says. "It is a woman named Grace Sinclair from Montreal. She is being deputized to do this by MindGeek."

Grace's attack is just the start of escalation of new waves of humiliation and intimidation. Within hours Sofia is doxed, her real name is exposed by an anonymous online attacker called "JC." This person is relentless, and he possesses the videos of her rape, which he wields as a weapon to terrorize and silence her.

I get a message from Sofia.

"Sorry to bother but if you could report this Twitter account. He posted a video of me and he's threatened to post videos of me being raped."

I go to the page, and under the blog link she shared, I see a video of a young girl undressing with a post reading "One of your infamous strip tease fails. Nothing can top those videos of you screaming and being tied up though."

Underneath the post, Sofia replied: "What the hell you sick fuck. I was a fucking 14 year old."

"I have your more fun videos. I sent one to you, you look so good."

Then I see another post from "JC" that is an all-black screen with audio of a girl screaming.

"This audio is my favorite," he writes. "The visuals with it are just so much better."

I message Sofia back right away and tell her I am reporting the account and links to the National Center for Missing and Exploited Children. I tell her I am also reaching out to security professionals, organizations, and law enforcement on her behalf, but she strongly protests.

"I don't want to involve anyone else," she says. "He told me he knows where I live and my full name, school, and I don't want that getting out."

With her own parents complicit in her abuse, I understand that if mistakes are made things can get much worse for her. I don't want to push her to do something she feels will make her more unsafe. My mind races trying to figure out what to do to help. I reach out to Brad to get his assistance with trying to pursue asylum for Sofia in the US and I update the local anti-trafficking organization working in her region and ask if they can help assist Sofia safely.

18

THE FIRST MILLION
SIGNATURES

Moments after midnight on June 8, 2020, I am awake with my laptop open on the living room coffee table watching the live counter on the petition scroll higher and higher. We are now at 995,959 signatures from 192 countries and more people are signing each minute. I struggle with my sadness and anxiety over Sofia's situation, and at the same time my excitement grows as the petition to shut down the site that immortalized her abuse approaches one million signatures. I get up several times throughout the night to check so I don't miss it.

A press release I drafted waits to be sent on the newswire the moment we hit one million. My circle of friends and advocates in parts of the world that are in daylight hours buzz with excitement. We text back and forth as the number keeps rising closer and closer to the goal.

At 3:30 that afternoon, while I'm playing with my kids in the living room, I begin the countdown of the last ten signatures. When the petition hits one million, I jump up and down around a floor full of toys and shout out in celebration. I swoop down and pick Jed up to do a victory dance, holding him in my arms and twirling him around and around as he laughs in delight, having no idea what we are celebrating. Then I hug Lily Rose and kiss her head as she plays with her dolls on the floor and looks at me with amusement as I make a fool out of myself.

I never could have imagined this moment just a few months ago, but now it has become real. One million people from 192 countries have signed my petition to shut down Pornhub and hold its executives accountable.

After I hit send on the press release, I have another idea. There is a journalist that I have had in the back of my mind for months. I can't imagine a better person to do a deep dive on this story and get it out to the world. His name is Nicholas Kristof, and he is a two-time Pulitzer Prize–winning journalist with *The New York Times*. Throughout his career Kristof has powerfully and compassionately written about the issues of child sexual abuse and sex trafficking. I was particularly impressed with his reporting on child victims who were being sex trafficked on the website Backpage.com.

I find his email from some old emails where other anti-trafficking groups had written to him. I copy and paste the press release into the email with a note.

> Hi Nick,
>
> I wanted to bring this to your attention. I know you covered what happened with Backpage and this is even bigger and more insidious than Backpage. Would you be interested in covering this campaign to shut down Pornhub for complicity in sex trafficking of women and minors? See my statement below about hitting one million signatures.
>
> Thanks!

Recalling that Brad knows Nick Kristof personally, I call Brad to ask if he can also reach out to Nick about this. As an all-star in the anti-trafficking field, Brad's endorsement could go a long way. Brad agrees.

I need a moment alone to reflect on what has happened today, so Joel takes the kids. I jump in the car and drive to the grocery store down the street, where I buy some prepackaged sushi and sit in my car in the parking lot with phone in hand reading the headlines. Texts and messages with virtual high fives and celebratory social media posts are going out and coming in every couple minutes.

Petition to Shut down Pornhub for Hosting Rape and Sex-Trafficking Videos Gains One Million Signatures

The news stories covering this moment are fantastic and Pornhub isn't happy.

19

MEET THE MODERATOR

I have been working on a short, two-minute explainer video about Pornhub for months with the organization Exodus Cry and an animation company. It is released on June 30 and instantly starts to go viral across social media. Celebrities and influencers such as Terry Crews, Rosanna Arquette, Mia Khalifa, and Chris Kattan are sharing it along with nearly every person who sees it. In just a few days it has over thirty million views. Because of this viral moment, the petition nears two million signatures, and my inbox is exploding like never before.

As the video exposing Pornhub continues to gain momentum, I sit in my yoga pants and a Traffickinghub T-shirt on the living room couch going through a flood of emails, social media posts, and texts. My hair is in a disheveled top knot, the sink is overflowing with dishes, and I am bouncing Jed on my hip to keep him calm while Lily Rose is playing with my mom in the room down the hall. I see a notification of a new message on Twitter from an account with no picture and an anonymous name.

"Hey Laila. I've been working for MindGeek for a long time now. They made me sign many legal documents which frankly, I do not understand, so I decided to use a throwaway account to contact you.

"My title is very vague, but I am basically a moderator for Pornhub and many of their websites. I am uncertain of the legalities of what we do here. If you need some kind of proof please let me know." He tells me his moderator position is called a referral source review agent, which is so opaque it suggests a deliberate attempt by MindGeek to obscure the role. These are the "expertly-trained human reviewers" Blake the Fake was talking about. For months I have been wanting so badly to talk directly to a Pornhub moderator. I am amazed that it's suddenly happening.

"What time is it in Cyprus?" I type into Google, quickly learning about the small island in the Mediterranean where this new whistleblower works. He tells me I can call him Alexios or "Alex."

"How long have you been with MindGeek?"

"A little more than 2 years," he replies. Then adds, "They make it pretty hard to go against them."

I thank him for taking the risk to reach out and get right to the question I have been pondering again and again.

"Can you tell me how many moderators work at MindGeek?"

"There are three shifts. We used to be around thirty people in Cyprus for all sites before the controversy and now they started trying to hire more. They also have a really high turnover just because of the job that we have to do."

"Thirty moderators for *all* MindGeek sites including Pornhub?" I ask.

"Yes, about ten agents work per eight-hour shift for all MindGeek tube sites."

The number is ridiculously low.[1] Mind-bogglingly low. It surprises even me. The math makes no sense. At the end of 2019 they had 6.8 million videos uploaded annually to Pornhub. That number has now increased to 9.1 million videos uploaded to Pornhub alone each year,[2] not counting millions of images, or the millions of videos uploaded to RedTube, YouPorn, Tube8, GayTube, Xtube, and all of the other MindGeek porn tube sites. It doesn't add up.

"Can you tell me about how many are dedicated to Pornhub, or how does it work?" I ask.

"The more experienced people work at all sites at the same time. Everyone works on Pornhub just because of the sheer volume of videos we get every day." He tells me he has an internal document he will share with me showing the names of the moderators, their schedule, and shifts, proving what he is telling me.

Incredulous, I ask him how many videos he had to watch per shift before Pornhub recently started being exposed in the news.

"The official number was around seven hundred to eight hundred Pornhub videos per eight-hour shift, but it was really expected that we do at least nine hundred on Pornhub and then more for the other tube sites."

"So how many total?" I ask.

"Well, the more experienced moderators did around one thousand videos on Pornhub and around one hundred and fifty to two hundred videos from other tubes."

"My God. So up to twelve hundred videos per shift. Wow . . ."

I pause to try to wrap my head around how any person could view twelve hundred videos in eight hours minus breaks for the bathroom, cigarettes, and lunch. It's mathematically impossible even at much lower numbers. So when he tells me he knows a veteran moderator who reviews over two thousand videos per shift, my mind is blown.

"How many videos have you personally seen during your time at Mind-Geek?"

"I have seen over a million," he says.

"I am sorry, that must be difficult. It sounds like a tough job," I say.

"Well it is and honestly I would rather do anything else, but the pay wouldn't allow me to live."

I am pained for Alex as he says this and feel a sense of solidarity knowing what he has had to witness so many more times than I have.

He opens up a little more, telling me that it has been especially traumatic for him because he was sexually abused as a child.

"I'm so sorry, Alex."

I can tell he knows that I mean it.

He changes the subject by letting me know that there were over thirty thousand videos on average coming in on a daily basis for MindGeek's porn tube sites.

"That doesn't include images?" I ask.

"No," he says. "That is only videos."

"Can you tell me how videos of children under eighteen are getting on Pornhub?"

He explains how videos immediately go live on the site and then get put in a queue for later review.

"There are numbers that we have to hit every day, and a very heavy load of videos to watch. We are overworked and asked to do many videos every day, which would mean less time viewing each video and way more mistakes."

There is a pause.

"Now I know that we had videos that were very underage being approved because I know a few of the people that approved such videos. It was mostly them trying to hit the numbers they were being asked and not viewing some videos at all."

Very underage children being approved . . . by people he knows at MindGeek . . .

"We get many illegal videos every day, mainly from China," he says. "The rules are not defined. The rules are not very clear. If it seems to the moderator that the video contains someone underage, they should decline it but . . . well, we are supposed to hit high numbers."

Then he adds, "But just recently we have been told to be more careful with the videos."

"Recently?" I ask.

My interest is piqued. I ask him to tell me more.

"Well, the company got in trouble with Mastercard and that is why."

"Really? When?"

"Yes, the rules that we follow had a major overhaul around the tenth of June," he replies.

This is encouraging news. Mastercard appears to be reacting to the conversations I have been having with them.

Next, I inquire about whether they were provided any training and how they attempt to detect underage videos.

"We have some clues in the videos, titles, tags, and usernames."

He goes on. "If the camera quality is bad—underdeveloped breasts—unkempt appearance or, like, not painted nails . . ."

I press him for more answers.

"There are many videos that are close-ups of hairless private areas where you don't even see a face or body," I say. "How do you tell if these are victims or who is underage?"

"There are other things you could look out for, like toys, nails, room, clothing."

"What about when they have braces and pigtails and underdeveloped bodies," I ask. "How could you tell if someone was under eighteen, which is a felony, or over eighteen?"

"We didn't have strict rules, we just follow the rules. We were overworked. And at the age between seventeen and eighteen, the company doesn't care."

The company doesn't care. But that certainly doesn't hit a limit at seventeen.

Painted or unpainted nails? Camera quality? My three-year-old has me paint her nails sometimes. What about underage teen boys? How are they trying to guess which boys are fifteen and which are eighteen years old? Not even a pediatrician could guess correctly on a consistent basis. No one can. MindGeek knows this. Anyone with half a brain knows it. Yet they refuse to verify the age of those in these videos before upload, because doing that is bad for business. What Alex is telling me right now is that MindGeek is playing a game of Russian roulette with children's lives. This is nothing more than a guessing game for moderators, if they even actually take time to look at the videos.

"I want to understand more about how so much obviously illegal content gets through," I tell him. "Recently there was a video of a totally unconscious woman being sexually assaulted."

"I'm assuming it's Asians in the video," he suggests.

"There are numerous videos like that involving different races, but many are Asian."

"We were told not to be as strict on these videos. Something very important to understand is that every time our rules change, we don't actually remove the videos from before that went against the new rules. So many videos are still live today that wouldn't be approved today but would have been last year."

I let out a breath. "I see. So if they were drunk or on drugs, was it okay to leave it?"

"Yes."

"What other kinds of videos were allowed to stay on? What about torture?"

"If the video doesn't have blood, we are OK with it," he says. "They also do something called mummification."

I understand this as a reference to numerous homemade videos I have seen on Pornhub involving mostly Asian women who are subjected to vacuum bag torture. Their arms and legs are tied up and their heads and naked bodies are put inside a plastic bag. The air is completely sucked out of the bag to the point where they start suffocating from lack of oxygen. I have witnessed women in these videos screaming, gasping for air, and jerking their bodies as they are suffocated. Sometimes it's unclear if the women survived the torture since the video is cut off before it ends.

"How could a moderator be sure it was a porn actress in the videos versus a victim if MindGeek doesn't verify ID or consent?"

"Well, if someone used a good camera, it would be OK."

"But these days all iPhones have good cameras," I protest.

"Yes, and generally we were lenient on these."

"Did anyone monitor comments? There were twelve million comments on Pornhub alone in 2019. Many of these comments indicate that the video contains rape or child abuse."

"No, they don't review comments," Alex says. "They only review the ones that are spam and flagged by the system. For example, comments that are advertising something over and over are flagged as spam and the accounts posting them are removed after a review."

I am disgusted by what he just told me. MindGeek set up a system to detect *spam* comments but not comments shouting that a video contains *child rape*? I want to know how rape videos that literally say they are "rape" videos get onto the site so easily.

"So do most moderators just speak English and your native language in Cyprus?"

"Yeah, just English and Greek, a few speak Russian, too," he answers.

"On Pornhub, the tags, titles, and comments are often in many different languages. How would you be able to detect the words 'rape' or 'child' or 'drugged' in other languages like Chinese or Spanish or Arabic?"

"Well just a couple of months ago we started using Google Translate but before that we didn't care."

Of course. A couple months ago, Mastercard quietly confronted Mind-Geek after our call.

20

HOW TO PROFIT
FROM A BLACK BOX

H i, how are you? Pornhub uploaded videos of my rape as a minor that I have been trying to get taken down. I've filled out the form to take the videos down, but they haven't gotten in contact with me yet and the videos are still up. Do you have any advice for me?"

Messages like this from victims have now become routine. I would never have imagined a year ago that it would become my normal day-to-day to be interacting with victims of child abuse who can't get their rape videos off Pornhub.

She goes on. "I'm 19 years old and I just want those videos to be gone."

Her name is Lilly, and she has been speaking publicly against Pornhub online. When I type her name as I am writing back, I am reminded of my own daughter Lily Rose, and it's haunting. I tell her she shares the same beautiful name as my own daughter and ask if she would like to talk on the phone. I give her my number and tell her she can call anytime. I see an unfamiliar number that night after the kids are in bed and answer.

In contrast to the confidence she displayed in her posts and messages, the girl speaking on the phone is so timid and soft that I have to be still to catch all of her words. Her voice quivers and sounds on the verge of tears.

When she tells me that she is from Montreal, I mention that is where MindGeek's headquarters are located. I let her know that as a first step I can help her get the videos taken down and reported to the National Center for Missing and Exploited Children. Next, I ask her if her abusers have been prosecuted and she tells me she hasn't been able to take legal action against them yet. I tell her if she wants to speak to a lawyer about the various options to pursue justice to let me know and encourage her to reach out anytime she needs support.

A few days later Lilly sends me a screenshot of a text message a man sent to her. She blacked out her naked body but left the rest visible. She says it's her rape video from Pornhub. "You liked it rough," the man told her. "Might pay you a little visit." In one photo her face was contorted as she was screaming, and someone's hands were around her neck. In another she had her hands tied behind her back.

"Why do people do shit like this?" Lilly asks me rhetorically. "I got an email from Pornhub earlier today, they told me they would 'review' the videos. Why would they need to review them? I don't understand.

"Sometimes I think it's fucking impossible to win. I can't understand what they get out of having those types of videos on their site. I've spent years trying to forget what I've been through."

The next day she tells me that Pornhub finally removed her rape video. "I threatened them with legal action," she texts. "I hope you don't mind that I said I was in contact with you."

"Not at all," I reply. "I'm glad they finally took them down."

"I guess they got scared I would actually go through with it and sue them or something. I would love to have a phone call with you, there are some things I don't really know how to say over text, please let me know when you have time."

That night Lilly calls and confides to me more of her story and tells me she would like to be connected to a lawyer to pursue legal action against MindGeek. I soon put her in touch with Mike Bowe.

———

For a while an anonymous email account has been sending links to me on a daily basis of suspected child sexual abuse videos that are live on Pornhub along with troves of comments from users flagging illegal videos.

When I'm home sorting through an inbox full of unread emails, I see two more that come in from the same anonymous account that emphasize a particular video they say I need to pay attention to. They tell me it was uploaded by two different users and they flagged the videos to Pornhub multiple times, but they haven't taken them down.

I click the links and am taken to two identical poor-quality, homemade videos of an *obviously* prepubescent child being tortured. The girl's hands are tied down to the bed posts and she is being anally raped by a man who doesn't show his face on-screen. The child is recoiling, struggling, and crying as she is sadistically abused. I instinctively slam the keyboard to pause the video and a big advertisement pops up in the middle of the child's rape for a dating website that says, "Fuck Now."

For a moment I press my palms against my eyes, trying to process what I just witnessed. I rub my face and gather the courage to look back at the screen. The video is listed under the Pornhub official categories "Amateur," "Anal," "Big Dick," "Bondage," "Old/Young," "Small Tits," and "Teen" with the tags "petite," "young," "daddy," "daughter," "abuse," "punished," "tiny," and "torture." I immediately send the links to the National Center for Missing and Exploited Children (NCMEC) and document sending in a takedown notice to Pornhub. How long will it take for them to remove it? Every minute on the site is a minute too long. The glaring download button ensures that this victim's trauma will live on as the view count continues to rise. I know that many of the people who are watching this video are downloading it so they can reupload it again and again. Both actions are felony crimes.

Day after day goes by as the video remains on the site. I check a few times a day to see if it is down yet. One commenter says, "This is fucking C***d porn." The view count is steadily rising into the thousands and then the tens of thousands—the ads in and around the rape video still raking in money for Pornhub. One of the ads I see above the child's assault says "WARNING: Delete your history after clicking here." *How do even the advertisements on this video cater to pedophiles?*

Soon I can't wait any longer, so I phone Brad for help.

"Brad, there is a video of a child being raped and tortured on Pornhub. Multiple people have done takedown demands, but it is still up. Do you have a contact at the FBI I can send this to?"

Of course he does. He quickly puts me in touch with Leonard Carollo at the FBI in Washington, DC, who works at a senior level in the crimes against children division. He tells me to send him the links. Brad also helps me get in contact with the leadership at NCMEC. They get millions of reports per year, but I need this one to be prioritized. The contacts at NCMEC communicate with the FBI directly and finally, two weeks after I initially got the links sent to me, the video is taken down. NCMEC confirmed that it was indeed a child and sent a takedown demand directly to Pornhub.

I go back to the original email and click the link to verify that the video was removed. Yes, the video is gone, and in the black box where it used to be are the words "Video has been removed at the request of NCMEC." Yet the title, the view count, the tags, and the URL are still live. Around the video that was taken down are "Ads By TrafficJunky" for things like "teen cams."

Why would Pornhub remove the video but leave all the data and links up that are associated with this child's rape? Then suddenly I realize this must not be the only child abuse video where they have done this. I go to

Google and type in the words "Pornhub removed at the request of NC-MEC." Pages and pages of results come up, each result showing that there was a confirmed child abuse video on the site that Pornhub finally removed after NCMEC confirmed it and reached out to force them to take it down. But each time they left the URLs, titles, tags, and views live on the site. But why?

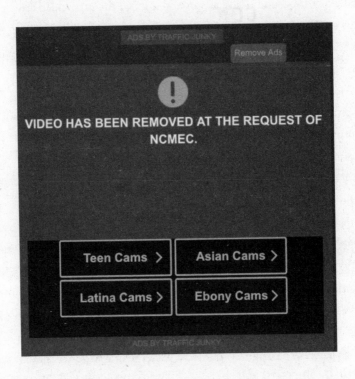

21

CONTENT IS KING

Mateo, a four-year MindGeek veteran from Montreal, tells me he's been keeping up with my Twitter posts. This isn't surprising. Another employee told me that moderators and management now keep my Twitter account open on their devices to monitor what I am sharing. Mateo says he found my claims to be factual but could tell I didn't understand everything about MindGeek. He tells me he wants to be an "information tool" to help fill in the gaps but asks me to keep his true identity private. On our first phone call he starts off by saying the negative headlines don't surprise him.

"MindGeek's a company that grew too fast, the managers are completely incompetent, and they are put in charge of things that can harm people's lives," Mateo tells me. "That's why I'm not surprised when I read this stuff about Pornhub, I'm just like 'Yeah, that makes sense.'"

Mateo has spent time in almost every major department at MindGeek, but has the most experience in their search engine optimization (SEO), marketing, and compliance departments. With a mind that races trying to figure things out, he suffers from insomnia, and most of the time it drives him crazy. But in the case of understanding MindGeek, it proves helpful for me. He knows a lot about why MindGeek does things and how they do them.

"The headlines you are sharing and the campaign you started, it struck a chord in my conscience. I don't think there is malicious intent on the lower levels of the company, but at the executive level they are clearly complicit. They are not controlling the content and it's for the sake of revenue. It's just money. One hundred percent. Management just sees numbers—let's be honest, it's like any other company but they are trading with people's lives."

His speech is accented, but I understand all too well what he is telling me.

"This is a race for Google search results between Pornhub and its biggest competitors like Xvideos," Mateo says. "Google is where Pornhub lives or dies. They all fight for the rankings and it's just crazy. And that's the thing, this search engine optimization, it's not about the big searches, it's about the long searches . . . whichever site has the most content, and the most diverse content, wins. For free porn tube sites content is king."

The most content . . . the most diverse content . . . whatever that content might be.

"Were we planning any efforts to stop the illegal content? Absolutely not. Because of views. Every time you put an extra layer of control on what goes up, you lose content. And content is more web pages, and more web pages are more Google results, and more Google results are more paid views."

As he speaks, it finally clicks why MindGeek took down the Pornhub child abuse videos that NCMEC demanded they remove but left up the black box saying "Removed at the request of NCMEC" along with the titles, tags, views, comments, and URLs. It's because of the race to be number one on Google. More information is more searchable data, which leads to more traffic and more profit. I ask Mateo to confirm; I am correct.

"Absolutely. If you can still search it, that means more Google search results. And when you go to the video, you can't see the video, but you can still see ads, right? They don't want to remove any content from the site; they need it to drive results in Google. It's all about getting found on Google. That's the whole business. I think the video itself is irrelevant for them. It's another excuse to bring you to the site. When they buy content in bulk, they don't even care about the quality, they just need references—inventory. It's about URLs. Right?"

I stop him. "Wait, what did you just say? MindGeek buys videos in bulk and uploads to Pornhub themselves? Are they doing this pretending it's from individual users?"

"Oh yes. Pornhub buys bulk. They get a butt ton of videos, I don't even know where it comes from most of the time. I mean, eastern countries, South America, we don't know where. And they just buy bulk and throw it in."[1]

I'm stunned as I contemplate the possible criminal implications of MindGeek uploading bulk "user-generated" porn videos from developing countries that are not verified for age or consent.

Mateo goes on. "Because in the end, let's be honest, the video content by itself, they don't care what it is. There is no product placement there, they don't care about the content, they don't care if it's one minute, two minutes, five minutes, they don't care. Because what they want is ad impressions, because that's what they charge for. It's ad impressions, ad impressions, ad impressions."

"But do they need all that nonconsensual content? They could have made the choice to not be that type of company. They could verify the people in the videos to make sure they are consenting. You'd have to wait one or two days for it to upload and you might have less content, but that's the price you pay for being a clean site. Right? But they don't want to pay that price."

He explains MindGeek's mentality.

"The problem with this company is they don't think about the future.

They focus on how much money they can make today. Right? They take risks because today it's going to give them a dollar. If they have to change their practices next month, well, they'll get there. But right now, this is making more money. That's the type of mentality behind the decisions they make. 'What's going to help me make more money?' That's it."

That's exactly it.

That is why getting Visa and Mastercard to cut them off is going for the jugular.

I ask what he knows about MindGeek's moderation of the porn tube sites.

"They are not watching every Pornhub video. They just scroll through them. Should they be looking at their own site for child porn? Sure. Yes, they should. But they don't have the bandwidth because they don't want to hire the people and put in place the policies, because it's a headache they don't want to have."

He goes on with a tone of contempt.

"And the stuff they actually do put a focus on? It's always the weird PR bullshit written by a guy using a fake name. So, even from the inside, it's so ridiculous. Behind the social media memes they've got a lot of shady shit, and they're okay with it. And that's one of those things that upsets me so much about the brand. They don't do all those nice campaigns for like planting trees or whatever 'because they care.' They don't care. It's just another reason to be in the media. They are obsessed with mainstream media. They want to be there, they want to be talked about. They brag about the media attention they get."

I laugh to myself thinking how their PR department must be losing it because of all the bad press they are getting now.

Before we get off the call, he emphasizes one more thing. "TrafficJunky is MindGeek's advertising arm, it's how they make most of their money from Pornhub's millions of free videos. If you get the credit card companies to cut off Pornhub but not TrafficJunky advertising, you will not devastate Pornhub's revenue. Don't forget TrafficJunky."

I tell him I want to stay in touch so I can ask him questions as they arise. He tells me he is happy to keep talking.

"Mateo, there is also an attorney I want you to speak with. You can trust him to keep your identity safe. He is building a big case against Mind-Geek on behalf of many victims. His name is Mike Bowe."

I'm glad to hear him agree. I end our conversation with a final question. What does he think needs to happen to MindGeek?

Mateo answers without hesitation. "Should they be held accountable for the content they post? One hundred percent. Should they be held accountable for the content they should have blocked, but they didn't? One hundred percent."

After Mateo and I end our call, I am going over our conversation in my head when I see something I never imagined I would: The former owner of Pornhub and MindGeek, Fabian Thylmann—"The Zuckerberg of Porn"— just sent me a message.

22

THE ULTIMATE INSIDER
REACHES OUT

Fabian Thylmann's initial approach is amicable even as he seems slightly annoyed.

"Considering your followers are complaining to me about a business I sold seven years ago, I thought I would contact you and see if you are willing to talk . . . maybe I can help your cause, which I am much more in line with than you might think . . ."

As soon as I see it, I follow him back and he messages me again.

"Thanks for adding me! This shit would not fly if I would still own the company, very sad." He types in a sad face to emphasize his dismay. "So I am genuinely interested to see if I can help somehow."

I'm not buying it. I recall witnessing some of the worst rapes I have ever seen on Pornhub, and the time stamp showed they were uploaded while Fabian was still in charge of the company. Fabian is the man who mainstreamed, popularized, and took Pornhub to a global level. He made the machine that has churned out countless victims, shredding their lives into pieces that are impossible to put back together.

But I want to engage Fabian, and this is my golden opportunity to get vital information from the top. I try to respond in a way that will keep him talking.

"Hi Fabian, I am surprised you reached out to me but interested in speaking. I understood you had completely divested from the company. Some say that is not true, but I am not sure there is a way to tell. Are you still involved at all?"

"Not involved one bit," he says. "Obviously I cannot prove that, but considering I am talking to you at all should be a hint I would guess . . . I do not agree with the way Pornhub is ignoring this subject, which is why I contacted you." Given what I know about the Zuckerberg of Porn, I'm not buying this. But I continue nicely.

"Thanks for reaching out. Why do you think those at MindGeek are ignoring the issue and in what way were you thinking you could assist?"

"They believe they are correctly removing content that should not be there and anything that falls through the cracks is just 'how things are.'"

What I know, and what he must know, is that those "cracks" exist by design, so MindGeek can keep profiting from unrestricted amounts of content.

He continues. "I think they also believe that in most cases if someone claims they were underage when the video was done it is just an excuse because of a bad decision in life they now regret."

This explains why MindGeek has been relentless in forcing victims to show proof in order to get their abuse videos removed. Victims have said over and over that in instances where Pornhub replies to their video takedown requests, they will demand identification and proof that they were underage in the video or that it was nonconsensual. MindGeek's mentality is that *all* victims are liars.

Without my asking, Fabian tells me his personal view on the matter.

"I think any reason someone wants a video removed should be granted . . . as long as their identity can be verified."

I'm repulsed that Fabian thinks that a victim should have to *prove and verify* their identity to get their rape *off* Pornhub, but no one has to prove or verify their identity to upload the rape *onto* Pornhub.

"In order to see if I can help you, I need to know what your goal is, though," he continues. "As I said, if it is a general 'porn is bad' stand then I disagree with you. I do however agree with you that people are misused in this business, like they are in any other business, and that for sure should not be allowed."

I tell him the truth. This is not an "anti-porn" or "porn is bad" campaign; this is a Pornhub-is-complicit-in-the-global-distribution-of-filmed-rape campaign.

"I don't believe any company, or any person, should be allowed to benefit from another person's trauma, rape, and abuse . . . Pornhub is a major issue when it comes to sex trafficking and assault of women and children and that must change."

My answer seems to satisfy Fabian.

"Ok so there are two things," he says as he starts to offer his biggest pieces of advice. "First, the easiest way by far to get content removed is via a copyright claim. So, if next to Pornhub doing the right thing and banning this kind of content, you want content quickly removed, use the copyright claim route. It is too risky for them not to react."

I have never thought of telling a victim to try to copyright their assault videos. I can hardly wrap my mind around such a concept, but here we are. Unbelievable.

He goes on. "Second, there is one important thing to understand: They do not care about your campaign. The only thing they care about is money. You can however use this to your advantage. The absolute worst thing that can happen to MindGeek is that they lose their ability to charge customer's credit cards."

I can hardly believe it. The former owner of MindGeek just encouraged me to go after the credit card companies. He confirmed they are the Achilles' heel of Pornhub. In this moment I can't help but wonder why Fabian wants to help me attack the company he used to own.

Fabian's comments both encourage and annoy me. He affirmed that pursuing the credit card companies is the most effective path to take, but how can he say MindGeek doesn't care about my campaign? This work has brought me to my limit. Is it my pride that is hurt by that statement?

I realize I'm bothered because I believe I'm getting through, and that if MindGeek didn't care, it wouldn't be reacting with attacks, smears, and denials. But Fabian is right. The only reason MindGeek cares is because of money. Big money. All the bad press, the widespread awareness of wrong-doing, and the victims emboldened to come forward is bad for business.

I text Mike Bowe. "Fabian is speaking with me right now, what should I ask him?" Mike responds quickly. Like a seasoned Wall Street attorney who has gone after many big fish, he displays no emotion, excitement, or admiration for my new connection. He simply says, "Ask about ownership and company structure."

Of course.

My heart picks up speed as I ask Fabian the burning question.

"So, who owns the company now? Is it really Feras and David, or are there others who actually own it?"

23

THE SECRET OWNER
REVEALED

Fabian doesn't seem to flinch as he immediately answers my question. He reveals to me that David and Feras own a portion of the company, but he confirms there is one more secret majority shareholder.

"He owns most of MindGeek," Fabian says. "Very hard to find the guy. I know very little about him. Lived in the W hotel in Hong Kong when I sold it to him. First name Bernard, last name Bergemar. But this name is virtually unfindable on Google, which hints toward it being fake or modified. It is listed in a court document *Cammarata v. Bright Imperial.*"

He sends me a link to the court document.

"Bright Imperial was the owner of Redtube," he tells me. Redtube merged with MindGeek when Fabian sold the company, so this makes sense.

I want to call my media contacts immediately and tell them what he just revealed to me, but I am confident I'm the only outsider who knows this information. If it is leaked to the press, Fabian will quickly know exactly where it came from and might stop talking to me. I want to maintain this new relationship in order to get as much information and insight as I can, so I hold back. I will expose this when the timing is perfect.

"So what happened to all the other equity in the company?" I ask. "As I understand it was bought for 360 million in 2011 and then sold to Tassillo, Antoon, and Bergemar for 100 million, but did others own it with you to make up the other 260 million? Who owns that share of the company or what happened there?"

"The numbers are not true. It was sold for 360 million, period. It was just not all paid at once."

"I see. So Bernard bought you out basically and gave Feras and David some of the equity?"

"Well, Feras and David bought me out, Bernard gave them money so they could. But I guess the other way is more or less the same."

"Do you stay in contact with David and Feras?" I ask.

"No. Not at all. Very hard to reach anyone at the company."

Fabian's denial doesn't ring true to me. I am sure if they saw the former owner of MindGeek's name on their caller ID, they would answer. Employees tell me Feras usually gets back to their emailed questions or calls within fifteen minutes.

I realize I need to be careful with what I say as any of it can be shared with MindGeek and their lawyers, who are certainly on high alert right now.

"Got it. Thank you," I reply. "I have done some research into the company and am curious why there are so many associated entities. Do you have any insight regarding that aspect?"

I hadn't just done *some* research. I have been obsessively investigating the company, but Fabian doesn't need to know that.

"MindGeek itself?" he asks.

"Yes, it seems like a complicated structure of many different companies all over the world but all tied together."

I know it is for tax evasion and money laundering, but I want Fabian's answer.

"Ah. I guess some of that is my fault," he types back to me with a smiley face. "But mainly this is because of mergers and acquisitions . . . it looks very complicated, but it really isn't. It would have big tax effects if assets would be grouped together. Another reason on top of that is litigation safety I guess. They don't want Brazzers to die because one site is attacked. Or an attack on YouPorn to affect all tubes. So, some things are split apart on purpose."

There is a pause.

"But again, one thing they cannot efficiently split . . ." He then types another smiley face for emphasis. "Payment merchant account companies."

The credit cards.

Fabian is emphasizing again that the credit card companies are how to hit MindGeek the hardest.

Fabian goes on to give me an example of the influence the credit card giants have on MindGeek.

"Very recently there was a flood of content removed from Pornhub which related to incest storylines . . . The reason this was suddenly banned is because of Visa and/or MasterCard complaining to MindGeek about it."

This information matches up precisely with what the moderator, Alex, told me about Mastercard recently demanding a change in rules after the conversations I had with them. Fabian's knowledge about Mastercard's intervention proves he was lying when he told me he isn't involved with the company anymore. Someone who is not involved with MindGeek wouldn't know about these kinds of internal changes happening recently.

This realization makes me uneasy as I try to game out Fabian's motives for "helping" me. He could be using me to get information to give Mind-Geek, or to use against MindGeek for his own purposes.

I bring up the issue of moderation and ask why MindGeek doesn't verify the identity, age, or consent of those in the videos and images on Pornhub.

"If Pornhub had to ask for ID information, it would lose a TON of content uploaded by people that do not own it." Fabian continues, "It doesn't make sense to allow user-generated videos without verifying in a reliable way the age and the consent of those in the videos from a safety and child welfare perspective."

His answer baffles me. Pornhub operates the exact same way for uploading user-generated content as it did when he was in charge. He is merely pretending it is different now. Does he think I don't know?

"I had a question regarding a comment you made previously . . . you had said that if you still owned the company you don't think these abuse videos would be on the site and my question is why? What was different 7 years ago?"

"Different culture in the company. It was not all about 'as much money as possible.'"

I push him a little more. He is skirting my questions with vague insinuations that when he was in charge he wasn't putting profit over people. I know what he is saying isn't true but I don't want him to get defensive, so I let it go. We end the conversation with some niceties, and he tells me I can reach out to him again whenever I want. And I plan to do exactly that because the former owner of MindGeek has just become my best informant.

———

After disconnecting with Fabian, I am energized. I call Mike Bowe right away and tell him everything, most importantly the name of the secret majority shareholder, Bernard Bergemar. I also emphasize that Fabian confirmed going after the credit card companies is the right move to bring MindGeek to its knees. "Good stuff," Mike says. Fabian's comments reinforce Mike's plans to sue both Visa and Mastercard along with MindGeek. Mike's strategy has been spot-on, which is not surprising for someone who has spent their career in the ring with the wealthiest financiers and companies in the world. He knows it's money that moves them.

Not long after connecting with Mike about Fabian, I have a call with *Financial Times* reporter Patricia Nilsson. She is doing an investigation into MindGeek. We've been in touch and I've been sending her information that I'm gathering on the company. I suggest that she speak with Mike Bowe. I let her know that he has been investigating the company and is preparing to file a major lawsuit against MindGeek. When Mike speaks with her, he offers many bits of information, but the most important thing he intentionally mentions is the name Bernard Bergemar.

"Bernard Bergemar is allegedly the majority owner of MindGeek," Mike tells her. "You should look into it."

Considering how well Bernard has kept his identity and ownership of MindGeek hidden for all these years, it's highly unlikely Patricia has already uncovered this information. This is the perfect way to leak Bernard Bergemar's identity to a major press outlet because I am not the one revealing it and potentially compromising Fabian's trust in our conversations. If he were to ask me if I told a journalist, my simple and truthful answer would be no.

24

A MEETING WORTH
GETTING DRESSED FOR

This meeting might be the most important one I will ever have.

Brad has leveraged his relationships on my behalf and landed a big briefing with the decision makers at the US Department of Justice. After joining the video conference call, Stacie Harris is the first to sign on. She is the DOJ human trafficking and child exploitation coordinator and helped set up the meeting. One by one more senior officials from the DOJ sign on.

As Brad does an introduction to the meeting, I feel the pressure of the moment. A petition with millions of signatures won't put MindGeek's executives in prison, but the people I am speaking to right now can. Whether they will is a different question. I have to convince them to pursue this case.

Everyone on the call stays attentive for the whole hour as I share my screen and walk them step-by-step through the Pornhub crime scene. I reveal vast amounts of information including conversations I have had with whistleblowers from inside the company and even with the former owner, Fabian, himself. I show them the internal company documents I possess and other evidence exposing MindGeek's criminal negligence and knowing complicity in sex trafficking, as well as information pointing to money laundering and tax evasion. I also share over two hundred examples of criminal content on the site and dozens of cases of child exploitation and trafficking evidence I have gathered, including testimonies from dozens of victims who have personally reached out to me.

After I am done, instead of jumping off the call, they stay on and ask questions. It's clear from their questions that they have been listening intently and with interest. They thank me for presenting the information and tell me they will circle back with follow-up questions.

Next up is an online briefing with the US ambassador that is the head of the US State Department's Office to Monitor and Combat Trafficking in Persons. He is appointed to oversee the country's efforts to fight human trafficking in all its forms. I use a shorter version of my presentation and it goes well. The ambassador expresses his support for the effort and says to call on him if there is anything he can do to be of help. I later take him up on the offer and call to ask if he will join the Justice Defense Fund's advisory council. I am grateful when he agrees without hesitation.

During COVID I'm accomplishing more than I thought I could virtually. But Brad has secured me an upcoming meeting with Heather Fischer, the White House special advisor for human trafficking, and it needs to be in person. This will be the first time I've been away from Jed overnight since he was born, and I have mixed emotions. He still needs me at night, and I am worried that Joel won't be able to comfort him back to sleep like I can.

Flying to Washington, DC, I recall the early days of my advocacy career, before having children. Back then, I spent over half the time traveling country to country meeting with politicians in the ornate halls of governments around the world to try to convince them to adopt more effective trafficking policies. Washington, DC, is a ghost town in July 2020 because of the pandemic, so I find a deeply discounted, but safe, hotel room one block from the White House and book it.

I do feel the working-mother guilt, though, when I FaceTime Jed and Lily Rose at bedtime and it makes them miss me more. They cry and cry, and we finally have to cut off the call. But as I sit on the crisp sheets at the edge of my bed I can't help thinking of the young woman being raped at knifepoint in a dingy hotel room. I am doing this for her and all those like her. I assure myself it is worth being away from my kids, even if it's difficult for them.

My first meeting starts early and I'm anxious that my alarm won't go off, so I end up waking myself up every couple hours to make sure I don't sleep in. When Brad greets me in the morning in front of the hotel his smile is welcoming and his enthusiasm for the day is contagious.

We walk from the hotel past the White House West Wing to the Eisenhower Executive Office Building next door. "EEOB" is a large and impressive building with elaborate French Second Empire architecture that includes four-foot-thick granite walls. It takes getting through a few layers of security before we are escorted to an ornate room in the Secretary of War Suite.

Heather and an associate join us, and we begin without small talk. My experience with politicians and officials has taught me to get right to the point in tightly scheduled meetings like this. I walk her through my presentation, with visuals I printed and brought with me. Like a seasoned diplomat, she shows no emotion, even during the most disturbing parts. When I am done, Heather asks one question.

"So, what would you like us to do?"

I'm prepared with a specific ask, which I've learned is essential in public policy discussions: "I met with those in charge of these issues at the Department of Justice a few days ago and they seemed interested in this case. *Please communicate to DOJ that the White House wants to see a criminal investigation launched.*"

Heather doesn't respond or show any expression to let me know what she is thinking, but she doesn't say no. I take that as a good sign.

Brad and I head out into the sweltering summer heat to a briefing for the House Committee on Investigations followed by appointments with various members of Congress. I am not used to wearing heels and my feet are killing me, so I hold my shoes in my hands and walk barefoot between our sessions. It has been months since I have had an in-person meeting. I've gotten used to wearing yoga pants and sandals during video conference calls while all the camera sees is a nice black blazer.

When we finish our last meeting, I give Brad a big hug, thanking him for everything he has done, and then head back to the airport. I get home at 3 a.m. to find Jed and Lily Rose sleeping on either side of a snoring Joel. Their faces are dirty and they're half in pajamas and half in day clothes. Exhausted, I lie down at the foot of the bed and let myself crash.

25

THE OTHER LILLY

I get a congratulatory message from Lilly, the victim from Montreal. She has been watching the petition and the headlines and is encouraged by it all. I ask how she is, and she says her barista job is going well but she's been disturbed when a stranger has come to her work asking for her by name and she doesn't know who he is.

"That's really concerning," I say. "Please be extra careful, especially now that you have been speaking out publicly against MindGeek. And because MindGeek is based where you live."

I tell her I have a few people I can put her in touch with for security advice and she agrees to take me up on the offer if she ever needs it.

"I decided to sue MindGeek," she says next. "This isn't about money, because no amount of money could make what happened to me go away. I don't want this to happen to anyone else and they need to be held accountable for what they've done."

She tells me she has been in contact with Mike Bowe since I introduced them and has become a client of his.

"That is amazing to hear, Lilly. Honestly—advocates like me can shout from the rooftops all day long, but it's the voices and actions of survivors that will make the biggest impact."

"I hope so." She pauses for a moment, then continues to text. "You chose a good name for your daughter."

She adds a smiley face to the end of her message. I browse to find a photo of Lily Rose that will make her laugh. I am usually private with my family—I don't ever post pictures of my kids or family online anymore, but I want to share this with Lilly. I tell her these days whenever I say my daughter's name, I think of her.

"Laila, can I ask you a question?"

"Of course."

"This may seem like a silly question but, what is it like to be a mother?"

That is a question I didn't expect from Lilly.

"It's the most wonderful thing I have ever experienced, but also one of the most challenging things I've ever done."

"I am sure you are a wonderful mother," she says.

I am moved by her comment. There have been so many times since this intense fight against Pornhub began that I have felt like I was failing Jed and Lily Rose. As I look down at my phone to type back, I feel a stab of guilt when I realize I have more screenshots of Pornhub evidence on my phone than photos of my children. A heaviness comes over me as I realize I haven't fully been there for Jed in his first year of life.

"Thank you, Lilly, that means a lot to me," I reply.

"I have always wanted to be a mother," Lilly says. "I felt so much hope and joy when I thought I was going to be, but I lost my babies."

I'm moved with compassion as I read her words.

"I had miscarriages because of the sexual abuse and all of the trauma it caused."

"I am so sorry, Lilly. There are no words to express how sorry I am that happened to you . . . I also know what it is like to lose a baby."

"You do?" she asks, prompting me to offer more.

I have Jed and Lily Rose, but I have been pregnant five times. One of the babies I gave birth to in the hospital, but she was already gone. I remember holding and kissing Samantha, putting a tiny knit hat on her head, and taking a picture of her tiny, lifeless body. It was two days before Christmas the year after my dad died.

"I know losing a baby is one of the hardest things to go through because it's not just the loss of a child but also a loss of dreams and hope for the future. It's a huge loss. I'm so sorry that happened to you."

"You do understand," Lilly says. "It has been so hard to go through all this, but I'm not losing hope that one day I can be a mother like you. I am going to keep remembering the losses you went through and how you now have two sweet children. Thanks for talking to me about this, I really appreciate it."

It is late for me but even later for her, so we decide it's time for bed. As I lie there before drifting off to sleep, I think about the conversation with Lilly. I wish I could go to her and be there to support her day by day through this difficult period of her life, but I know that is a completely impractical thought.

One thing is certain. This fight for justice isn't just about a website and pixels on a screen. It is about real, living, breathing, feeling human beings—people who have been severely harmed by those who abused them, and by the men running this website that is immortalizing their trauma. This is about Lilly.

I lie in bed staring at the ceiling as my mind goes in circles thinking about all the moving pieces of this complicated battle. A thought comes to mind, and I know it is one I want to hold on to. In order to sustain this fight until the end, I have to be fueled more by the love I feel for survivors like Lilly than the hate I have for her rapists, Pornhub, and the executives behind it. We can fight hard for a short time because of hatred for abusers, but we can fight long because of our love for the abused.

26

THIS HELLHOLE OF RAPE

For a moment, I take a break from the nonstop intensity of work as I sit in the sun on the steps of the front porch watching Lily Rose and Jed laughing and playing with the garden hose. Their world is so innocent and full of joy, such a contrast to the dark reality I'm wading in.

My break ends when I see Brad's name on my caller ID. When I pick up his voice is full of energy, and I can tell he is smiling.

"Do you have a minute? I have some exciting news!"

"Of course! What is it?"

"Well, Nick Kristof from *The New York Times* just called me," Brad says. "He said he is exploring the idea of writing a major piece about Pornhub for the *Times*."

I am elated. There is no better journalist to tell the stories of the victims I've been talking to. I remember a piece Kristof wrote in 2005 about Darfur, Sudan, where one thousand people were being killed every week and tribeswomen were systematically raped. Before his piece landed in the *Times*, the average New Yorker wouldn't pay attention to the headlines. After the piece was published, everyone was outraged—and many were inspired to act.

"He said he wants to speak with you and see your presentation with all of the information you have compiled."

"Oh my God, Brad—this is incredible!"

"This is significant, but don't get your hopes up too high because anything could happen. We should stay measured about it until it officially has the green light and is published, but still, this is cause for celebration."

He sounds confident as he continues.

"Nick said he is going to email you soon to set up a time to talk."

He wasn't kidding that it would be soon.

At 5:45 that evening, I see an email appear in my inbox. It is from Nick Kristof. He responds to the email I sent him after the petition hit one million signatures. His email looks like he typed it out on his phone.

> Laila, I would like to do a good piece on Pornhub, so would love to chat. Not particularly urgent, but today or tomorrow works if good with you,
>
> Cheers, nick kristof

This is really happening.

Kristof says hello to me as if he is greeting a friend, and it makes me smile. As he speaks, his nasal voice strings sentences and words together with lots of ums and ahs. This surprises me because his writing is so smooth and punchy. I picture him sitting in a leather chair in his farmhouse home office in Yamhill, Oregon, wearing an argyle sweater vest with professor glasses dangling on a chain around his neck.

We talk for over an hour, and I answer many of his initial questions about who MindGeek is—how Pornhub operates, how content is uploaded, how it is monetized, what motivates users to upload, what kind of content is on the site, and much more. As we speak, he asks question after question and listens intently to what I say. I can tell he is intrigued, but I can't tell if he will definitely do the story. I end the call by saying he needs to witness firsthand what I am describing to him. I tell him I will send some key-words, hashtags, and links that he can explore for himself.

Not long after my call with Kristof, a porn producer I have been in touch with sends me a message.

"Hi Laila, I am going down a rabbit hole with Pornhub illegal scenes. I'll send you to a profile who has a playlist of unconscious girls and a guy molesting them."

She sends me a link and I click on it, landing on a profile of a twenty-eight-year-old man from Rio de Janeiro, Brazil. His "About" section says "Like sleeping past out. Limp. Drugged. Drunk girls." His page is full of videos of passed-out girls being criminally abused. The Pornhub algorithm immediately activates and takes me down the dark path of illegal content until I get to a video that is one of the worst things I have ever witnessed on Pornhub.

A young Asian girl is lying on a hotel room bed. Her body is limp and she is completely unresponsive. Her assailant wears a black full-face mask to hide his identity and only his eyes and mouth are visible. He takes his time to record her completely unconscious state, going so far as to lift her eyelids and press his finger several times onto her exposed eyeball to prove she has no reflex or reaction. He tickles her feet to show no response. Then he proceeds to rape her, flaunting again and again to the camera that she is unresponsive. The title of the video is in Chinese, so I copy and paste it into Google Translate.

"dead pig half-opened eyes after being drugged"

The horror doesn't end with this video. The Pornhub algorithm now serves up more videos of other unconscious women being raped. One of the videos shows a close-up of the victim's vagina with the drug needle used to attack her inserted into it.

I take a deep breath and force myself not to click away before I document how far the trail of crime goes. I need to hang on just a few more moments. Pornhub's suggestions lead to a shaky homemade video of a naked young Asian woman who is brought out to a dirty balcony at the top of an old apartment building. As she cries they throw her into a large plastic tub of freezing water full of ice cubes, then grab her hair and plunge her under as she struggles. When they let her up for air she pleads for them to stop, but they don't.

This is not acting, and inside I'm panicking for this girl.

If they continue this for one moment more she is going to die from lack of oxygen and hypothermia.

Finally they throw her down on the dirty, wet cement. Her body is shaking as they gather around, open their pants, and urinate on her face as she whimpers, having given up trying to struggle. Then it's over. I click to exit Pornhub, reeling from what I saw.

I don't know what happened to that girl next. Is she even alive? I feel as though I experienced a form of secondhand trauma by merely witnessing what these victims went though, and I can tell my cortisol level is through the roof. I don't know how much more of this I can take.

But even that very thought makes me angry and guilt-ridden. How could *I* ever feel like it's too much to take when these *victims* had to actually live through the pain of these violent attacks? And they continue to relive it day after day, because they know their abuse has now been immortalized online and the trauma will *never* end.

I don't know how Nick will react to seeing these videos, but like I said on our phone call, he needs to witness the reality of the Pornhub crime scene for himself. I send him a message listing titles, descriptions, keywords, and links for him to look into that will take him straight into this hellhole of rape and criminal torture on Pornhub.

Nick opens my email and begins to follow the keywords and titles I suggested. They take him down the same rabbit hole of rape and torture that I just went through, and he sees with his own eyes the horror of Pornhub. In that moment he decides he has no other choice but to do the story. I soon get an email letting me know he is moving forward. He will spend the summer on his investigation and will release an extended column for *The New York Times* in the fall.

27

PLAUSIBLE DENIABILITY: PRICELESS

Unlike Mastercard, Visa has been unresponsive since our initial interactions. They had promised to respond to my presentations of evidence, but I can barely get a reaction from them, aside from brief emails expressing their "concern" and "frustration" over the issue of sex trafficking while making it clear they aren't going to do anything about it.

I see a new headline about an underage girl from Alabama who was raped on Pornhub. The local reporter breaking the news reveals the Pornhub username of her trafficker, who had just been arrested. As I am investigating his account, I realize the reporter failed to notice that the girl's rape videos were not only being monetized with ads paid for by Visa and Mastercard but also being *directly sold* as pay-to-download content to Pornhub customers. Pornhub and the credit card companies were earning a cut of each sale.

I shoot off an email to Visa with the news story of the arrest and evidence of the account.

Dear Elizabeth and Martin,

As a response to your letter attached where Visa wrote to me "we do not believe Visa should be in a position of imposing restrictions on lawful goods" even after being sent evidence of unlawful child pornography and trafficking being distributed and monetized by Pornhub, I want to present new evidence . . .

I follow this email with another to Mastercard's VPs, alerting them to the news. True to form so far, Visa ignores the message. But my email sets off another phone call with the executives at Mastercard. The senior VPs and general counsel from my first conversation join the call: John Verdeschi, Paul Paolucci, and Thibaut Gregoire. Verdeschi, Mastercard's senior vice president, begins the conversation.

"Thank you for joining us today, Laila. I asked for this discussion based on the recent memo you sent us . . ."

He explains how a big part of their role at Mastercard is to ensure that their customers follow their rules, meet their standards, and only conduct legal activities.

"I know we've had discussions with you in the past and explained to you that we have some strong standards around what is considered unsuitable from our perspective when it comes to the world of pornography. Things like bestiality, things like rape, are just not tolerated in our ecosystem. Implementing that can be challenging sometimes. You provided us with information. I wanted to let you know we take that very, very seriously. We certainly take it serious enough that we have engaged these entities and they've come back to us and explained how they are looking to remediate this. I wanted to convey that to you. So with that as a backdrop, let's open it up to discussion."

I quickly jump in. "Sure, I appreciate you taking this seriously. This certainly is not the only instance. We have victims of rape and abuse and trafficking on Pornhub that are coming forward on a very regular basis.

Most of them were underage teens or tweens. I have personally spoken to women who were being drugged unconscious and raped on the site for profit.

"As another update, I've been talking with the US Department of Justice about this. You should also be aware that there's going to be a pretty significant journalistic piece coming out in the immediate future. I've been sending a lot of this evidence to Nicholas Kristof of *The New York Times*, who has taken great concern viewing the evidence and speaking to victims."

John speaks up. "I want to really stress to you that when you engaged us and when you provided us with specific issues, we have demonstrated to you we will not only engage but force action on their part. Keep sending us that information."

His tone sounds slightly condescending.

"John, thank you," another voice says politely. "Laila, this is Thibaut. I think it's helpful to continue cooperation. Obviously, you have access to some information which we don't, right? So it's important you keep us informed . . . I just want to echo what John mentioned so we can continue to walk hand in hand, so that hopefully what you do and what we can do is going to result in some efficient measures."

It's interesting that they are requesting more information when I have sent them so much already. Is this a stalling tactic so they can keep doing business while they talk out of both sides of their mouths?

"I just spoke last week with yet another victim," I say. "She was trafficked in Colombia and two American men videotaped her exploitation as a child. It was child trafficking, and her abusers were arrested and put in prison in Las Vegas and Brooklyn. These are very solid adjudicated cases and there's an abundance of them. There's just so much. Do you want me to individually send you each one of these instances I come across?"

Thibaut answers. "At the end of the day, look—I agree with you. The real issue is how can we prevent that from happening, right? We have to work with the tools we have. Just like you have your own tools. More information could be extremely helpful to us."

"Sure," I reply, feeling frustrated by their insistence on "continued dialogue" and "more information" when what I want is *action*.

"Let me just add to it too," John chimes in again. "I want to emphasize you just pointed out several instances where trafficking or abuse was going on. We're not privy to that. We're in the payment card business and we don't have access to the information you have. So when you share that information with us, we do something with it. We apply pressure. I want to convey the same message that Thibaut is conveying to you. We see this as a working relationship. If you are coming to us and providing us information, we are committing to you that we are going to act on it."

Even though I am losing my patience, because either they didn't care enough to read my emails or they are pretending they didn't, I remain calm and composed as I speak.

"I definitely appreciate that, John. I think so far, I have sent you examples of about one hundred and eighty documented instances of children being exploited on Pornhub in addition to dozens of examples of rape, trafficking, and nonconsensual content. I sent you my presentation months ago. Did you all have a chance to review it?"

"I'm sorry, you said you sent us what?" John asks.

"I sent a presentation that had an abundance of evidence of these cases I've been referencing. Have you had a chance to review that?"

"That was a while back and it's not in the full center of my memory right now," John replies.

This is not a response one would expect from a motivated individual. I am gathering that John isn't serious at all about addressing this issue.

"What I would say to you is this, though," John says. "It's difficult for us to do something about something that happened in the past. What is much more helpful for us is something that is happening now."

I rebut his comment. "One month, six months, or a year ago is not ten years ago. These things are also happening in real time. I have been sending that information to you already. But my question is when do you say, 'Okay, this is enough. This is enough for us to do more than just to bring it to Pornhub's attention.' When do you say we can't continue a relationship with a company that is knowingly engaging in profiting and enabling this abuse to go on? Is there a point where you say 'This is enough, we're not seeing the needed changes and we will not allow our card to be used on this site anymore'?"

"You are asking a great question, and unfortunately, it's a bit of a hypothetical question," the senior VP says. "I don't have an answer for you on at what point, how many videos, or how many times, or how many days . . . I can't give you a hard and fast answer because every situation is different. We are going to take it as it comes. That's the best I can say to you. We will take it as it comes and that's our commitment to you."

"Okay, that's helpful," I reply, feeling deflated at the ambiguous nonanswer.

Before the call is over, I have another point I need to make.

"I also need to inform you that due to the pressure you have been placing on MindGeek about this issue, they have made changes. But these changes have made them more complicit in abuse. I have documented evidence that they removed words from the titles of their videos, like 'drunk' and 'drugged,' but they have left the illegal videos up. To me, just hiding and covering over illegal activity is not a show of goodwill that they want to take this down. It's even worse than not doing anything at all."

The short pause feels longer than it should.

"Laila, you have engaged with the Department of Justice," Thibaut says. "Do you have any news or information to share with us about what law enforcement is doing?"

"Sure. I was able to have a briefing with the DOJ where I shared a seventy-nine-page presentation with evidence I have of child exploitation and trafficking and of MindGeek's complicity. They came back with very specific questions, asking for certain pieces of evidence and additional data that I was able to provide. They opened an online portal for me so that I can continue answering questions and sending more evidence to them. They won't tell me as a civilian if they opened an investigation yet, but they have certainly indicated they are pursuing this in a very serious way. I have also briefed the White House, the US Senate Committee on Investigations, the FBI is aware, the Organization for Security and Cooperation in Europe has had a special briefing. I could go on and on. I'm also engaging state attorney generals, and civil attorneys are mounting lawsuits.

"I want to make sure you are aware of all this, because without the ability to process credit cards on this site, Pornhub isn't able to do business. I know you don't like me to say this, but from the perspective of where I'm sitting, Mastercard is enabling these illegal transactions to take place. Transactions where there are profits being made off of the immortalization of the trauma of child trafficking victims, and things of such an egregious nature that I think they deserve action."

"Yeah, so we appreciate you making us aware, right?" John says.

I continue. "It's not ambiguous at this point. It's not a one-off case. This is not one bad apple—it's a tree of bad apples and there is nothing that is being done to create meaningful change."

They just told me they want more examples and I figure there is no better time than right now.

"For another example, there is an abundance of spy cams. Nine women sued Pornhub in March because they were filmed nude in a locker room without their knowledge. There was a young woman named Tiziana Cantone who actually died by suicide in Italy because her abuse videos were uploaded against her will. She is dead now because of this, but I recently found her videos on Pornhub."

Thibaut respectfully interrupts me.

"Laila, thank you, thank you. I think we got the point, I hear everything you just said."

John concludes the call.

"Look, I certainly, on a personal level, I admire the work you are doing. It's important work. Again, it's important to raise these issues. I hope to be hearing from you in the future. Listen, I'm inviting you if you have information about illegal activity that is happening right now, please send it our way. We will act on it."

It's clear to me from all this doublespeak that the credit card companies don't want to admit they know what they know. They really, really don't want to give up MindGeek as a customer.

28

SERENA STEPS FORWARD

I wake up to another batch of Pornhub headlines. Most are about their latest nauseating PR stunt to sell a new Pornhub Premium subscription for couples called "Premium Lovers." This subscription means that for $9.99 a month, users can masturbate to porn *or* to real rape, assault, and trafficking of victims without the nuisance of distracting advertisements placed all over the crime scenes.

I keep scrolling through the headlines until I see one about Pornhub's trafficking problem and I read Pornhub's response to my petition, clearly honed by a public relations executive with expertise in nondenial denials: "Pornhub responded to Mickelwait's petition, saying: 'Pornhub has a steadfast commitment to eradicating and fighting any and all illegal content on the internet, including non-consensual content and child sexual abuse material. Any suggestion otherwise is categorically and factually inaccurate.'" After all I have seen and learned, these public denials infuriate me.

The next thing I read is someone alerting me to a video they found on Pornhub they think is child abuse. I click the link and see a face that looks so young, she can't be older than thirteen or fourteen.

The young girl clearly looks distressed as she is repeatedly being hit by a man as she is sexually abused. The video has over a million views and the comments indicate that many users believe the video is illegal. Acting on anger and impulse, I screenshot a close-up of only the girl's face, then write an email to Mastercard's VPs John Verdeschi and Paul Paolucci that includes the live link to the video, a screenshot of the child's face, and the comments.

> Hi Paul and John,
>
> I come across illegal content on Pornhub daily, here is a video I woke up to this morning. Also see attached screenshots of user comments flagging the video as underage criminal child pornography yet it has been on the site for 2 years with 1.5 million views, monetized and made downloadable.

I hit send and then click over to Twitter. In the vein of posting missing children's faces on milk cartons, I post the screenshot of the young girl's face with the following caption: "This is clearly an underage victim on Pornhub! If anyone can help identify her, please reach out. She needs help!"

Within just a couple minutes, I get a message from a random user. The stranger tells me she knows the girl in the photo and will tell her to contact me. I immediately take down the post.

How did that happen so quickly? What are the chances?

I receive a message. "That is me. I am nineteen now, but I have been fighting to get these videos of me as a child off Pornhub for years. Every time I get one down, they just pop back up and I have given up."

I ask if I can call, and she agrees. She tells me her name is Serena and that she has had videos of her as a young underage teen being abused on Pornhub over and over again. She goes on to share her story of being an innocent fourteen-year-old girl who was a straight A student. She had never even kissed a boy before, but she had a crush on a boy a year older than her. Her crush convinced her to send him nude images and videos that he then shared with his classmates against her will. Soon they were uploaded to Pornhub, where they were viewed millions of times, downloaded, and then uploaded again and again. She explains how she went into a downward spiral of depression and despair and tried to take her own life multiple times. She eventually got addicted to drugs in an attempt to alleviate her pain and finally dropped out of school because of the shame.

By now I have heard so many victim's stories, but as Serena speaks it feels like I'm hearing of the abuse for the first time. I tell Serena how I have been trying desperately to hold Pornhub accountable and offer to connect her with Mike Bowe for legal assistance in demanding the takedown of her videos. I also let her know that he can advise her on her legal options if she is interested.

"Yes, I am very interested. Pornhub has ruined my life. When can I speak with him?"

The urgency is real. Every minute her video stays on Pornhub is another minute it can be downloaded by users from around the world.

I ask her to hold on for a moment as I text Mike, hoping he is available.

"A victim of underage abuse on Pornhub wants to speak with you. Are you free to speak with her?"

He texts back immediately.

"Tell her I will call her in five minutes, I am in a meeting, but I will step out for the call."

After they talk, Serena tells me how grateful she is to be connected with Mike and lets me know that she is ready and willing to share her story with any journalist I think can be trusted.

I quickly put her in touch with Nick Kristof.

By this point the constant barrage of illegal Pornhub links being sent to me from around the world is becoming unbearable—but I can't bring myself to ignore them. I feel I have a responsibility to the victims to open each one and report them to the proper agencies and document their existence. Tonight, as I go through my messages, I experience a new level of heartbreak: the exploitation of homeless teens. "Teen Screams While Getting Fucked in the Ass" and "Homeless Teen Pussy" are videos uploaded by a user called "jakim658." I go to his account, and it says he is from New Jersey. I see he's uploaded many more videos along these lines. "Young Thot Afraid of Dick," "First Time Anal She Screams It Hurts," "I Don't Care if Your Ass Hurts" with the tag "stop my ass hurts." Underneath the videos, Pornhub *promotes* the search term "runaway teens."

Everyone in the anti-trafficking movement knows that teens who have run away from home and who live on the streets are at the highest level of risk for sex trafficking. As I think about these homeless teens my mind flashes back to the faces of the beautiful people I came to love on the streets of my hometown so many years ago.

Even though I've seen a lot on Pornhub by now, this hits harder.

A man who never shows his face films himself penetrating the girls' anuses as they protest. I see his hands with dirty nails pressed on their skin and their hands reaching back to push him off. I hear his disgusting voice moaning with pleasure as his victims yell and cry out in pain, then their quiet sobs and whimpers of defeat because he won't stop.

My instinct is that I want to shut the videos off and smash the screen, but it feels like if I turn away, I'll be letting these victims down. I am compelled by the realization that there needs to be a witness to these crimes. Someone has to face this and be able to say it really happened—to say "I saw it happen. It was wrong, and every abuser needs to pay."

Overwhelmed, I weep as I hold the recorded trauma of these girls in my hands, unable to stop it. How can someone be so cruel as to see a vulnerable, hungry, young homeless teen girl and instead of offering her help, he rapes her as she screams—all for a bite to eat or a night's shelter from the bitter cold. I just can't comprehend it.

It's almost 1 a.m. now but I have one more thing to do before bed—send Nick Kristof an email with these links. It feels like a therapeutic exercise as I hand the crime scenes to someone who I feel will be able to help bring true justice to these girls and accountability to their abusers. Abusers like Feras Antoon, who decided it was a good idea to immortalize and profit from their pain.

29

THE ATTACKS TURN PHYSICAL

I get a message from Lilly telling me people have been leaving notes on her car while she is at work. Disturbing and frightening notes. They list her home address and speak of her sexual abuse. She shares a photo of one of the intimidation letters folded up and placed on her windshield. "I want to get into a new apartment," she tells me. I want a security professional to investigate this threat, but before I am able to I get another message from Lilly: she was physically attacked in the parking lot outside of her work at night on the way to her car. She says her assailant mentioned her rape videos while he was attacking her. Thankfully he ran away before she had any serious injuries. Lilly feels it was to intimidate her and wonders out loud if it was tied to her speaking publicly about Pornhub.

As I scramble to get Lilly connected with people who can professionally assess the situation, I encourage her to file a police report as soon as possible.

Then, like a bad dream, Rose reaches out next telling me that she was also just physically attacked outside of a relative's house and a knife was stabbed into her father's car tire. She sends me a photo of the knife and describes how they roughed her up enough to scare her and left. I am relieved she is okay, but my mind is spinning with fear for these victims.

I soon get a notification that I have a new message from yet another victim. Sofia.

"It wasn't that bad. I bruise easily."

The text I receive from Sofia late at night reveals a selfie that tells me otherwise. The young teenager's pretty face is marred by a dark, swelling bruise below her lip and across her chin. Her large brown eyes appear dazed as she stares into her phone's camera. I am deeply concerned as I carefully reread her whole message.

"Hi Laila how are you? I wasn't going to mention anything because I didn't know if it was relevant, but I got jumped at a park. I'm alright just have a nasty bruise."

Sofia is now the third girl this has happened to in the last few days. The third underage victim of Pornhub who has gone public with their story who reached out to tell me they were physically attacked by a stranger.

What is happening? Is this real?

Are these back-to-back attacks just a crazy coincidence? The skeptic in me wants to believe that's the case, but the questions about whether there is something more sinister going on are unrelenting.

I text back. "I am so sorry this has happened to you. It happened to two other Pornhub survivors in different parts of the world. What happened? Did they say anything to you?"

Sofia immediately messages me back. "It was one guy. He called me a little slut and I'm not sure how to translate it in English, but he said some really nasty things.

"This is really freaky," Sofia says.

I couldn't agree more.

Everything is happening so fast, it's hard to process. I have spent years doing policy work, not police work, and I feel like I'm in over my head. I know we need law enforcement involved in each of these cases, but the victims have had horrible experiences with the police. Each has had encounters with officers who disregarded them, blamed them, shamed them, and failed them. They are refusing to reach out to the police, and I can understand why. I don't want to push them to do something they don't want to do—they have had too many people in their lives doing that, and I won't be one of them. But I am terrified for their safety and well-being.

Sofia finally agrees to get further help, not from Guatemalan law enforcement, who she thinks are bribed, but from the organization I have been in touch with that has trained intervention staff in the region where she lives. They connect with Sofia, and I feel some relief knowing that she now at least has a lifeline. Brad has been in contact with other agencies asking if they can help her with asylum in the United States. But this is the summer of 2020, and the world is battling a pandemic, so nothing seems to be functioning as it should.

"We also spoke with agencies about asylum," I tell Sofia. "They said it is impossible in the US right now but we are going to keep trying."

Sofia suddenly stops responding to my messages. Days go by and I don't hear anything from her. I check in with the intervention organization and they haven't gotten responses in a few days either. My level of alarm over the situation is increasing as the days tick by.

Then I finally get a response.

"Laila I can't talk much, even doing this is not a good idea for me but in case anything happens to me, right now I'm not in Guatemala anymore. I'm in the neighboring country Honduras in a city called San Pedro. I don't know much about the address. I'm trying to get away. It's gotten so much worse."

Sofia thinks she is in serious danger now.

"I'm running from here," Sofia tells me. "I don't know how yet, but I need to. They have me working in this brothel sort of place. The name is Pink Pussycat."

I mention the name Pink Pussycat to the rescue organization who works in the region and to my surprise they know it right away. It's a strip club, they tell me, but it operates as a notorious brothel for selling young girls. They say they aim to someday find a way to shut it down, but it's difficult because local law enforcement is bought off to keep quiet. When I see online photos of the club it makes me feel sick. There are black cage bars on each of the windows of the run-down building, ostensibly to keep the club safe from intruders, but the cage bars also ensure Sofia can't break out.

The organization quickly moves to try to coordinate an intervention for Sofia, but they lose contact with her again. I keep checking in with them to see if they have had responses, but they haven't heard from her. I feel helpless in the face of these circumstances. No matter how much I want to, there is nothing else I can do for Sofia right now to take her out of this nightmare. Each day I wait to hear something—anything—about her. I try to remind myself again and again that *this* is the reality of anti-trafficking work. It isn't always a dramatic rescue and a happy ending. Sometimes it's silence and failure. But it's hard to face. I do my best to charge ahead despite being haunted over Sofia's dire situation, taking some solace in knowing a skilled organization in the region is ready to help her find a way to freedom, if only they can get back in contact. Despite this, the weight of too many unanswered questions is piling up.

30

DEMONIZING THE CRAZY
AMERICAN WOMAN

From the start of this battle with Pornhub, I have mostly held back from connecting victims to journalists, even though I am being asked all the time. The reason is that I don't trust those journalists with something so sensitive and potentially harmful to victims if it isn't done right. But I trust Nick Kristof because he has consistently told victims' stories with care and compassion, and I have been in touch with him quite a bit lately. I connect him with brave survivors who tell me they want to speak out and am encouraged by the positive feedback about him: "He didn't push me for details I wasn't ready to share."

"He was easy to talk to."

"He was respectful."

Some even said, "He is amazing."

It's not only victims I'm putting Nick in touch with but also MindGeek employees who have reached out to me including Alex, the moderator from Cyprus, and Mateo from Montreal. Nick tells me he hasn't had any luck getting Fabian to talk to him. I try to help from my end, but it appears Fabian doesn't like speaking to journalists.

One evening Nick tells me that he has some questions for me, and we get on a call. He says he has had a few conversations with MindGeek's spokesperson over the course of his investigation, and I remind him the spokesman is likely Pornhub's VP Corey Urman using a fake name. Nick goes on to say that on the last call the spokesman mentioned Lilly to him.

"They called her 'Lovely Lilly,'" Nick says, revealing they also told him not to believe anything Lilly told him.

"She is lying," the spokesman from MindGeek said as he told Nick that she is uploading her own child abuse videos to the site.

The spokesman also said they found Lilly's specific location using her IP address and he claimed her abuse videos were being uploaded from an IP address in the same place. The idea that MindGeek is admitting to knowing where to find Lilly is highly disturbing. They obviously don't realize that they admitted once again that child abuse videos were on their site.

They told Nick the same thing about Sofia—that she was uploading her own videos to Pornhub. This was the same attack that MindGeek's @EyeDeco used when going after Sofia on Twitter, until Sofia shared a screenshot of proof from her abuser that shut down the attack.

This line of attack has become MindGeek's modus operandi. I was told by Alex that the middle managers at MindGeek's Cyprus moderating office told the employees during meetings that they must never speak to me because *I* was the one uploading child abuse videos to Pornhub. Trying to make themselves out to be the heroes, they told the moderators that MindGeek upper management were the ones finding and taking down the child abuse videos I kept putting on the site and claiming they were uploaded by others.

"Did any of them actually believe that nonsense?" I asked, completely taken aback and disgusted.

"Well, some of them," Alex said. "It's because they want to demonize you. They are afraid they will lose their jobs if you succeed, and they need the money. At first everyone was just mocking you in the office, saying there is this crazy American woman trying to take down the world's biggest porn company. It was a joke. But it's becoming less of a joke as time goes on."

———

It is a dreary, cold day in late November 2020. We are still with my in-laws and I am appreciating all the hands available to help take care of Jed and Lily Rose. As I am driving to the grocery store, I see Nick Kristof's number on my caller ID and pull over to take the call.

He chuckles as he says, "You have a PhD in Pornhub, so I wanted to ask you a couple more questions before publication."

He then takes on a more serious tone.

"Why do you think that there have been so few reports of child abuse on Pornhub when it's so easy to find illegal content on the site?" he asks. "I have my own theory, but I wanted to know what you thought."

"They aren't reporting to any of the agencies," I reply. "Pornhub doesn't want anyone to know the site is full of underage teens because it damages their brand. They are purposefully hiding it."

Then Nick tells me what I have been waiting to hear for many months.

His article is finally going to be published Friday, December 4, and printed in *The New York Times Sunday Review* two days later.

I text Mike Bowe the publication date. Mike says he will get the "preservation letters" ready to send the morning the article goes live. These preservation letters are formal legal notices being sent to MindGeek, Visa, and Mastercard letting them know that Mike is about to sue the hell out of them, and they better not destroy any evidence that could be relevant to the case.

I also learn that Serena decided to use her real name and photo for the article, and I am concerned for her safety, especially considering what has happened with other victims recently. As her attorney, Mike is aware of her decision and has talked through it with her. He says he and his team will be on standby as the piece goes live in case anything happens after her identity is revealed.

I call Serena to check in and I stress that if she has second thoughts about using her image and real name, she has the power to revoke permission at any point before publication. Serena assures me that she is confident about her choice. No matter how uneasy I am, I know Serena is a smart adult with agency who knows what she wants to do. She tells me she is hopeful about the impact and feels that revealing her identity will enhance the effectiveness of the article. She isn't wrong—putting a name and a face to a story is a powerful way to make people care about issues they might otherwise overlook. I tell Serena that she will get many more people who support her than who attack her, but those who attack can be vicious.

That evening I get a distraught message from a high school administrator in Belize. There is a video on Pornhub of one of his fifteen-year-old students having sex with a boy and she is suicidal because of it. "Can you help us take it down?" he asks in desperation. I am told her real full name is in the title of the video along with the name of her school and the city where she lives. He gives me the information and tells me if I search for her on Google, I will be able to find the Pornhub video. He is correct. I also find her Facebook account that has photos of this clearly underage girl being a young teen, and my heart is broken knowing this could happen to anyone's unsuspecting child.

I first send the link to the National Center for Missing and Exploited Children and then to Nick Kristof, explaining what has happened. He immediately sends the link to Pornhub demanding that they remove the video, and they listen to him immediately. I wonder to myself if MindGeek is shaking in their boots knowing that Nick is fully aware of what is going on and abundantly armed with mountains of verified evidence.

The next day I send an email with the information about the victim to Mastercard's executives along with a screenshot of the child's face from Facebook so they can see for themselves just how young she is.

"I was made aware of yet another minor who became suicidal after finding out explicit videos of her underage were uploaded to Pornhub. 'High School' was in the title of the video along with her full real name, school name, and town. There were ads placed before the video. It had thousands of views and was on the site for a month with a download button. I have attached screenshots of the video information including the title and tags. The child is fifteen years old. This is yet another example of so many. I was speaking with a Homeland Security prosecutor just this week about a new case of child pornography and trafficking on Pornhub that he is handling. The perpetrator is Victor Galarza, who is now in prison in New York."

Mastercard does not respond.

How will they react once Nick's article is released on Friday? It's exciting to imagine the impact, but I check myself. Is it just wishful thinking to imagine this will hit like an atomic bomb? The truth is I really don't know what is coming. Kristof has written articles about child exploitation in the past and they were met with little fanfare. It's entirely possible that this article will not get much traction at all. It could end up being just another in a long line of hundreds of articles written over the last ten months about victims being exploited on Pornhub.

I hear my dad's words:

"We shall see."

———————

Moments before midnight, I am counting down the hours to the release of the article. My anxiousness isn't going to allow me to sleep tonight, so I sneak quietly downstairs to the guest bedroom. A huge picture window reveals a view of the beautiful Northwest forest, with giant cedars creating a silhouette against the cloudy night sky illuminated by the light of the moon.

For a few minutes I stand there in silence thinking about and remembering all that has transpired over the last ten months. The reality hits me. Pornhub had almost eleven million videos on the site when this all started. Today it has almost fourteen million videos. Their site traffic is better than it has ever been, and so is MindGeek's bank account balance.

I feel such a deep longing in my heart for Nick's article to be a significant hit to MindGeek, one that pushes this fight forward in a powerful way. In desperation, I do something I haven't done in years: I get down on my knees. I remember doing this on many nights as a young child, kneeling in front of the large window in the bathroom adjacent to my room that came down almost to the floor and staring up at the starry night sky. I would clasp my hands together so tightly that they would tremble. In my child's mind I believed the tighter I clasped my hands, the more effective my prayer would be. I would look up at heaven with tears pouring down my face as I talked to God about what I needed from him as a nine-year-old.

Tonight, as I look out the window to the sky, I don't clasp my hands. But I do whisper a few words to heaven.

"If you care . . . If you can . . . Please, *please* help bring justice to these victims."

At 5 a.m., my phone starts to buzz. In the group text threads where I first connected Nick with different survivors, I see a message from him to them.

"Here is a link to the article, thank you for sharing your story with me."

I click the link and am stunned by the power of what I see.

31

THE CHILDREN OF PORNHUB

December 4, 2020

A huge and haunting picture of Serena stands next to the harrowing title: "The Children of Pornhub."

Nick details the stories of victim after victim in one of the longest columns he has ever done for *The New York Times*. He exposes MindGeek's exploitative business model, the negligent upload process, their reckless moderation practices, and so much more. The centerpiece is Serena's horrific story of underage abuse and how her videos continued to show up on Pornhub again and again, eventually driving her to drugs, dropping out of school, and attempted suicide.

After I read the article, I write to Nick expressing my gratitude for the incredible work he has done. I tell him that I'm going to send it to every member of Congress and Parliament in the US and Canada, credit card companies, banks, every possible changemaker I am in touch with in the US, Canada, and beyond.

The weightiness of the article is tangible. The careful choice of words, the haunting realism of Serena's images, and the narrative of the article are moving in a way that I have never seen before. The article ends with these words:

The world has often been oblivious to child sexual abuse, from the Catholic Church to the Boy Scouts. Too late, we prosecute individuals like Jeffrey Epstein or R. Kelly. But we should also stand up to corporations that systematically exploit children.

With Pornhub, we have Jeffrey Epstein times 1,000.

I can immediately tell that the impact of this piece will be huge. The sun isn't even up in Washington, yet the internet is already exploding with the news of the bombshell exposé. It's difficult to keep track of how many news outlets around the world are reporting on it since there are so many. First it is hundreds doing follow-on stories, but quickly the numbers move into the thousands.

Nick is calculated and strategic in what kind of impact he wants to get from his article. He mentions the need for legislation to provide more legal recourse for victims against websites like Pornhub, and he calls out the Canadian government and Prime Minister Justin Trudeau by name, demanding an answer to why he tolerates a company that "distributes rape videos to the world." He asks Mastercard and Visa why they are still doing business with Pornhub when PayPal stopped a year ago. He even makes specific recommendations on what Pornhub needed to immediately do to help put an end to further exploitation. In a subtler way, he also encourages the filing of lawsuits.

Within twenty-four hours, Canadian prime minister Justin Trudeau is on national Canadian television responding to the article, saying he is "extremely concerned" and telling the country he is committed to taking necessary actions to protect children from exploitation. Members of the Canadian Parliament are now up in arms on the floor of the house quoting the article, expressing their outrage. One Canadian liberal MP, Nathaniel "Nate" Erskine-Smith, puts forward a motion to conduct a full parliamentary investigation of Pornhub and MindGeek, which is unanimously approved.

Two bipartisan bills are immediately introduced by senators in the United States that will require age and consent verification for porn sites and give victims more recourse to pursue legal action against offending companies like MindGeek.

Mike sends me a text as soon as he reads it letting me know the preservation letters will be in the hands of MindGeek, Visa, and Mastercard lawyers soon.

Journalists from major news outlets around the world are reaching out to Visa and Mastercard demanding answers to Kristof's question to them:

"Why are they still doing business with Pornhub?"

Every one of these things is being extensively covered in the news. The original article is like the gift that keeps on giving. The news cycle is on global repeat as each of these events triggers a new cycle of stories, and it doesn't stop.

At the same time, other forces are coming into play. Nick is deluged by readers who want to help in various ways. Lawyers in Canada and the US are reaching out to Nick, who after reading the story are now interested in filing lawsuits. He tells them they should speak to me and gives them my contact info and I am setting up numerous phone calls with these attorneys and firms. It's like sharks are smelling blood in the water and I love it. I let them know about my organization the Justice Defense Fund and how we support attorneys and courageous victims through the process of filing strategic lawsuits. I also tell them I'm happy to share research and evidence to help bolster their lawsuit complaints. They want to take me up on the offers and make it clear they are interested in getting connected to victims who want to pursue lawsuits. I am still betting on Bowe, but seeing MindGeek die a death by a thousand cuts is extremely appealing. I tell them my organization will help in every way we can.

One reader has an idea to open a GoFundMe for Serena. I think it is a fantastic idea, so I immediately start it and Nick makes an announcement on social media. The donations start flooding in and I quickly transfer ownership of the fundraiser to a specialized, survivor-led victim services organization to see it through.

As I relish what is happening, I go back to the article and scroll through the readers' comments. My moment of satisfaction at seeing the outraged responses is quickly extinguished when I see a message from Nick in the group text with Serena.

"Serena, someone called @EyeDeco on Twitter is sharing screenshots of your accounts before they were closed, to try and embarrass you. It's an account in Canada, so it may be someone working for Pornhub. I just want to prepare you for this. Your story threatens some people and they will try to discredit you. It may be painful. But you're strong and the love and support so many people show you will carry you through it. Let me know if I can help in any way."

Of course it is @EyeDeco attacking Serena. Nick has no idea who this person is, but his guess is correct. I go to @EyeDeco's account on Twitter to see what she has been doing to Serena. Somehow, she has gathered a whole array of photos of Serena taken from her various online accounts. They are of Serena being a typical teenager posing in some ways that are silly and some that are sexy. It's @EyeDeco's interpretation of the images that is disturbing to read. She posts all these photos under Nick and *The New York Times*'s social media posts.

"Serena seems like she knows and has known for quite some time exactly what she is doing aka #grifting. Grabbed these screenshots before she sealed up her social media. Lots of pictures . . . lots. Case in point. She likes GoFundMe types of grifts . . ."

There is a screenshot of Serena doing modeling poses, and a screenshot where she asks followers if they would donate on Cash App to help her get her dead dog cremated. Another post by @EyeDeco on Kristof's account of Serena in modeling poses says, "Here are a few more of alleged 'victim,'" and she uses the hashtags #Pornhub and #MindGeek. Her other posts are along the same lines, trying to paint Serena in a bad light by trying to attack her character and question her status as a "real victim."

I text back to the group.

"EyeDeco is associated with MindGeek. This account always attacks survivors and uses the same lines the MindGeek spokesperson uses. They have doxed me in the past, she is from Montreal, I have her real name."

I share screenshots with Nick and Serena of when @EyeDeco was lashing out to attack Sofia and Lilly online in a similar way.

Nick responds. "I'm sorry Serena that you are being targeted in this way." Then he calls me.

"You think this account is MindGeek related?" he asks.

"I do."

I tell him that the @EyeDeco account was unmasked as Grace Sinclair from Montreal and that she is deputized by MindGeek.

Since the moment the article went live and started spreading, Nick has been getting a deluge of death threats. He has even been receiving intimidating calls to his cell phone that are eerily originating from his own home phone in Oregon and his own office phone in New York. How that is possible, no one can guess. But Nick is thick-skinned after an entire career of reporting on some of the most volatile and dangerous situations in the world, so this doesn't bother him or his wife much. However, people like @EyeDeco attacking a victim like Serena has clearly gotten under his skin. He tells me he is going to call MindGeek right now and personally confront them about this.

Suddenly, just minutes after he calls MindGeek questioning them about @EyeDeco and point-blank asking if they deputized this person to attack Serena, @EyeDeco locks her account down for the first time. She then proceeds to delete the posts she made attacking Serena, Sofia, Lilly, me, my family, and others. But I have already preserved them and have given them to Mike Bowe and his team. Her actions right now are more proof she is communicating with MindGeek. It took an intervention by a *New York Times* journalist to finally shut her down.

32

A BILLIONAIRE ACTIVIST
INVESTOR GETS ACTIVE

The morning after Nick's article is published, a fifty-four-year-old father of four girls reads it while catching up on the news in his luxury Manhattan residence. He becomes incensed and turns to Twitter to voice his anger.

"Please read this and in your mind replace the victims with your daughter or son. We could fix this problem by making it illegal for porn sites to allow content to be posted before review by a monitor, and ages and consents of participants validated."

The man posting this isn't any ordinary parent expressing his outrage on social media. It is billionaire William "Bill" Ackman, the founder and CEO of Pershing Square Capital Management, one of the biggest US hedge fund management groups with over $10 billion in assets. But Ackman isn't your ordinary billionaire either. He has been known as an "activist investor" who isn't afraid of controversy and taking tough stands. Ackman most notably attempted to take down the billion-dollar company Herbalife by short-selling it and exposing it as a "pyramid scheme" to the public and regulators. Although Ackman was unsuccessful at tanking the company, Herbalife ended up paying a $200 million fine to the Federal Trade Commission and was forced to reform its practices.[1]

Bill reaches out to Nick to tell him how he was impacted by his article and offers to pay for Serena's schooling.

But he doesn't stop there. The activist in Ackman is compelled to do more. He continues to leverage his weight of influence by calling out the credit card companies. "VISA and Mastercard should immediately withhold payments or withdraw until this is fixed. PayPal has already done so. Owners of this site should be criminally prosecuted if this continues . . ." Then he ends by saying "Pornhub likely makes hundreds of millions of dollars. It can stop this now. Our humanity depends on it."

Many others would have left things there, but Ackman knows there is more he can do. He texts Ajay Banga, the CEO of Mastercard, who he knows from the tennis circuit. "Ajay, please read the above," Ackman writes as he shares the article, adding that Mastercard is "facilitating sex trafficking" and needs to immediately stop working with Pornhub.

"Call to discuss if you disagree," Ackman says.

Banga doesn't take long to reply. "On it."

A day later, headlines around the world on CNN, *The New York Times*, BBC, and hundreds of other outlets announce that Mastercard is "investigating" the claims in Kristof's article. Visa echoes Mastercard in the press. It's amusing to me to see Mastercard and Visa acting surprised, like they are just hearing about these issues for the first time when they have known for such a long time. But that is irrelevant now because all I care about is whether they do something about it.

My excitement is tempered by a reality. If they "investigate" and then decide not to act, the whole effort is doomed because they will never walk back that decision once it's been in the press. There is no other option now but for them to cut off Pornhub.

Mastercard needs a strong shove in the right direction right now, so I send their senior VP John Verdeschi and their lawyers two emails. The first has links to some of the worst, most blatantly illegal rape videos of unconscious women live on Pornhub, and the second has an offer to put them in touch with victims to hear their stories directly.

The next day Bill Ackman makes a phone call to a contact he knows is a prominent anti-trafficking leader in Washington, DC: my friend Brad Myles. Bill shares what he wrote on Twitter and the messages he sent to the CEO of Mastercard. But he wonders what else he can do and wants to learn more about MindGeek. Brad fills him in on the whole situation and tells Bill about the work I have been doing.

Brad quickly connects me with Bill and we jump on a phone call. I notice Bill's measured and intentional voice. It's clear that he is extremely knowledgeable and powerful, yet he maintains a quiet, low-key conversational tone. I thank him for his involvement and quickly fill him in on what has happened since Traffickinghub launched.

———————

Mastercard's reply finally arrives two days after I reached out.

December 9, 5:15 p.m.

Laila,

Thank you for sharing this additional information.

We hope you appreciate the seriousness in which we've taken our conversations over the past several months, including our investigation into these latest allegations.

I know you understand that the website is massive in size, so if you can direct us to the illegal content that is currently present, it would be very helpful. While we have searched the

keywords specified in the NY Times article, we have not found
the illegal content.

Thank you and regards,
John Verdeschi
Senior Vice President
Franchise Customer Engagement & Performance

I shake my head in disagreement and disgust as I read his message.
Now I'm really pissed off. Since the *Times* piece was published five days
ago it has been circulating around the world. MindGeek *obviously* already
removed the keywords and videos Nick mentioned in the article. But the
site is still infested with illegal content including the unconscious rape
videos I sent to Verdeschi as links just days ago. I take a screenshot of the
email and text it to Bill Ackman.

It's almost 4 a.m. when I respond to Mastercard, and this time I don't
hold back my disdain and frustration for how they are handling all of this.

December 10, 3:44 AM

Hi John,

I sent you two unconscious real rape videos live on the site
days ago and I have been sending you actual evidence and
information about child exploitation on Pornhub since May 1. If
you were conducting a real investigation since I first spoke with
you in May and made it crystal clear that both MindGeek and
Mastercard are profiting from the sex trafficking and abuse of
minors among other crimes, you would have easily turned up
an abundance of illegal videos on your own by this point. The
fact that you are still asking for these things from me clearly
indicates that there has been no real serious investigation into
the site. It also seems clear you have recklessly and/or willfully
ignored the information I have been sending you.

I copy Mike Bowe on the email as well as Nick Kristof. I hope John is ashamed at his impotent and irresponsible response. Exactly four hours later, at 7:44 a.m., John responds to me privately and copies only Seth Eisen, Mastercard's media spokesperson.

Laila,

We want to confirm that we have received and reviewed the two video links that you shared on Monday. We will share an update with you shortly.

John Verdeschi
Senior Vice President
Franchise Customer Engagement & Performance

I am suddenly in a three-person text group with Nick Kristof that Bill Ackman created, and Bill shares a screenshot of his text from Ajay Banga, CEO of Mastercard, that he got three minutes ago.

"Hi Bill . . . we just informed our banks that we are terminating the use of our cards at Pornhub . . . Ajay"

In the screenshot Bill responds, "You are doing the right thing. Thank you for jumping on top of this."

"They just told me too," Nick writes back. "They told me I could tweet it, so I just did."

I remember the MindGeek employee Mateo's words of warning from months ago. He said if the credit card companies acted without including TrafficJunky, the arm of MindGeek that places the ads on Pornhub, it would not devastate MindGeek.

I quickly emphasize to Nick and Bill that we *must* be sure they are also cutting off payment processing for TrafficJunky. "This is how they generate the most profit, through the ads. I know you know this, Nick, but Bill may not."

Bill responds with two words. "On it."

33

THE CREDIT CARDS
DROP PORNHUB

Bill Ackman just leveraged his power and relationships to help push Mastercard to a decision I never thought possible. They announce they are officially breaking up with MindGeek: "Our investigation over the past several days has confirmed violations of our standards prohibiting unlawful content on their site. As a result, and in accordance with our policies, we instructed the financial institutions that connect the site to our network to terminate acceptance."[1]

Minutes after Mastercard's announcement, Visa follows suit. "We are instructing the financial institutions who serve MindGeek to suspend processing of payments through the Visa network."[2] Visa clearly felt the pressure after Mastercard's announcement.

Bill Ackman isn't satisfied, however. Six hours later, he puts the pressure on Discover, who is now the lone major credit card company who hasn't cut off Pornhub publicly. He issues a challenge to Discover on Twitter.

"Does @discovercard intend to be the exclusive payment system for Pornhub or will they ban Pornhub like @Mastercard and @Visa?" Ackman asks the world. Since Ackman is such a compelling public figure in the world of finance, headlines are covering what he is saying.

I am alone in the drafty room off the garage that I recently turned into my office. I haven't slept properly since Nick's article was released seven days ago, but adrenaline and coffee are keeping my energy soaring. I have spent dawn to dusk here each day in my pajamas and a sweatshirt, answering a nonstop whirlwind of calls and emails from victims, journalists, lawyers, and colleagues. This is when I see the headline that Discover Card has also cut ties with Pornhub and I read their official statement.

"Discover has terminated card acceptance at Pornhub.com . . . When Discover determines merchants are offering prohibited activity, we promptly terminate card acceptance . . . "[3]

I slump down in my chair near the window and stare outside for a moment in stunned silence as I process the weight and meaning of all this. I remember the struggle of the past year and the lingering fear that it might be impossible to get the credit card companies to stop business with Pornhub.

But it just happened.

As I sit pondering all this, I feel deep gratitude for what Nick Kristof has done; he has gone to the darkest corners of Pornhub and has been a witness to the horror. He has compassionately spoken to so many victims, honoring their experiences and giving them dignity even as they recount their trauma. And it has had blunt-force impact. I realize that I love Nick for what he has done, in a very real sense of the word. None of what is happening now would be possible without him. I relish the moment, feeling a sense of deep peace and satisfaction knowing that real justice may finally be coming to these monsters who have gotten away with their crimes for too long.

I go to Pornhub.com and screenshot Pornhub's payment options that now only list cryptocurrency.

MindGeek has just been struck with a devastating blow. What will become of them now is still unknown, but I have no doubt this will bring Pornhub to its knees.

34

FERAS GOES FOR BROKE

The Montreal headquarters is now in absolute chaos, and I'm told by insiders that four hundred employees have suddenly quit. The entire human resources department is gone along with half of the engineers. Four of the six MindGeek lawyers have jumped ship. MindGeek has been dropped by their financial auditing and accounting firm Grant Thornton, the banks are calling to get rid of them, and their mainstream advertisers are rapidly canceling their accounts.

Feras and David are being sent legal notices that they are being dropped from their car insurance, home insurance, rental property insurance, and business insurance effective immediately because they have just been nationally blacklisted throughout Canada as a "moral risk." David suddenly can't drive his Lamborghinis and Ferraris anymore. Karim El Marazi, the MindGeek CPO, has started selling his luxury cars and Feras is trying to get his forty-seven condos on the market as soon as possible because he is being dropped by his lenders and insurance companies. Reporters are swarming everywhere including all over Feras's neighborhood and the site of his new mansion. Feras, David, and Corey have also just been notified that they are being subpoenaed by the Canadian Parliament to be publicly questioned in front of the world.

"It's like a hurricane has just hit MindGeek," one employee tells me.

All of this has made Feras sick. I am told that he is hardly able to leave his house or get out of bed, not because he is physically ill, but because he is in such emotional distress about being exposed, blacklisted, shamed, and cut off from the credit card companies. He can't handle the mounting pressure. A close family insider quotes multiple exchanges that Feras was having with his family during that time. At one point Feras emerges and sits down at the breakfast table with his mother, Lailah, and she tries to console her son.

"It isn't your fault, Feras," she tells him. "You pay people good money to be taking care of those things for you and they weren't doing their jobs. Don't worry, most of the victims are probably fake anyway."

Feras's father, George, chimes in. "I told you that you should never have gone into this porn business." Then as the type of Catholic who has a shrine of religious figurines in his house, George adds solemnly, "But God will see us through this."

The only thing that matters to Feras right now is convincing the credit card companies to come back. When the card companies announced they were investigating the site, Feras made the quick decision to start verifying video uploaders to appease them. Afterward he lamented to a friend, "Today we get 25,000 uploads a day. With this new rule, we will get 2,000 studios and model videos, maybe."[1] But now Feras knows changing the upload process and removing the download button, as MindGeek has done in response to the pressure, won't be enough. There are 13.5 million videos on the site and forty million images, most of which were uploaded without checking whether they contained children or rape victims.

Feras decides he has no choice but to go for broke: MindGeek must remove all unverified videos and images from Pornhub and all of their other porn tube sites. The thought makes Feras feel as if he will faint. Reducing the amount of searchable data on the sites is the worst thing he could ever do to MindGeek because it means site traffic and revenue will plummet. But it's either this risk or certain financial ruin. He is going to pull the plug on his own company and hope he can reboot it.

Feras sends out the order, and the number of videos on the site starts to drop, and drop, and drop. People across social media are in an uproar and shocked journalists around the globe start reporting on what's happening. They share in real time how many videos are left, as the search bar counter number decreases every second.

I can hardly believe what I'm seeing.

In less than twenty-four hours, *eighty percent* of the entire site is gone.

A stunning 10.6 million videos and over 30 million images have suddenly disappeared from Pornhub.

The tenth largest website in the world has just been cut down to a stump. Not to mention most of the content is also gone from MindGeek's other porn tube sites like YouPorn, Redtube, Gaytube, Xtube, Tube8, and more. MindGeek also got rid of entire Pornhub partner channels like Asian Street Meat and Exploited Teen Asia.

News stories are calling it one of the biggest takedowns of content in internet history, and I am receiving nonstop calls from overwhelmed victims crying tears of relief and joy. For the first time in years, their rape and abuse is finally gone from the internet.

———

On December 16, three days later, the *Financial Times* drops the next bomb. As I hoped she would, Patricia Nilsson unmasks the majority shareholder of MindGeek:

". . . MindGeek towers over the pornography industry . . . Despite this, basic facts about the company are largely unknown. That includes its main owner—a businessman called Bernard Bergemar, whose name is almost completely invisible on the internet but who has a claim to the title of the world's most successful porn tycoon. Until this *Financial Times* investigation, his identity was secret, known only to a small circle of MindGeek executives and their advisers . . ."[2]

"And me," I add as I laugh to myself.

Well, me and Mike Bowe.

I am astonished as I watch the dominoes fall, one after another.

35

FUCKING STUPID

It looks like you really did it," Fabian messages me.

There is a long pause as I soak in his words.

I don't say thank you.

"Now I hope you attack the other tube sites the same way," he adds.

"I am hearing things from various sources," he continues. "They look very bad. More to come in the next days I am sure."

"Look bad for who?" I ask.

"For the whole company. And Feras and David."

Fabian asks if I told the *Financial Times* journalist that Bernard Bergemar is the secret majority shareholder.

"Actually no. She discovered that on her own," I say, smiling to myself.

I feel like me saying this gives him a boost of confidence in the security of our conversations.

"Can we talk?" I ask Fabian, which he agrees to. Then I take it further by asking if I can have a lawyer that I work with on the phone. I want Mike Bowe on the line with us.

"No," Fabian says. "No lawyers. Because if you have lawyers, I have to have lawyers and then it gets so complicated that what's the point?"

"Ok no problem. Talk soon."

When we talk, the main thing I want to get from him is whether he would be willing to cooperate with civil attorneys and federal law enforcement when the time comes. I tell Fabian about the briefing I did with the Department of Justice and that it appeared there was interest in pursuing a case. Now with all the global attention on Pornhub, the issue may have a high enough profile that the feds will act. I hint that Fabian will want to be on the right side of things if, and when, they go down.

I share Mike's email address and Fabian says he will have his lawyers reach out after he wraps up a business deal he is currently working on.

We next talk about the lax moderation, and he asks me if I know how many moderators they had working at MindGeek. He knows how many they had, but I can tell he is trying to figure out if I know. Nick reported eighty moderators in comparison to Facebook's fifteen thousand, but that is the number MindGeek has now after a year of intense scrutiny and negative headlines. They have been frantically trying to onboard more moderators to clean up the mess.

"Yes, I know how many they have because I have seen the internal Mind-Geek documents including the names of the team and the schedule. It was only 30–31 per twenty-four hours for all MindGeek porn tube sites as of early this year."

Fabian seems a bit uncomfortable with the fact that I know this specific information. I don't care if he tells this to MindGeek. I would be glad if they know they can't hide it because I have the evidence.

"Why did they do that, Fabian? They had the money. Why would they only hire ten people per shift to be looking at those millions of videos when they knew they weren't verifying age or consent? Is it because they are cheap and didn't want to spend the money?"

"They are not cheap," he says with a thick German accent. "They are stupid. Fucking stupid."

He tells me he is perplexed by the fact that they had put the download button on every video. He says that having a download button that transfers content to users' devices for payment compromised their Digital Millennium Copyright Act status. I don't understand what he means, but I will try to figure it out after the call.

"So you didn't have the download button when you were in charge?" I ask.

"No, this is something Feras added after he took over."

"Do you realize that the download button has made him liable for transferring and distributing countless videos of child sexual abuse, and each instance is a federal felony crime?"

"They are idiots, plain and simple," Fabian states. "They handled this all wrong from the beginning. They should not have attacked you; they should have engaged with you like I have these past months instead of being defensive and ignoring the problem. They brought this upon themselves because they are fucking stupid."

No, they aren't stupid.

They might be a lot of things, but these men aren't stupid. Feras is objectively an intelligent man. He has a degree in engineering and his employees call him a mathematical genius. He knew exactly how many videos and images were being uploaded, and he knew exactly how many moderators he had working for him. Feras knew how much of the content on his sites was illegal. In fact, he had admitted in the past that he himself was an avid porn user who would go to Pornhub for his "appetizer" then to his paid subscription sites for his "main meal."[1] Feras knew it all. He just didn't care as long as money was coming in.

Perhaps that's another definition of fucking stupid.

After getting the kids to sleep, I walk quietly down to the guest bedroom again, close the door, and drop down onto the carpet. Overwhelmed with relief and gratitude, I exhale a huge breath, cover my face with my hands, fall forward onto the ground, and let the dam break. The last time my face was pressed into the carpet like this with tears running down my cheeks was the moment my sister told me the words "Daddy died." After wiping my face, I look down at my damp hands and see my dad's signature in Arabic tattooed in white ink on my palm. His face comes to mind like it has every day for the past six years. I see his smile and feel his affirmation in my heart.

Can this be over now?

The question overwhelms me. I don't know the answer, but the thought of this being the end, or close to it, makes my chest ache with a combination of relief and pain. Relief that I may finally be finished with this madness and pain that it ever had to begin in the first place. We are only here now because of the incalculable and unfathomable trauma of countless victims.

And it turns out, we are nowhere close to done.

36

PORNHUB ON TRIAL

February 1, 2021

ended up trying to kill myself many times. I ended up in mental hospitals."

As Serena speaks at this high-stakes virtual hearing, she remains confident and convincing.

The Ethics Committee of the Canadian Parliament has just commenced their investigation of MindGeek and its owners.[1] For the first time in over a decade of hiding in silence, Feras and David along with Pornhub's VP Corey Urman will be called out of the shadows to answer to the public and to the Canadian government for their actions. First to be called to testify is Serena, the centerpiece of Nick Kristof's exposé. Since Mike Bowe is Serena's lawyer, he was also invited to speak as a witness.

Serena continues. "There were instances where the video would have literally 2.7 million views, and it would still be on Pornhub despite hundreds of comments saying: 'Oh, this is definitely child pornography. That girl can't be any more than fourteen, thirteen.' And yet Pornhub still wouldn't take it down, even when I messaged them multiple times, it would take forever. And then, when I did get a response, they would hassle me for all these other details and I would have to go through the whole process of sending them pictures of me with my face next to my ID, over and over again, to prove that, yes, that video is child pornography. And even then, even after I proved all of that stuff, it would still take a while for them to take it down, which would gain hundreds of thousands more views."

Mike is up next. I notice his father's Ladder 36 firefighter's helmet on the bookshelf behind him is in the frame. I remember how Mike wanted to be a firefighter. I'm glad he became a trial lawyer instead.

"First, I want to talk about what it is we're really here about. This is about rape, not porn. It's about trafficking, not consensual adult entertainment... I think everybody can agree that no industry should be commercializing and monetizing rape, child abuse, and trafficking content. And I think we all expect that any legitimate business or industry wouldn't do so . . ."

He draws the audience in. His words are conveyed with power and authority even as his tone is deadpan and factual.

"I'm raising this because for the last year, when public scrutiny started to be focused on MindGeek, a Canadian company, about the fact that it, in fact, knowingly commercialized and monetized this type of content, instead of acknowledging the problem and aggressively dealing with it, what it has aggressively done is conduct a gaslighting campaign in the media and social media to discredit victims and deflect . . .

"But this is a real problem. It's real in the sense that it happens, it's not isolated, it's awful, and it's significant. It is not one or two people here or there, certain things that slipped through the cracks. As I'll explain in a minute, this type of content is part of the business model.

"We have been investigating Pornhub and MindGeek for about a year. Included in that investigation are hundreds of accounts that are similar to Serena's . . ."

Mike slips on his glasses to read a number of his clients' horrific stories.

He shares about a child trafficking victim under ten whose videos were distributed on Pornhub. A fifteen-year-old secretly filmed via computer hack and extorted to do other videos that were monetized on Pornhub. He describes how many victims considered suicide.

He shifts next to explaining MindGeek's complicity.

"MindGeek essentially became the Monsanto of porn, in that it would just simply not put any limits on content . . . The fact of the matter is they knew about the problem of illegal content on their site and decided not to do anything about it. And how do we know that they knew? The evidence is overwhelming. Put simply, in terms of knowledge, a search engine optimization company like MindGeek knows as much about what's on that site as NASA knows about what's going on in the space capsule. That is to say, everything that's going on. And it optimizes that knowledge on a real-time basis."

The Monsanto of porn . . . As much as NASA knows . . . This is brilliant.

"At the center of all this is an algorithm . . . And for people who would search for child pornography, MindGeek itself would begin directing the user to more and more and more of that content."

Mike explains how MindGeek's publicly stated that they review every video before it's uploaded and how this is an admission of active complicity.

"And their treatments of complaints, comments, and red flags . . . To say MindGeek was nonresponsive does not accurately characterize it. It was hostile, it was discouraging, it was designed to make people go away.

"The other evidence of their knowledge and intent, to a trial lawyer like myself, is what they did over the course of the last year when all of this finally got the public scrutiny it required. As someone who advises companies who sometimes end up in a jam because their company did something that they shouldn't have done—well, we all know what the right formula is. You acknowledge the problem, you indicate that you are going to fix the problem, you hire whoever it is from the outside and give them whatever resources you need to, and then you go ahead and fix it. That's what real companies do. That's what responsible companies do. But that's not what happened.

". . . despite the fact that nobody knew what was on Pornhub better than MindGeek, they have run a gaslighting campaign that has denied this was a problem, denied its extent, discredited victims, discredited advocates, and essentially attempted to silence everyone and deflect . . . All the while, saying not only that this stuff isn't true but that the people who are saying it are intentionally misleading, that they're lying. But they're not lying.

"The astroturf campaign that has been run has ended up doxing people. People have been hacked. We were representing a victim in Montreal who felt threatened, who felt for her safety . . . I have other examples like that. That's what's going on behind the scenes.

"This industry has to begin acting like a real industry, like a real business industry that actually cares about what it is it's peddling. As opposed to some chemical company from the seventies that didn't care that it was making money poisoning people. There's a reason MindGeek is called the Monsanto of pornography, and what needs to be done by everybody is make that an impossible position to maintain in this industry."

Immediately after the session I call him.

"Serena did amazing."

"Yes, she did," he replies.

"You weren't bad either, Mike. Actually, you were incredible."

"Ha. You sound like my mother."

"I can't wait to see you do this in the courtroom."

"I won't lie," he says. "Gonna be fun knocking the bullshit out of these fucks. Doesn't mean it will be easy."

———

Feras and MindGeek's lawyers were watching the hearing closely. They must have been impressed with Mike Bowe, too, because shortly after

Mike's presentation they reach out to him with an offer to settle all his cases before he has even filed them. But Mike and his clients aren't going to settle for anything less than significant financial justice and a complete transformation of MindGeek's business practices and executive leadership.

Mike isn't playing games. When MindGeek realizes it, they quietly back away.

37

FERAS AND DAVID
TAKE THE STAND

Feras and David are about to take the virtual stand for the second parliamentary hearing. They are being forced to show their faces publicly and answer for what they have done. Since the moment Feras and David found out they were being subpoenaed by Parliament, I've been told by insiders that they have spent hours a week with their lawyers being advised on how to answer questions.

I stare at Feras's face for the first time as it appears on the screen. His olive skin, dark brown eyes, and salt-and-pepper beard seem familiar to me even though I have never seen his face before, except for one old photo of his younger self. I suddenly realize that his Arabian affect reminds me of my dad, and it's unnerving for both to be overlapping in my thoughts.

I see COO David Tassillo as he stares downward, with his lazy eye drifting to the side, and Corey Urman, the VP of Pornhub, or Blake the Fake, sitting there smugly, not looking at the camera. His smugness will be short-lived because he is about to be removed from his position at MindGeek.

"MindGeek is one of the largest, most well-known brands in the online adult entertainment space," Feras says with his distinct Middle Eastern accent. "Our flagship website, Pornhub, is among the top five most visited websites on the internet . . ."

Lily Rose crawls up onto my lap in her Princess Elsa dress to see what I am watching on the computer. "Mommy, who is that?" she asks. I take a quick moment to think of how to answer. Lily doesn't understand anything about what is going on, besides knowing that I have to be away from her sometimes because there are some bad people doing bad things to kids and I am trying to stop them.

"That is the bad guy, sweetie. The one that mommy has been working really hard to lock up because he is hurting lots of kids."

"I can get him, Mommy!" she says as she stretches her hands toward the screen and begins zapping Feras with her freezing ice superpowers.

He continues his introduction. "MindGeek is a proud partner of the National Center for Missing and Exploited Children and reports every instance of child sexual abuse material when we are aware of it so that this information can be disseminated to and investigated by authorities across the globe . . ."

He starts off with a provable lie. Pornhub hasn't been reporting to NCMEC.

"Has MindGeek or any of its at least forty-eight subsidiaries ever monetized child sexual abuse and nonconsensual material?" begins Shannon Stubbs, a smart, fiery forty-something-year-old member of the committee.

Feras nervously answers. "Sexual material and, uh, child abuse material has no place on our platform. It makes us lose money. When you see this kind of material on our website, it completely ruins the brand that we have been trying to build for over a decade—"

"I would agree," she interrupts. "So, I think that's exactly why it's concerning that there is public knowledge of such videos. On Monday this committee just heard from a witness who tried to get two explicit videos of her on Pornhub when she was thirteen years old removed. I guess it is the case, then, that MindGeek or any of its at least forty-eight subsidiaries has indeed monetized child sexual abuse and nonconsensual material?"

Feras stutters as he tries to answer. What she said was a factual statement.

"W—we . . . we lose money with every view, a user leaves forever. The user is disgusted and never comes back."

Shannon presses him to publicly admit the truth we all know.

"So do any of the websites run by your extremely complex corporate structure currently have child sexual abuse or nonconsensual material on them?" she asks.

"We should have zero child sexual abuse material on our website. And if there's—"

"How do you know?" she interjects.

"Because every single piece of content is viewed by our human moderators . . ."

Shannon snaps back. "But then why, for example, does Pornhub's terms of service say, and I quote, 'We *sometimes* review content submitted or contributed by users?'"

With Feras now in a bind, David jumps in to intervene.

"Ms. Stubbs, uh, I'd like to add to what Feras was mentioning. I'm not too sure where it says that in the terms and service, but I can guarantee you that every piece of content is reviewed before it's actually made available on the website . . ."

"Do they watch it with the sound on?"

"Uh, sometimes they do, sometimes they don't. The—the agents—"

Shannon doesn't let him continue.

"Sound would be extremely important to decipher consent?" she says rhetorically. "You said those formatters view and approve every single video and approve each piece of content. So, do you agree that MindGeek viewed and approved every example of child abuse and nonconsensual content?"

Neither Feras nor David answer her question. The chairman interrupts.

"Thank you very much, Ms. Stubbs. Your time is up. We'll turn to Mr. Erskine-Smith."

Nathaniel Erskine-Smith is the thirty-eight-year-old liberal MP from Toronto who initiated the entire hearing. He has two young children. Before getting into politics, he graduated from Oxford with a degree in law and practiced at a commercial litigation firm. His pro bono work included fighting public interest matters in court, and it shows.

He asks Feras about Serena. "Is it fair to say that Pornhub and MindGeek failed to take all actions they could have taken a number of years ago to prevent that instance from happening?"

Feras tries: "So maybe if I can step back and just explain the first time ever we heard the name of Ms. Fleites was a couple of months before the *New York Times* article . . ."

Nathaniel interrupts Feras.

"Pause, pause there, Mr. Antoon, because your company *did* hear from her when she asked for that content to be taken down. Is that correct?"

"For now we only know her name and last name," Feras says nervously. "And we do not have enough information to, to, to, to see if she ever contacted us or not . . ."

Feras is immediately cut down.

"Don't you think that's *worse* that you have no idea if she contacted you? She says she did. You are a company that is making millions of dollars and here's a woman who's been victimized on your platform and you don't even know, sitting here today, that she's contacted you when she was thirteen? Don't you think that's even worse?"

David Tassillo sees that Feras is being humiliated by Nathaniel, so he tries to jump in to help.

"Mr. Smith, if I could jump in, I, I—"

"Oh, no, my question is for Mr. Antoon," Nathaniel retorts.

"Uh, with the information we have today, we cannot find anything from what Mrs. Fleites is saying . . ."[1]

"So, I will say, then, it *is* worse," Nathaniel concludes.

He then asks Feras what he has to say to victims who were abused on his site, but Feras avoids any apology.

"You say one instance is too many?" Nathaniel continues. "So, let's talk about how many instances . . . Let's just pick a year . . . how many times in 2020 did individuals reach out to MindGeek and say 'I want content taken down because I did not consent to it being put up'?"

Feras won't answer.

"Okay, so let's pick 2019, then . . . how many in 2019?"

Feras looks down, almost like he is in a panic. "Uh, from the top of my head, uh—David I don't know if you know the number from the top of your head?"

David's eyes look nervously from side to side. "No, at the top of my head, I don't have the number and, um, and I apologize for that."

A smirk of disbelief and disdain spreads over Nathaniel's face.

"Yeah, it's a worthwhile apology. Although when I asked you what you would say to victims, I would have expected an apology there too, but at a minimum, coming prepared today, you would have thought you would receive this question. So, you *don't know* sitting here today, how many in 2017, 2018, 2019, how many times people reached out to you?"

"I respectfully disagree," says David. "I actually think we do have all those facts. I just don't have all the facts, uh, with me—"

"At a public hearing, with members of Parliament, you don't have . . . ?" Nathaniel cuts in condescendingly. "Okay. So, *do* provide those facts to this committee at the earliest opportunity."

Feras and David are being questioned as though they are on the stand at a criminal trial, which is appropriate considering the facts.

"Mr. Antoon, are you familiar with a recent article in the *Globe and*

Mail 'Lifting the Veil of Secrecy on MindGeek's Online Pornography Empire'?"

"There's no secrecy about mine," Feras says, seemingly losing his patience.

"*Are* you aware of the article?"

"Uh, I think I read it quickly, but there are so many lately."

He isn't kidding. There are so many articles exposing MindGeek lately. Thousands.

"So, in reading that article, did anything stand out to you?" Nathaniel asks.

"I mean, media articles are not facts. It's journalists writing whatever they want." Feras sounds angry.

Erskine-Smith snaps back. "Well, in this case, a journalist *isn't* writing 'whatever he wants.' He's actually reporting on something that two individuals who worked for MindGeek and Pornhub had told him. Did you read that section?"

"I don't recall," Feras says.

"Well, if I was a CEO of a company and I was very concerned about 'any single instance of harmful content' on my platform, I might've taken this a little bit more seriously, because in that article employees flagged content so egregious they recommended contacting the police. But they were discouraged by managers from doing so . . . Does that cause you any concern?"

"It's completely unfactual," says Feras, clearly upset.

"So, your response to an article like that is to shrug your shoulders and say, 'journalists make up anything'?"

Feras isn't faring well.

"We'll now turn to Mr. Viersen," says the chairman, interrupting Nathaniel because his time is up.

"Thank you, Mr. Chair . . . In 2019 there were no reports of child sexual abuse material from either MindGeek or Pornhub, can you confirm that?" Arnold Viersen asks.

"Not at this juncture," David answers. "I don't—I don't have any information, I had . . . as I said, this has been a constant evolution of our company, it's been at the core of what we've always wanted to accomplish. But in some ways, we are a start-up still, and we are still going—"

The owner of most of the world's largest mainstream porn sites and brands that has been in business for fourteen years, with over one thousand employees, and nearly two hundred related corporations, raking in hundreds of millions each year, is a . . . *start-up*?

Viersen looks a combination of disgusted and genuinely amused.

". . . Are you familiar with the mandatory reporting of child internet pornography legislation in Canada?"

"Yes—yeah," David answers.

"Under this law you would have to report illegal child abuse content to the child protection agency . . . failure to do this would result in jail time. Are you aware of that?"

Feras mutters a statement about following their lawyers' orders on reporting. Soon the chairman turns the questioning over to the next member.

". . . If your system and standards do not work, why are you continuing? Is it because it's too lucrative for you?"

David answers. "I actually believe that if Pornhub was to shut off its lights tomorrow, I think it would be a horrible situation for people around the world . . ."

"How do you sleep at night when you think about all of the parents and victims?" says Ms. Marie-Hélène Gaudreau, the female member of Parliament from Quebec, in her thick French accent.

Instead of a contrite apology, Feras arrogantly says, "I can tell you and tell the committee, we are very proud that we built a product that gets one hundred and seventy million people a day . . . We created a very good product that I am proud of, that our eighteen hundred employees who have families and children are proud of . . ."

Feras went too far in saying that his employees and their children are proud of MindGeek. Hundreds of his employees already quit over this and more are leaving all the time because they are terrified of having the name "MindGeek" on their résumé.

MP Han Dong is next with a question. "How much do you make, Mr. Antoon?"

Feras is stunned by the question. "Um, sorry, you want me to tell the panel how much I make?"

Han isn't buying the drama. "Yeah. What's your salary? What's your income last year?"

Feras gives a nervous chuckle and says, "Well, obviously this is a very private matter that I would not like to share with the committee." He laughs awkwardly again. "I get paid fairly, like any other CEO of a, of a . . . company."

Han doesn't flinch. "How much worldwide gross profit did your company make last year, and how much the year prior?"

"I don't have exact numbers but, uh—"

"You don't know how much your company made last year? Seriously?" Han asks.

"This is a private company, and I don't understand the relevance of what a private company makes has to do with this case."

"You file taxes?" Han says, pointing to the obvious answer.

The chairman, keeping track of time, pivots to Charlie Angus—the former lead singer of a Canadian alternative band and now a member of Parliament.

"Mr. Antoon . . . You say that you have no record of Serena Fleites, who was a thirteen-year-old girl trying to get content taken down from your site. Either you're suggesting Ms. Fleites lied, and that would be a dangerous thing to do, because in seventeen years of my experience with testimony, I found her a very strong witness. We're talking about criminal activity here. So, under your legal obligations in Canada, do you have a record of reporting *anything* from that time to the police of a thirteen-

year-old girl who said that her images were being used on your site? You'd
have a police record, wouldn't you?"

"Mr. Angus, if I can jump in, I just want—" David begins to say.

"It's for Mr. Antoon. Did you report it to the police?"

"You—you—there's an insinuation that, like, we . . ." David stutters,
trying to interject even though Charlie insists on Feras answering the
question.

Charlie goes for the next question, asking about the child pornography
found on the site.

"Pornhub's position was that they were 'conspiracy theories,'" Charlie
says. "That was repeated again in December . . . To say that this was
conspiracy theory is a real disrespect for the families who've gone through
this . . . Your link searches included '13 year old,' '12 year old,' multiple
variations of 'middle school.' And in Canada, middle school is grades seven
to nine; 'runaway teen . . .'"

Clearly Charlie did his homework.

"So, each of these videos would've been viewed by your team of experts
and given the flag to go ahead. Section 163-3 of the criminal code says that it
is an offense to transmit, make available, distribute, or advertise and sell child
pornography in any of these forms, and it is a fourteen-year sentence. At
any point when you were promoting these links, of twelve-year-olds and
runaway teens, was there a conversation that you were actually breaking
Canadian law?"

David can't help stammering. "I'm not—I'm not—I'm not—"

"We have examples," Charlie cuts in. "I'm not making this up, sir."

"I'm not insinuating that you're making it up," David says with frustration.

"The issue is that we're talking about criminal behavior here, the criminal
code, your obligations to protect people . . . it strikes me that you show a
staggering level of recklessness that's just been made apparent here."

I enthusiastically nod at the screen as Charlie continues his powerful
indictment.

"We asked you about Ms. Fleites. She blew your business model apart . . . You made her give you her pictures . . . You've dragged this child out and destroyed her life. And then you showed up at our committee after you had to flush eighty percent of your content down the toilet because it was either nonconsensual or possible criminal behavior, and you *shrug*? And you're asked about your own staff, whose job it is to protect people, and you didn't even bother to know what those allegations were? I think, sir, you are extremely negligent, and we're talking about possible criminal acts here."

The committee members have done a phenomenal job at drilling down into Feras and David. Feras is coming out of this in-person hearing looking much worse than he ever has on paper. David is not faring any better.

I would have given anything for the chance to confront David and Feras face-to-face and call them out on every untruth, every twist of the timeline, every line their lawyers fed them to avoid admissions of guilt. But that wasn't in the cards.

A few days after the hearing I get an email. I click the attachment and see the gold-and-blue emblem decorated with red Canadian maple leaves on a formal letter.

> Hello Ms. Mickelwait,
>
> The House of Commons' Standing Committee on Access to Information, Privacy and Ethics would like to invite you to appear in view of its study of Protection of Privacy and Reputation on Platforms such as Pornhub . . .

I immediately accept the invitation. But as soon as my name is listed as an upcoming witness on the Parliament website, Feras springs into action to try to stop me.

38

MY TURN TO TESTIFY

eras sends a letter signed by him and David on MindGeek letterhead to the committee:

> We understand that tomorrow the Honourable Committee will
> hear from additional witnesses, including Laila Mickelwait . . .
> At the outset, it is important to say that MindGeek applauds
> the victims of child sexual abuse and non-consensual material
> who are willing to appear before this Committee and tell their
> stories. However, we want to address the testimony of Laila
> Mickelwait.

They tell the committee members I am a "far-right" and "intolerant" woman on a "crusade to end legal adult entertainment." Then they warn the committee that if they give me a platform, they will be guilty of promoting these views. The inconvenient truth is I don't fit into the boxes MindGeek is trying to put me in. I am politically moderate, and my focus is illegal content, but the truth has never mattered to Feras.

MindGeek and their shills have been successful at deplatforming other

organizations and individuals who have tried to speak against them. I
have seen them get big donations rescinded, advocacy events canceled,
and invitations to speak recalled. It's a genuine possibility that my invitation will be revoked and I won't get the chance to expose MindGeek's lies
to the Canadian government.

———————

Three more brave victims open the hearing the next day with their powerful and heartrending testimonies of abuse on Pornhub. And because Feras
didn't win, I testify next. This is my opportunity to put the truth I know
about MindGeek into the permanent parliamentary record.

I first want them to hear the words of more courageous survivors. They
are who this hearing is about. I have met hundreds by now, but since I only
have six minutes, I quote a powerful handful of them.

I provide a sample of titles and suggested search terms that Pornhub
intentionally promoted to its users. "Punished teen," "Middle-school sex,"
"real hidden camera," "voyeur," "spycam shower," "stop fucking me," and
"rape" in Chinese are among them. Then I give examples of the thousands
of comments on the site flagging illegal content like, "Isn't this technically
child porn?"

I bring all of this back to David and Feras's blatant lies.

"David Tassillo told this committee that 'child abuse material has no
place on our platform. It makes us lose money.' But that is *not* true, because child sexual abuse *has* made its way to Pornhub in a significant way.
And *every single video* of a child that is found on Pornhub is heavily
monetized . . . and *any minor* used in a commercial sex act is a victim of sex
trafficking, according to international and domestic law.

"I also want to make it clear that Pornhub added insult to injury by
adding an intentional download button to their system, where over a hun-

dred million users a day had the ability to commit the federal crime of downloading and possessing child sexual abuse material, because Pornhub *built* that feature into the *design* of their website.

"Feras Antoon said to this committee, 'The spread of unlawful content online, and the nonconsensual sharing of intimate images, goes against everything that we stand for at MindGeek and Pornhub.' But on September 24, you could search the initials GDP for GirlsDoPorn, which is a known sex trafficking operation, and turn up 338 results of these sex trafficking victims on the site."

I can see committee members furrow their eyebrows and shift in their seats as I detail the uncomfortable facts.

"Videos were titled 'Fucked Sister Hard in the Ass While She Was Drunk and Sleeping' and 'Drunk Girl Gets Handcuffed and Abused Next to the Party.' Other titles were 'Hidden Camera: Girls in the Toilet at Prom,' and 'CCTV in Changing Room: Full Naked Hockey Team.'

"When pressed on the allowance of these kinds of nonconsensual and illegal videos on his site, David Tassillo said to this committee, 'We are a start-up still.' He said that about a site that is the tenth-most-trafficked website in the world.

"Lastly, I want to point out that VP Corey Urman has said that they have a vast and extensive team of human moderators viewing each and every single video before it is uploaded to the site . . . but I have evidence that, as of early 2020, Pornhub had under ten moderators per eight-hour shift reviewing content on the site, in Cyprus. They had only thirty to thirty-one employees per day looking at content, and that's for all of MindGeek's tube sites."

I bring it to a close.

"On behalf of two million people from 192 countries who have signed the petition to hold Pornhub accountable, I want to thank the committee for taking this issue seriously and for conducting this investigation."

The chairman calls on Ms. Shannon Stubbs for the first round of questions.

"Laila, you addressed a number of issues regarding MindGeek's testimony and proved many of their claims to have been false . . ."

Proved many of their claims to have been false.

As I hear these words, a sense of relief washes over me.

After Shannon's questions, the camera focuses on Charlie Angus. He is sitting in the Parliament chamber holding up a white piece of paper.

"I thank you for that, Ms. Mickelwait." He smirks as he begins his statement. "Um, I guess new stuff happens every day with this committee, stuff I have never seen before in the history of the committees that I've been on for many, many years. We got a letter today from . . ."

Charlie pauses for dramatic effect. The former lead singer for the Grievous Angels has retained his entertainer's skill set. In a sarcastic and amused tone, he holds up a letter for all to see, wondering who it's from and acting as if he is reading it for the first time.

"Feras Antoon and David Tassillo wrote us a letter . . . a personal letter about you . . . warning us that . . . well, it's weird . . ." He lists some of their attacks in such a way that you understand he isn't taking any of them seriously. "They sent us this letter prior to the committee hearing. I've never had people being investigated send us letters about people who are giving us witness testimony."

Charlie enjoys this moment of making them out to be the fools they are, and I do as well.

"Do you have anything to say about this letter that we received from the heads of MindGeek?"

He is sending me a pass. I catch it.

"That is standard procedure for them to try to distract, to try to defame, to try to discredit those who are telling the truth about what is going on," I say, explaining that everything I've shared is from the testimonies of survivors who personally reached out to me. The evidence I shared is documented and is factually correct.

"Okay, so is this them gaslighting you?" Charlie asks.

"Absolutely."

That felt good to say.

Charlie Angus jumps back in. "My concern is we have laws in Canada that are very strong, yet we've never had a prosecution against Pornhub—MindGeek . . . what's the problem?"

Charlie is headed exactly where we need to go. Criminal prosecution.

"I think it's important to speak to MindGeek's distribution of illegal content. I want to give the committee two brief examples because I am a witness and I want to tell the committee the information that I have on hand, that I documented . . ."

The hair stands up on my arms as I say the unplanned words "I am a witness."

My mind involuntarily flashes to a collage of traumatic moments—sitting alone, watching the horror, cradling my phone as if it was some vicarious way to comfort the victims inside the screen. Unconscious bodies being raped, children screaming in pain, men moaning with pleasure, boys crying as they are bent over, dollar signs, women gasping for oxygen, blood, blackmail, suicide—*I am a witness.*

After detailing the accounts of criminal content, I add a closing statement. "The truth of the matter is that once a video gets on a site like Pornhub, the victimization and trauma lives on forever. That is why we need laws that require the verification of every single person in every single video on every one of these porn sites. We also need accountability. Because when a site like Pornhub has engaged in this kind of behavior, a slap on the wrist for them is a slap in the face to the countless victims whose lives have been destroyed over the past decade by this predatory company."

I take a breath.

"Thank you."

Days later the heads of the National Center for Missing and Exploited Children and the Canadian Centre for Child Protection take the stand. They both testify that MindGeek was never a "partner" as MindGeek deceivingly said. Not only that, but both agencies testify that MindGeek had *not submitted a single report* of child sexual abuse to them in over thirteen years. MindGeek only began reporting after they were globally exposed when the Traffickinghub petition went viral.[1] As was emphasized in the hearings, it's against the law in Canada for a company not to report known instances of child abuse.

In response to what was exposed during the hearings, a group of organizations comes together to pen a joint letter to the parliamentary committee outlining the criminal behavior of MindGeek and demanding action by the minister of justice. The letter is signed by 525 organizations and 104 abuse survivors from 65 countries.[2] We then send the same letter to the US Congress. The response from Canadian lawmakers makes headlines across Canada as seventy members of Parliament from eight political parties write a joint letter to Canada's minister of justice demanding a criminal investigation of MindGeek.[3]

Employees later testify in court depositions, confirming that MindGeek's executives made the decision to hide child sexual abuse they knew about from authorities for over a decade.[4] As I hear this I ache inside wondering how many children could have been rescued all these years had Pornhub's executives not kept the abuse from law enforcement.

Emails and text messages between Feras and his VPs are also uncovered in further legal proceedings that expose the fact that Pornhub had only *one person* working five days per week to review videos flagged by users for terms of service violations, including criminal content.[5] The emails expose that there was a backlog of 706,425 flagged videos and an internal policy not to put a video in line for review unless it had over fifteen flags. This means a child rape victim could flag their abuse fifteen times and it wouldn't even qualify for review. In the email exchanges Feras said the flagged video review policy was "good and reasonable."[6]

39

FABIAN'S SURPRISE INTERVENTION

During the ongoing hearings, a Canadian cannabis entrepreneur named Chuck Rifici signals he wants to purchase financially distressed Mind-Geek.[1] He recruited a criminal defense attorney named Solomon Friedman to join him as his right-hand man along with the former director of the Royal Canadian Mounted Police Organized Crime unit.

"Of course you need a criminal defense attorney and the head of Canada's organized crime division to run a criminal enterprise like MindGeek," I tweet mockingly, but with a serious purpose. I don't want Chuck Rifici or anyone else to buy MindGeek and attempt to whitewash it—that would only make it more difficult for victims who are pursuing lawsuits.

While investigating Solomon Friedman I learn that he has a history of defending pedo-criminals in court who have possessed and distributed child sexual abuse videos. A Pornhub survivor alerts me to a video of Solomon lecturing other criminal defense attorneys on how to represent abusers in possession of filmed child rape. As he speaks about his work defending these criminals, he laughs and jokes, eliciting laughter from the room.[2] I am particularly disgusted by two posts he made on Twitter[3] where he publicly congratulated another criminal defense attorney for sinking a massive Canadian child pornography case on a technicality. The case involved a pedophile who had 7,730 images and videos of child rape on his devices.[4] The police reported that over 2,000 of the images were of grown men assaulting infants, and yet Solomon patted this attorney on the back for keeping the pedophile out of prison. This all seems in character for a man who would be involved in purchasing Pornhub. Maybe Solomon has plans to try to get Pornhub off the hook in the same way.

I am putting the names and faces of Rifici, Friedman, and their team on social media, and major news outlets in Canada are starting to call them out publicly. They aren't happy about the negative attention. Soon Fabian, the former owner of MindGeek, reaches out with some surprising news. He tells me I am not the only one who wants to stop the deal. He is also hatching plans to intervene.

"The group looking at buying is going to make this site worse and destroy the company, and not in the way you would want . . . I believe this guy is going to bleed it out of cash as fast as possible, making as much money as possible as close to the law limit as possible. This is what these cannabis guys do. It's a tight group of people, they start companies, bloat them, and cash out their shares, insider shit, tons of lawsuits . . . And at the same time they rip off little people that invested in these companies, these are not legit businesspeople."

No surprise there. I could never imagine that any "legit businesspeople" would be interested in buying a criminal organization like MindGeek.

Fabian tells me the deal is supposed to close in four weeks. "So, I am trying to slide into the process, I am trying to derail it," he says.

"It seems to me an investor would have to be insane to buy it at this point," I reply.

"You caused them a big problem and they lost a lot . . . but nobody would be insane to buy it. The site can easily be cleaned up," he says.

Why didn't you clean it up a decade ago? I'm thinking but not saying.

Fabian then starts probing to learn my disposition toward a "cleaned-up"

Pornhub. He is clearly indicating he wants me to end Traffickinghub. But why does he care if I continue?

Then it hits me.

Is Fabian planning to buy back MindGeek? I ask him point-blank. "Are you trying to buy it back?"

Fabian replies with a question.

"Would you prefer me having it over someone else?"

"Maybe."

I'm not lying. Because if Fabian bought it, he would be back on the hook legally for this monstrosity of rape that he himself created, and we could hold *all* of these men accountable.

"You seem more reasonable than Chuck Rifici."

That was pure flattery.

"Do you see yourself getting back into overseeing the site and managing it?" I ask.

"Maybe. What would you think about that? Would you work with me to make it better?"

Work with Fabian to make Pornhub better? That would feel like working with Jeffrey Dahmer on trying to reduce instances of murder. I tell him it's a loaded question and change the subject.

I can hardly believe what he is saying. I take a moment to digest the news and another light bulb goes on. I *finally* understand why Fabian was helping me attack Pornhub. He wanted to drive down the price of MindGeek so that he could scoop the company up at a major discount, rehabilitate it, and make a killing—again. We have been using each other. At least I don't need to wonder about Fabian's motivation anymore.

"How much are they selling for? Do you know the number?" I ask.

"If I understand correctly, they are basically trying to make a profit on the sale amount from me," he says.

I pause a moment and then reply.

"It would be a crazy twist in all of this if you were to buy back MindGeek, regain control of the company, and try to repair its reputation. If you really want to meet in person to discuss these issues, I would be open to that."

"Look, I really would like to meet," he says. "I will come to meet you in L.A. once COVID restrictions are lifted and travel is possible again."

As he says this, I imagine meeting with Fabian face-to-face at some café in Hollywood, and the FBI showing up to arrest him.

"Sounds good," I tell him.

40

FERAS'S MANSION ABLAZE

To say this work has taken over my life is an understatement. I have been so wrapped up in this battle that I missed Joel's fortieth birthday. He didn't even mention it to me until weeks later when I heard him chatting on the phone, laughing with a friend.

"I am getting old," he joked. "I am forty now."

"No you're not," I said from the kitchen.

But as the words exited my mouth, it hit me.

I completely forgot his birthday.

Weeks have passed and Joel never said a word. I feel horrible for missing it.

I am the type of person that normally makes a big deal out of birthdays, anniversaries, and holidays. Joel knows how sentimental I am and never misses them. But he understands what I have been going through; he has seen it all up close more than anyone else. When he says it's okay, I can tell he was a tiny bit disappointed.

As I pry myself out of bed this morning, I pick up my phone and see a text sent moments ago from Mike Bowe. "Call me." He also sent me a link to an article, so I click on it. My heart starts pounding as I read the headline.

MONTREAL MANSION OF PORNHUB OWNER
DESTROYED IN CRIMINAL FIRE

The large photo of Feras's home is shocking. I see an enormous orange-and-yellow blaze with smoke billowing upward and outward. The dark night combined with the brightness of the fire shows a silhouette of scaffolding and stone. Crumbled, black, charred beams of archways and structures stand alone amid everything else in ashes. The police were called at 11:30 p.m. when neighbors first noticed the fire, and it took eighty firefighters until 2:30 a.m. to get the 164-foot flames under control.

There is no question that someone skilled did this. The many news articles now covering the story are reporting that there were two figures seen on the property who set the fire. The two arsonists knew exactly what they were doing. They set such a powerful blaze that it razed the entire mansion to the ground in hours, yet the fire didn't touch any of the neighbors.

I don't know what to do or think. I am thankful that the Antoons haven't actually moved in yet. The house was still in the last phase of construction, so I am confident that no one in his family was hurt. Yes, I despise this man. I want to see him in prison and held accountable to the full extent of the law. I want him to pay for what he has done. But I *don't* need to see him dead or anyone in his family hurt, especially his wife or kids. Thankfully they aren't hurt. The only thing that is hurting is Feras's bank account, as twenty million dollars just went up in flames unless he can recoup the money from his insurance policy, which had been canceled after Nick Kristof's piece ran. Feras's assistants worked hard to pull a subpar policy together so he wasn't completely uninsured, but with his precarious position, I doubt he did this to himself for insurance money.

A haunting thought comes to my mind.

What if they try to blame me for this?

The timing of the fire is disturbing. Only twelve days ago, *Vice* published a widely circulated article falsely claiming that I was inciting "neo-Nazi" "extremists" into acts of violence in the name of the Traffickinghub movement. They even specifically said that I was inciting violence against Pornhub's executives. I feel a rush of anxiety as I contemplate the possible implications, not just for myself but for the whole movement to hold Pornhub accountable. Will they leverage this to try to turn the story around? Will they use this to claim victimhood and make me and my followers out to be the criminals responsible for arson?

"What should I do, Mike?"

"Nothing. Don't do or say anything. There is no benefit for you in commenting on what has happened."

I take his advice and keep my head down and stay quiet as I read headline after headline. Journalists start emailing me asking for a statement about the fire. Some of them are tying the claims in the *Vice* article to this arson attack and asking me to give comment on whether it was Traffickinghub "Nazi extremists" who did this to Feras's house. I refuse to answer even one of them. I won't feed a false narrative that is a boon to Feras and his cronies. I won't comment on a lie.

But who did this? Numerous people are talking about Feras's "Mafia Row" neighbors. But Feras also has enemies in the porn industry. He destroyed the traditional porn industry with the domination of his free porn tube sites and made scores of enemies because of it. I am certain he is also being blamed for MindGeek's woes by Bernard, the majority shareholder, who is now at risk of being further exposed and criminally held accountable because of what has happened. Someone's head needs to roll for it. This mystery man knows that if the movement to expose MindGeek isn't stopped, someone might actually find him.

41

LOCATING BERNARD, ER, BERND

Bernd Bergmair. Apparently that's the real name of the majority owner of MindGeek we all thought was named "Bernard Bergemar." He concocted a close rendition of his real name in court documents to hide himself, which is illegal.

Joe Castaldo with *The Globe and Mail* is the one who breaks the news[1] and uncovers additional details of this mystery man who has secretly partnered with Feras to dominate the global porn industry.

"Mr. Antoon, 46, isn't one to settle for small things . . . But there is another important figure most MindGeek employees have never seen or even heard about: an Austrian named Bernd Bergmair, who has listed China as his country of residence in corporate records." He describes Bergmair as "a man who has left so few traces of his existence he may as well be a ghost . . ."

Thanks to Joe, we find out where Bernd was born, where he went to school. He even shares one blurry, twenty-year-old photo of him—but no one knows where he lives. Mike won't be able to serve a lawsuit to a man with no address, and he is planning to not only sue the company MindGeek but each individual owner and executive by name. Feras, David, and Pornhub's

VP Corey Urman have easily been pinned down to a specific address, but not Bergmair.

———

Dear Laila,

We're investigating Pornhub and MindGeek and I hoped you may be able to help . . . We're currently looking into Pornhub's algorithms and trying to track down its secretive majority owner Bernd Bergmair. . . . But it'd be really interesting to get your thoughts on what Pornhub-related stories you think are worth investigating. Might you be free for a chat this week to discuss?

Best wishes,
Alexi Mostrous
Tortoise Media

I google Alexi's name and find out that he is a Cambridge-educated barrister turned investigative journalist from the UK with fifteen years of experience. He was formerly the head of investigations at London's renowned *The Times* and has been awarded Reporter of the Year and Scoop of the Year. He is now a partner at the innovative "slow news" organization Tortoise Media.

I write back right away, and we have the first of a series of video calls. The moment I meet Alexi I like him. He is sincere. I can tell he has a real concern for victims and a desire to help produce change. I encourage Alexi to go after Bergmair and tell him about Mike Bowe's forthcoming lawsuit. "It would be a game changer if you and your team could actually pin down Bernd's location."

A month later I get a message from Alexi.

"We found him."

He explains how his team was able to find Bernd's home because of location data called Exif data they extracted from his fashion model wife's blog photos. They took pictures and recorded the moment they confronted Bernd in front of his house. The podcast revealing it all will be released in a few days.

The day before Alexi's investigation goes live his colleagues from the *London Sunday Times* publish an article about Bernd's wife, Priscila Bergmair. Alexi told them the location of Bergmair's home and they confronted Priscila.

" 'THINK OF THE CHILDREN,' PLEADS WIFE OF PORNHUB TYCOON BERND BERGMAIR"[2]

Tracked down to London, the reclusive porn king is facing questions about his business—both from his critics and his model partner.[3] He is a secretive tycoon, accused of profiting from illegal content on Pornhub—a website that is more popular than Netflix and Amazon. Bernd Bergmair, 52, has long evaded scrutiny by keeping his identity under wraps . . . He is one of the world's most mysterious billionaires . . . But his wife—Priscila, a Brazilian model and fashion blogger—has 23,000 followers on Instagram. They are kept updated with glamorous photographs of her posing in jewelry from Dior, Chanel, and Cartier, and on luxury holidays in the Austrian Alps and on Italy's Amalfi coast . . . Speaking on the doorstep of their multimillion-pound rented home in London, Priscila said she "really hopes" that her husband will cut his ties with the empire he helped build.

The next day Alexi releases his investigation titled *The Hunt for the Porn King,*[4] a podcast about what it took to track down the secret owner of the world's largest porn conglomerate. For four months, Alexi followed Bernd's trail from New York to China, to Hong Kong and Austria, only to have the hunt end just minutes from Alexi's newsroom on one of London's most expensive streets, where homes cost up to thirty million pounds to buy or over eighty thousand pounds per month to rent.

Alexi describes the morning he showed up to Bernd's home.

"It's five thirty in the morning. I'm in an Uber on my way to a mansion that sits on one of London's most expensive streets. I take a walk up and down the street, and then I settle about twenty meters away from the house, and I'm watching for any movement, any twitch of a curtain, any sign that the man I've been looking for might come out."

Two hours later, Alexi recounts, with all the curtains still drawn, someone pulls up a window blind by a few inches. There's movement, and suddenly it's him. Bernd steps outside the door to smoke a cigarette and Alexi and his team snap photos of his face before the man notices anything. Then Alexi rushes up to him before he loses the chance. With his courteous British demeanor he launches into questions.

"Mr. Bergmair? Hi, I'm very sorry to disturb you at your house. I just wondered if I could ask you a few questions about MindGeek. Do you mind? We're producing a story about MindGeek, sir, and a lot of the victims on Pornhub are very anxious to hear what you think about how Pornhub allowed lots of horrible videos to be on their site. So, do you have anything to say—"

Bernd pulls up his hoodie, covers his face, and begins to walk away while Alexi follows.

"Sir, please don't walk away. Please answer my questions, Mr. Bergmair. How did you get into MindGeek, sir? What do you think about all the allegations against Pornhub? Do you have anything to say to the women? To the victims?"

Bernd continues his escape.

"No? Okay."

Later Alexi on his podcast, reflects on the encounter. "I hadn't quite believed that he really would be there. But there he was, standing in front of me—just another middle-aged guy, wearing a black anorak and dad jeans—refusing to answer any of my questions. And that . . . that was it. I felt weirdly deflated. But when I told Laila that we'd found him, she reminded me why this was such a significant moment."

Now Mike Bowe has an address where he can serve his lawsuit to the majority shareholder of MindGeek. Now victims can pin him down.

MIKE'S "NOVEL"

June 17, 2021

Sixteen months after I first met Mike Bowe, it's finally go-time. It's 3 a.m. on the West Coast.

Just as the sun comes up, Mike sends me the massive lawsuit complaint he is filing on behalf of thirty-four individual women, fourteen who were abused as children on Pornhub. Our team at the Justice Defense Fund has interfaced with hundreds of victims now. Most of the plaintiffs are victims who reached out to us asking for help pursing a lawsuit, who we connected to Mike. More survivors are in the wings preparing to file lawsuits, but this is the first group out of the gate. With time ticking away, Mike can't wait any longer and let important momentum wain.

Mike isn't only suing Pornhub and MindGeek, but also Feras, David, Corey, and Bernd Bergmair, all by name. He's suing those behind Colbeck Capital, the investment firm that gave Fabian $362 million to roll up the porn industry, and also Visa. Mike is planning to sue Mastercard as well, but taking on Visa first could drive a wedge between the companies and inspire Mastercard to enact proactive company policy measures to stop themselves from being sued.

My eyes burn as I sit in my pajamas in the pitch-black and stare at the bright screen. I get a rush seeing the mountains of evidence that the JDF team and I have sent him over the past year, incorporated perfectly alongside evidence he and his investigators dug up themselves. The landmark RICO, sex trafficking, and child pornography lawsuit complaint is 179 pages and I hang on every word. This isn't a lawsuit about a website; it is a lawsuit about a global criminal enterprise.

> MindGeek is a classic criminal enterprise carried out through wide-ranging criminal activities, including, but not limited to, human trafficking; child pornography; criminal copyright piracy; internet hacking, stalking, and doxing; blackmail and extortion; mail and wire fraud; embezzlement, bank and creditor fraud; tax evasion; and money laundering. The company's top management and shadowy international financiers and their investors are the "bosses" of this Enterprise and, together with their "capos," run its rackets and schemes. The vehicles for these rackets and schemes are an internet pornography platform led by the flagship website "Pornhub" and an international network of ever-changing sham shell companies. Through these two elements, the Enterprise secures hundreds of millions of dollars in illicit monies each year, diverts them to the Enterprise members without paying any taxes, and masks the criminality under the guise of legitimate adult entertainment and an impenetrable corporate structure. The Enterprise viciously defends its concealed criminal activities from exposure. When it senses a threat of exposure, the Enterprise responds like any lawless, rouge actor: it lies, attacks, smears, bribes, blackmails, extorts, and otherwise intimidates any perceived threat by any means necessary.
>
> According to whistleblowers with firsthand knowledge, the Mind-Geek Criminal Enterprise is run exactly like an organized crime family: "It's just like the Sopranos," described one insider. At the

head of that crime family is Feras Antoon, the CEO of the company. Feras Antoon and his select group of "made" men at MindGeek refer to themselves as the "Bro-Club." Bro-Club membership comes with the opportunity to make substantial monies participating in the Enterprise's criminal activities. Indeed, as one person close to members of the Bro-Club explained, "The only thing that mattered was how much money can you bring into the enterprise. That was the only metric for your advancement . . ."[1]

I feel like I am reading a true crime thriller written by a lawyer who could have a side career as a novelist. Mike knows this kind of complaint will not only capture a judge's interest but will also captivate the media. He hired a top PR firm to help with the rollout and they have set up an exclusive interview on *CBS This Morning* that will feature Mike and two of the victims from the case who are bravely facing the camera to tell the world their stories for the first time.

I text Mike: "This complaint is incredible. Better than I ever imagined."

At dawn the exclusive show about the case goes live on *CBS This Morning* and the case is filed simultaneously as planned. Then the media frenzy begins.

"LAWSUIT ACCUSES PORNHUB OF OPERATING LIKE A CRIMINAL ENTERPRISE"

"IN A NEW LAWSUIT, MORE THAN 30 WOMEN ACCUSE PORNHUB OF PROFITING FROM VIDEOS POSTED WITHOUT THEIR CONSENT"

"PORNHUB FACES LAWSUIT ALLEGING IT KNOWINGLY PARTICIPATED IN TRAFFICKING AND CHILD PORNOGRAPHY"

I rush to get myself ready because I know reporters will soon be calling for on-camera interviews. On some shows Mike and I are both separately being interviewed. Mike is in his Times Square office with a view of the New York City skyline, and I am in a new coworking space I rented when COVID restrictions lifted. I set up camp in its boardroom, but its glass walls aren't soundproof, so unsuspecting office workers are getting an earful about porn, rape, and sex trafficking.

By the end of the day the news of the lawsuit has spread around the world, being covered by over six hundred news outlets on almost every continent. When I get home, exhausted but still high on the adrenaline from the exciting day, I lie down for a minute and start scrolling through news articles. As I'm reading, I get a notification that I have a new message.

It's Fabian.

"I read Bowe's novel," he says, adding a snarky laughing smiley face to the end of his sentence.

"Fascinating story," he goes on mockingly. "Love the part about me too . . ."

I write back. "*The New York Times* mocked Bowe's lawsuit complaint against Steve Cohen as a 'John le Carre novel' but we all know what happened to Steve Cohen and SAC Capital after that." I send him back the same laughing smiley face.

If Fabian isn't already aware, I just directed him to find out.

SAC Capital was forced to pay two billion dollars, three managers and traders were sentenced to prison, and the company was shut down.

Fabian goes silent.

43

DEATH AT THE DOOR

When the word "Mama" shows up on my caller ID I answer it.

"I can't believe it. I can't believe what they just said."

My mom sounds stunned. She is calling from the hospital waiting room. After her brother Mario had lost his appetite for a couple days, thrown up a few times, and wasn't acting like himself, my mom took him to the ER.

"They did a CT scan and rushed him to the operating room," she says. I can sense panic in her voice. "When the doctor came out, he said Mario's whole abdomen is full of stage four cancer. He has a hole in his stomach they can't repair. He can't eat anymore. They said he doesn't have long to live—only a few weeks maybe. I can't believe it. I just can't believe it. How can this be happening?"

The irony is horrific. With his mental handicap that stunted his development to that of a young child, there isn't much Mario can do in life for fulfillment—he can't have a romantic relationship, he can't have a job, and deformities in his legs and feet make it hard for him to do any physical activity. For his entire life food has been the thing that has brought him joy. To have that taken from him now seems unfathomably cruel.

She and Mario are inseparable. Partly because he depends on her like a five-year-old depends on their mother, but also because they simply love each other deeply. They eat together each morning, afternoon, and evening, take every vacation together. They even sleep in the same room, watching cooking shows together late into the night.

My mom can hardly process what the doctors have just said.

"It's okay, Mama," I say. "I am going to come there right now. We will be with Mario through this. We won't let him suffer. Don't panic."

When we hang up, I find Joel in the house.

"We have to go to California right away. Mario is dying."

As the words exit my mouth, I feel a wave of nausea. I have always been grateful that my dad never felt pain in death. He didn't even know he was going to die—it just happened in his sleep. But I am afraid to see Mario die like this, to watch him slowly suffer out of existence.

The next morning we start the fifteen-hour drive from Colorado to California. On the way my voice starts getting hoarse and my nose starts running, but I don't think too much of it. The next day, however, it's worse, and we are finally almost to my mom's house.

What if I have COVID?

I can't risk letting Mario or my mom get COVID, so I find a clinic with rapid testing. After nervously waiting in isolation to see the results, they come via text message.

I'm positive.

Dread washes over me. Now it will be at least two weeks before I can get to Mario. The thought is crushing. The only thing I want to do is be with Mario in his last days.

I tell Joel the bad news, and we run through the available options. We make the decision to mask, roll down the car windows, and drive fifteen hours back home where I go isolate myself in my room. This feels like an intense flu—my fever is high, and I can't seem to get it down. My cough is so bad I can hardly speak without going into a painful spasm. I lie in bed tormented by the idea that Mario might die any moment and I won't be there to say goodbye, to comfort him in his last moments and help my mom through the loss.

While I'm locked away at home battling COVID, my phone buzzes. Someone has sent me a headline I never expected to read.

44

BEFORE YOU BREAK

"ONLYFANS TO BAN SEXUALLY EXPLICIT CONTENT OVER REGULATORY CONCERNS"

The website called OnlyFans is suddenly, without warning, shutting down all of its pornographic content. Unlike Pornhub, which is despised by those in the porn industry, this site is beloved by porn performers who sell content directly to their fans to earn money. Hundreds of thousands of porn performers are understandably shocked by the change. A leader of the porn industry lobbying organization, the Free Speech Coalition, funded by MindGeek and rabidly defensive about Pornhub, seizes this opportunity. He tells thousands of furious porn performers the OnlyFans porn shutdown was my responsibility, effectively placing a target on me.

Like stepping on a hive of killer bees, the swarm of attacks begins immediately. They are violent and furious. Death threats, rape threats, and people telling me to kill myself—to impale myself anally with a cross, people telling me they are looking for my home because they want to hurt me. Journalists join the fray, calling and messaging, asking for statements about my role in a seismic event I took no part in. To make matters worse, I can hardly lift my head and can't speak without violently coughing, so I am forced to ignore the media requests for comment.

The online porn industry spokespeople with strong ties to MindGeek use this swirl of outrage to launch a new attack against me. They begin to say I've been storing and uploading child rape videos to the internet and must be held accountable for my criminal actions. In the frenzy of the moment, this horrifying false narrative gains traction as people begin spreading and sharing this despicable lie online as if it were the shocking truth.

One of my supporters sends me a message with a screenshot. "I think you need to see this. I'm so sorry."

It's a statement from a small anti-trafficking organization in the US. They saw the attacks online and believed them without verifying the allegations. They release a public statement condemning me for the federal crime of storing and sharing child pornography. Elated, the instigators disseminate the statement as if it is "proof" I actually committed this crime.

After sending emails to the organization that go without response, I call up an abuse survivor ally that has worked with the organization. He tries to get them to take down the statement, but the director isn't budging. I can't let this lie be legitimized even by a small anti-trafficking organization, so I call Mike Bowe for advice.

"Mike, please help me," I say in a tone that he has never heard from me.

"Whoa. Are you okay?"

My voice is raspy and I'm on the verge of tears as I share with him what happened, trying to get the words out between coughing fits.

"Listen—calm down," he says. "I can hear you're not in your normal state of mind. I know you feel like this is the worst thing that could ever happen to you as an advocate against this abuse, but you need to put this into perspective . . ."

Mike helps me realize that the attacks only exist at the moment on social media. He says to monitor them but not to panic and assures me if any media outlet were to publish the false statements, they would be legally liable.

"Should I disable my comments on Twitter so I don't keep getting spammed with all this hate and the accusations, or leave them open?" I ask. As the words exit my mouth, I remember so many months ago when Pornhub turned off their own Twitter comments after being swarmed by Traffickinghub activists for *actually* distributing child sexual abuse. The irony isn't lost on me.

"Is that a win for them? Have you ever turned off your comments before?" Mike asks.

"It would be a win, and I have never done it."

"Fuck them. That will only encourage them. Post your new TV interview then post your new article about the moderators and keep pumping out content. Hey diddle diddle, right up the middle."

I laugh, and it feels good.

Mike then tells me he will make a call to the director of the organization who published the statement against me. I have no idea what he says to the woman, but immediately after his call I get a message from her.

"I will take down the statement if you assure me I will never hear from a lawyer about this again."

It's a momentary relief, but to my dismay the attacks don't stop there. My enemies start a public petition accusing me of committing the same crime. It demands that I immediately be removed from my leadership roles. They aggressively circulate the petition letter, trying to get signatures and even send it to many organizations who partner with me and the Justice Defense Fund, demanding that they publicly condemn me. No one complies. Instead, I start receiving messages of sympathy from allies and survivors.

"Hang in there, we know what is going on here."

"We see through these attacks, stay strong."

Morgan Perry, the Justice Defense Fund's cofounder, stays on social media day and night to monitor the attacks and document what is being said. I appreciate that my colleagues have my back, but the pain of being accused of the very crime I've given so much to fight is still hard to bear.

Not long after, as the momentum of the attacks continues to build, Joel comes home with a pile of mail from our PO box. I open a letter addressed to me in blue ink handwriting with no return address.

"You have beautiful children, Lily Rose and Jedidiah Wisam, who you call 'Jed.'"

It disparages my work against Pornhub and lets me know that the anonymous sender has my home address. They list my address, and say they are close by, watching my family. It ends by saying "You are going to get someone killed."

How do they know where I live? Who is this? How do they know my children's full names, something I've never disclosed publicly before?

I tell Joel and he plays it down, saying anyone who actually wanted to hurt us would just do it and not send letters about it beforehand. He says these are intimidation tactics, empty threats to try to scare me.

"Don't fall for it."

Later he sends me a text message of encouragement: "You have enemies? Good. You stood up for something, sometime in your life.—Winston Churchill"

I want to believe Joel is right, that I should take it all in stride as an indication of progress, but them mentioning the names of my children leaves me with fear I've never felt before.

That evening as I FaceTime Mario, tears pool in my eyes and spill down as I see how pale and weak he is, though I'm trying to smile as I speak with him. It's becoming difficult for him to even have the strength to hold the phone. Though he's in pain, he musters up the energy to tell me enthusiastically, with such sincerity, "I love you, Laya."

"Laya" is the endearing way he pronounces my name.

"Come visit me soon, okay?" he says with a weak smile. "Give Joel and the kids my regards!"

I can see his peeling, cracked lips, parched from the medication and lack of nourishment. Since Mario can't get out of bed anymore, my mom is beside him 24/7, changing his diapers, giving him medication, and trying to keep the pain at bay. My mom holds the phone and lies down next to him in the large hospital bed, moved into the living room where he will die. She puts her head on his shoulder and cries, kissing his face as I try to comfort her with empty words over the phone, all while my own heart is shattering.

I need to get there, quick. I have to get better so I can go.

That night sleep is out of reach because I can't calm my racing heart, in part because of my fever and partly from my anxiety. I have felt this way for days, yet it has seemed like weeks, and I don't know how much more I can stand. My thoughts are full of questions. Why is Mario suffering and dying? Why couldn't I be fighting poverty, or hunger, or cancer, or animal abuse? People working for those causes aren't attacked like this. I want to delete my Twitter account, shut down the petition, move on, and do something easier and lighter. I don't think I can maintain this level of intensity much longer.

As I search my mind for anything to bring comfort, I hear my dad's voice in my head.

"You have to be tough, Laila!" he would say, hugging me and rubbing the top of my head until my hair was messed up. He did this every time I complained about a heartbreak or was mistreated by a professor or faced some other upsetting situation. When he spoke these words with his Jordanian accent, I knew it was advice born out of experience. A few weeks before he died, my father recounted having to tell a young mother with small children she only had a few months to live. He knew about needing to be tough. I repeat his words over and over like a soothing mantra.

Three melatonin have done nothing to get me to sleep. Frustrated, I walk down the hallway and grab the plastic medicine bin off the top shelf of the messy linen closet. *Who has time to fold fitted sheets?* I rummage through the bin of remedies and grab two prescription-strength ibuprofens saved from after Jed's birth. I chug them with a big gulp of liquid NyQuil. Thankfully, there aren't any real drugs in the house, otherwise I would probably take them.

I shuffle back to the bed, lying as still as possible to calm myself down, but my heart rate is still out of control and my mind is spinning. I wonder . . . *Is this what it feels like before you break?*

It's a genuine question. I lie there, remembering the time when I was a young girl and my mom had a nervous breakdown due to a period of intense stress in her life. Her aunt, who had become her adopted mother, had just died, and she couldn't process the loss. This on top of the stress of taking care of Mario around the clock alongside three needy daughters and keeping a spotless house with meals on the table.

I recall the sadness I saw in my dad's eyes in the rearview mirror as he drove her to the hospital psychiatric ward. I demanded to go along and stay with her overnight because I couldn't handle the thought of my mother being there alone. Since my dad worked at the hospital, the nurses ignored protocol and allowed me to stay. I spent one night with her, trying to comfort her. Thankfully, she recovered quickly, but it was a traumatic experience I'll never forget.

I'm fearful that I might have reached my own limit.

And more is about to hit me.

45

NOW I'M THE DEFENDANT?

When I finally test negative for COVID, and Jed, Lily, and Joel look to be in the clear, we rush back to California. I am helping my mom gently roll Mario's heavy body onto his side so he can avoid bed sores when I get a call. It's from an unfamiliar number, so I let it go to voicemail as usual. But when I see the voice-to-text preview, I can't believe what I am reading. I click play just to be sure it didn't get translated wrong.

"Hello, this is Detective Kevin Mahoney with the county sheriff's office. I got a report about you that I am investigating. Please call me back as soon as possible."

That is *my* county's sheriff's office.

It suddenly sinks in, and my stomach tightens.

The security expert James warned me this would happen when this fight first started. He told me that if I kept gaining traction, at some point Joel or I would be criminally accused of possessing and distributing child pornography. I never really believed it could happen. Until now.

My mind begins to race with the possible ways this can play out. I imagine police getting paid off to falsely prosecute me or MindGeek calling in favors. I picture an officer being blackmailed by MindGeek about his own porn consumption and my imagination runs wild. It's the mental picture of getting separated from my children that strikes real terror in me. *How insane would it be if I'm the one who ends up in prison after all of this?*

I want to call the detective back right away to try to tell him they're all lies, to explain why they are attacking me, and to mitigate the situation, but I check myself. I have learned over the past year and a half to be more cautious than that.

When I call Mike and he doesn't answer, I try his partner, yet she doesn't pick up, either. So I text him and ask what I should do, attaching the audio file of the voicemail so he can listen to it. As each minute goes by, I obsessively check whether the text shows he read it.

When it finally says "Read," I feel relief.

"Don't call back law enforcement. I will have one of our lawyers call them back for you now."

He gets an experienced former federal prosecutor to make the call to the detective on my behalf. The attorney explains the situation and sets up a call in a few days with myself, him, and the detective.

———————

In the dim light of the living room, I see Jed and Lily Rose sleeping on the floor mattress I put down beside Mario's hospice bed. I have a feeling this might be his last night, so I told my mom that I would watch him through the night. I don't want her to go through the pain of seeing him die.

For a few minutes I make a playlist of Mario's favorite Frank Sinatra songs on my phone, then I place it on his pillow so he can hear the music playing softly by his ear. As "That's Life" starts to play, I give Mario a dose of morphine and Vicodin, which he takes as liquid drops on his parched tongue since he can't swallow anymore. I sit down beside him on a chair at the head of the bed, pull the railing down, get close, and take hold of his hands. He squeezes me tightly as he opens his kind, green eyes and we make eye contact.

"I've been a puppet, a pauper, a pirate, a poet . . ." Sinatra sings in the background.

Mario can't talk anymore, but he makes a moaning sound as he hears his favorite song; I can tell it's because he likes it. I lean down and kiss his cheek, then begin to whisper in his ear while holding back tears.

"I am right here, Mario. Okay? I am not going anywhere."

There is nothing I can say or do now to take his pain away, or to stop the inevitable.

"You'll be out of pain soon. Don't be scared, okay? I love you, Mario."

He makes a noise in response, and I know he understood what I said. I start to talk about all his favorite foods that he will get to enjoy soon, listing them one by one and describing them. As I am doing this, his oxygen level goes up to perfect and his heart rate monitor shows it has also gone into perfect range, something that hasn't happened in weeks. I am stunned. It's like his body entered into peace.

For a few minutes it stays like this, then his breathing slows down and becomes more spaced out. I feel scared and helpless, knowing I might be watching him take his last labored breaths. I scoop his head in my arms and press my face into his, with my tears streaming down onto his cheeks.

"It's okay, Mario," I say, despite my panic inside. "I love you. I love you. It's okay. I love you."

These are the only words I can think to say. My tears are flowing uncontrollably.

His jaw suddenly becomes stiff in my hands, and I see his chest stop moving. His skin loses any color it had left.

Then he is gone.

———

Everything in me wants to disengage from this battle against Pornhub for a while, to have some peace, some quiet, some time away from the madness. I want to breathe for a moment and grieve the loss of my beloved Mario because he deserves it. But as much as I want to, the circumstances of the moment have their way. This train is barreling ahead regardless of my feelings. I am on it, and I can't get off.

Anxious and feeling weak, I dial into the conference line to speak with the detective who is investigating me. I start by introducing myself and begin to give him a history of my work, but he cuts me off.

"I know all about you," the man says bluntly. "I have been investigating you thoroughly. I know all about your work. In fact, I spent days going through your entire online history, including all your social media posts. Even the ones you deleted I can access, and I've gone through them all."

He explains he also searched every database where child pornography images are intercepted, and he searched all the reporting databases both locally and nationally. He even went to my address.

He found nothing.

"There is nothing to support these accusations against you," he says.

"But I did learn quite a lot about MindGeek and Pornhub in the process," he adds wryly. He then tells me that he investigated the source of the false reports and sees they were made by a person who spends a considerable amount of time defending MindGeek and Pornhub online and attacking those who speak against them. Evidence is later uncovered showing the person who made the false report collaborates with MindGeek's marketing manager.

"It's bullshit," the detective says. "This is obviously because they oppose your work and I'm sorry it's happening to you. If there is any way I can help to stop these attacks in the future, let me know. I am closing this out and will send you a copy of the report."

He then adds, "We should meet up for coffee sometime when you are back in town. I'd like to see if our office can coordinate with your organization to protect children from online exploitation. We clearly have the same goals."

I take a deep breath after we hang up. That attack didn't go as they had planned.

But I am in for another nasty surprise.

46

THE CREDIT CARDS
SNEAK BACK

When I get back to my computer, an email from the name "MG Leaks" is in my inbox.

Hi Laila,

I commend you on all your efforts in fighting the MindGeek porn empire and fighting to help all victims of sex trafficking for many years. Given that I am a MindGeek veteran for many years, I can tell you that you must follow the money. More than 60% of their revenue now comes from advertising. I don't know if you know this, but Visa and Mastercard came back to MindGeek's advertising arm for Pornhub called TrafficJunky just a few weeks after *The New York Times* article. Since Visa and Mastercard cut off Pornhub Premium and all the paid content, they are focusing more now on advertising through TrafficJunky to make up for lost revenue. Exposing Visa and Mastercard for returning to Pornhub through TrafficJunky advertising will put more pressure on their main source of revenue today.

I am in disbelief and crushed by this news. I didn't have any idea that the credit card companies went back to processing Pornhub's advertising shortly after everything blew up in December.

I need to confirm this for myself, so I log in to MindGeek's TrafficJunky website, where advertisers go to purchase Pornhub ads. The tagline on the home page is "Your customers are on Pornhub so why aren't you?" The credit card logos were removed from the site last December and they are still gone. So how can I confirm this? I get an idea to pose as an advertiser to MindGeek's customer service team.

"Hi, I want to sign up for Pornhub advertising, but I am wondering if I can pay using my credit card?" I ask.

"Yes, you can."

"Visa and Mastercard both?"

"Yes."

"What about Discover? Can I use my Discover card?"

"Yes, you can. Is there anything else I can assist you with today?"

I am shocked and angry. How in the world am I supposed to do this all over again? We don't have the momentum of the petition anymore. Nick Kristof already released his bombshell article. The lawsuits are filed.

What am I supposed to do now?

I text the bad news to a Montreal reporter whom I've been in touch with since all this began, and he is shocked as well. "This is a big story."

A horrifying thought comes to mind. MindGeek's owners are desperate to sell. What if this gets out in the media and MindGeek spins it in their favor to attract buyers? I imagine the devastating headline: "Pornhub Wins Credit Card Companies Back."

No. I can't let that happen.

"Please don't report this yet," I tell the journalist I just confided in.

Full of questions, on the verge of tears, and feeling like pulling out my hair, I get on the phone with the new whistleblower who sent the email. He tells me I can call him "Bob," then he goes on to confirm everything he said in the email, only adding more color.

"After the *New York Times* article, when the card companies cut off Pornhub, Feras was begging them to come back but he didn't know if they would, so he made a private room in the office and the walls had lists taped up with the names of hundreds of employees that would be fired if the card companies refused to come back at least to Pornhub's advertising. They knew it would be the biggest devastating blow and they were panicking. But then a few weeks in, Visa, Mastercard, and Discover all went back to TrafficJunky, so the whole advertising arm of the business was going forward as usual."

I can't believe I didn't know this, but neither did anyone else. "Bob" goes on to reveal something else.

"Another thing they do is a credit card scheme they call 'rebill shift.' How it works is that many people use prepaid credit cards to sign up for porn sites because they don't want it to show up on their normal card statement. When the user signs up for a subscription for $9.99 per month or $19.99, it is renewed every month and it draws down the prepaid card until finally the card balance won't cover the cost of the subscription anymore and the subscription is immediately canceled. But MindGeek realized that these cards still have a small balance on them. So, what they do is keep billing the user in small increments to see what will go through. First, they try to charge something like nine dollars. If that doesn't work, they charge seven. If that doesn't go through, they charge five and they do this all the way down to one dollar. No one ever knows it happens because no one checks a statement for a prepaid credit card. Even if they did, who is going to go through the trouble of disputing a five-dollar charge on a prepaid card? I'm not a lawyer or a police officer, but that doesn't sound legal to me. They are making half a million dollars a year doing this."

"No, it doesn't sound legal at all," I tell him. "It sounds like credit card fraud, and I am going to run this by some attorneys. Thank you."

I send this information to Mike Bowe and the Federal Trade Commission's lawyers whom I have been in touch with. As disgusted as I am by the whole credit card scheme, I am not surprised by it. But I am shocked by the news that the credit cards are still processing Pornhub's advertising. How could they continue monetizing Pornhub's content when *they know* so much of it is illegal child abuse, rape, and sex trafficking?

I call Brad to tell him what happened, and he can sense the disappointment and distress in my voice. I ask him what he thinks I should do.

"This is so hard to believe—I'm so sorry. I think you should call Bill Ackman. Tell him what's going on and see how he can help . . . Next, I think you should investigate Pornhub's ad platform the same way you investigated Pornhub. You need to be armed with evidence. Third, I think you should write another article exposing all of this in a powerful way, framed the way you want it framed." Brad's advice grounds me in actionable steps and I'm grateful for it.

My first thought had also been to get in touch with Bill Ackman; he needs to know that Visa and Mastercard didn't do what they said they would. I send Bill an email explaining the gist of what's going on.

Early the next morning, I am startled awake by my phone buzzing under my pillow. Bill Ackman's name is on my caller ID.

47

MEET "FILTHY RAMIREZ"

When you get a call from a billionaire hedge fund manager you answer it, even at 5 a.m. I fling my covers off, leap out of bed, and run downstairs to the hall closet, shutting the door so I don't wake up the kids.

"Hi Bill, thanks so much for calling. I need to tell you what I just found out because I'm devastated about it."

"Sure, what's going on?" he asks politely but with his trademark reserve.

I explain how Visa and Mastercard went back to processing all the ads for Pornhub through TrafficJunky, which is how they monetize their content.

"I am sick about this, and wanted to know if you have ideas on how to get Visa and Mastercard to stop," I say. "If after all that's happened, Pornhub gets to recover financially and go on with business as usual, it will set a horrible precedent and embolden future abusers. They will think they can exploit victims with impunity. We *can't* let that happen."

The confidence in Bill's voice reassures me. "I get it. I can help. I know journalists who would want to report on this. It's a big story that they went back to Pornhub. I will also see if I can talk to Ajay about it."

Ajay Banga, who was the CEO of Mastercard in 2020 is now the chairman of the company. My spirits lift as Bill tells me this.

"Thank you so much, Bill, I appreciate it."

Next, I decide to pose as an advertiser and set up an account with Pornhub's TrafficJunky ad platform to see how their back end operates. Once I get into the system, I'm stunned at what I discover. TrafficJunky allows advertisers to choose keywords that will place ads on related illegal content.

Now I understand why I saw ads targeting pedophiles on child abuse content.

The keywords all have a traffic indicator bar that shows advertisers how much traffic they will get to their ads by choosing each keyword. As I type one keyword, Pornhub offers a list of high-traffic suggestions. After typing in "teen," Pornhub suggests to me "young," "teeny playground," "pigtails," "braces," then "baby," "hidden camera," "younger," "baby girl," and "extreme tight pussy." I take screenshots of each selectable suggestion. I am sickened when the traffic indicator bar is full when I see the keywords "14yrsold," "not18," "tiny girl," and "screaming teen."

Companies that pay to advertise on Pornhub went through this same process of selecting keywords and seeing suggestions like these? They saw all this, but no one said anything?

Next, I discover that MindGeek allows Pornhub advertisers to target users who speak different languages. "Rape" is a high-traffic keyword to choose in Russian, Arabic, and German. "Underage" can be selected in Chinese. I meticulously document everything in a visual presentation that I send to Mike Bowe and every other lawyer now pursuing lawsuits against MindGeek. Next, I tip off Montreal journalist Martin Patriquin and send him my Pornhub advertiser account log-in.

"Fuck," he replies when he sees everything for himself. Martin documents it all and gets an article ready to publish.

For my sanity's sake, I had stayed off Pornhub for several months. But when I turn on my VPN to mask my location and dive back into the site, it appears not much has changed. Yes, Pornhub now verifies uploaders' identification, but often those uploaders are the abusers and traffickers of the victims in the videos. Pornhub still refuses to verify the age and consent of the millions of individuals in the free and ad revenue–generating content, which constitutes most of the site. As usual, within minutes, I find women who are being filmed without their knowledge as they are passed out from alcohol and drugs.

"Birdman361" is one of the uploaders of these illegal videos and he discloses that his name is Ramirez and he lives in San Antonio. His entire Pornhub profile is full of videos of homeless women and girls. He flaunts the fact that they are vulnerable with titles and tags like "Filthy Ramirez Destroys Mentally Ill Woman," "Homeless Girls Sucks Me Good for Money," and "Homeless Black Girl Suck BWC for Ice." He tags his videos with "homemade" and "mentally handicapped."

One user asks him a question. "Love the videos, how do you meet/approach these girls?"

His answer is incriminating.

"I just say I have some things they can do around my apartment and that I'll pay them like $20 or $30," Ramirez replies. "Sometimes I only give them $10 . . . a little bit of food and a shower and maybe a place to crash, it doesn't take much. I do this daily."

Here is a man admitting publicly on Pornhub that he *deceives* vulnerable *homeless women and girls* by saying he has work for them to do around his house, and when he gets them there, he coerces them into sex for $10, a little bit of food, a shower, or a place to sleep. He films them and uploads the videos to Pornhub, which then partners with Visa and Mastercard to monetize their exploitation for profit.

I post the video comments on Twitter and tag Visa and Mastercard while emphasizing once again that sex trafficking is the commercialization of any sex act induced by force, fraud, deception, coercion, or where the victim is under eighteen. *This* is, by definition, a sex trafficking venture.

Next, I audio record a victim's voice in another homemade rape video (masking it with software so it's not recognizable) and post it with the words she is screaming: "Seriously! It hurts! Stop! That fucking hurts! Stop! Put it away! Put your goddamn phone away!" I again tag Visa and Mastercard.

Since Bill Ackman follows me on Twitter, he shares some of the posts. Soon he gets back to me with some good news. He sent my tweets about this directly to Ajay Banga. Then shortly after he shares even better news.

"Just connected with Ajay Banga. He is going to reach out to his colleagues at Mastercard about the advertising issue. I gave him your mobile."

Hours after Bill's message, I get an email from Mastercard's John Verdeschi. The last time I connected with John was December 2020 when he told me I would be hearing an announcement from Mastercard shortly— an announcement that they were cutting off Pornhub. Now it is February 2022, and we are having this conversation *again*.

John also loops in Tiffany Hall, the vice president and senior managing counsel of Mastercard and chief of staff to the CEO. John asks me for a meeting to discuss my tweets and update me on what they are doing to "prevent illegal activity and unlawful content."

I decide to respond in a way that will ensure when we get on the call there is no question in John's and Tiffany's mind that Mastercard is *still* monetizing illegal crime scenes on Pornhub. If they try to eat up the time with gibberish and fluff about all the steps they are supposedly taking to prevent this abuse, they will have to do so with full knowledge that they are lying to my face.

It takes me a full day to draft my sixteen-hundred-word email. I include links, titles, and descriptions of over a dozen obviously illegal videos. I also send my TrafficJunky presentation documenting how MindGeek suggests illegal keywords to their advertisers.

They don't respond.

I wait a few more days and they still don't respond.

I message them two more times asking for a date to meet but there is no response. I conclude they weren't interested in actually addressing their continued relationship with Pornhub. They just wanted to tick a box and tell me some meaningless words about their supposed efforts so they can tell Ajay Banga they spoke to me and move on.

But I won't have it.

Next, I quickly get to work writing my article that will expose what Mastercard and Visa have done. The proposed title is "Why Are Visa and Mastercard Still in Bed with Pornhub?" When I finish, I send the article to half a dozen news outlets, but they don't respond. It's a tough read with graphic descriptions. I didn't mince words in calling out Visa and Mastercard. The last outlet, *Newsweek*, gets back to me saying they liked it but that it was "too hard-edged." I am discouraged, but at this point, after all I have been through, there are few things that could deter me from pressing forward.

Back to the drawing board.

————

"I work for Pornhub. What do you want to know?"

After reading the subject line, I open the email. My cofounder and COO of the Justice Defense Fund, Morgan Perry, recently encouraged me to start a Twitter "truth campaign" to retell the stories of victims who have been abused on Pornhub. I follow her advice and my tweets hit over 100 million views in a few days. They also catch the attention of a new Mind-Geek insider who calls himself "BBJE." I answer immediately, thanking him for reaching out. Sparing no time, I list a series of questions I want answered.

"I can answer your questions," he replies. "I am not the average em-

ployee. I can send you information, but I want this to be a two-way relationship."

A two-way relationship?

It sounds suspicious. This might be a setup.

He sends me a photo that proves he is on the sixth floor of the MindGeek
Montreal headquarters—a floor reserved only for the top executives and
VPs at the company.

"I have access to all the financials. Past and present."

That's exactly what Mike Bowe needs in order to get at the money his
plaintiffs deserve. Maybe this insider knows that.

"Could you send them to me?" I ask.

He sends me screenshots of some financial statements to prove he is
telling the truth about his level of access. I ask him if we can switch from
email to text and he agrees. He says he is going into the office and won't be
available for a few hours.

The next thing he sends is a sideways photo of a man smoking a cigarette inside MindGeek's exclusive sixth floor. The photo shows a sterile
setting with high ceilings and recessed lighting. Glass is everywhere; the
furnishings are modern and new. As I rotate the photo and zoom in, I realize I am staring at a covertly shot photo of a man who tried to hide his
face from the public for years—Bernd Bergmair. BBJE confirms it's him.
This is gold for Mike Bowe's lawsuit because it's hard proof that Bergmair
isn't some distant hands-off figure without knowledge of what has been
going on in Montreal, as his lawyers are trying to argue.

"Where did the money go?" I ask. "The fear is the victims won't get paid
even if they prevail in court unless they can trace the money."

"You're right. The money is gone. It gets paid out in dividends to the
shareholders. The shareholders spend it on assets and leisure. The money
that stays in the company gets spent on expenses and new products. It will
be practically impossible to recover that money unless you go after the
shareholders' personal assets."

He reveals that he has troves of detailed evidence about how MindGeek's owners and executives have been comingling their personal businesses with MindGeek. This evidence could be the key to keeping the owners in Mike's case and holding them *personally* liable for MindGeek's actions.

"Can you provide info and insight on how the money flowed from the websites to the owners?"

"I can send you full documents," he replies. "However, once I download them Eddy will see a trace. If you can send me some insurance, I believe the documents will be very valuable to you. I am risking my position doing this."

I was hoping he wouldn't say this.

Eddy Di Santo is the CFO of MindGeek and BBJE is afraid he will find out.

"I don't want to put you in a place you are not comfortable with and I am not sure what you mean by insurance."

"If it ever comes down to it, I would appreciate your assistance in a whistleblower case. For now, I'm looking for financial insurance," he replies.

This is out of the question.

"I could not and would not pay for information, unfortunately," I tell him. "Maybe you could consider the benefit of knowing you helped these victims be vindicated and abusers held accountable. I am sorry I can't help you in that way."

He asks me about the status of the victims' lawsuits filed against Pornhub, so I send him links to multiple legal complaints where he can read the victims' stories for himself and see how the cases have progressed.

There is a pause in our conversations after I send the links. It looks like BBJE might be done now that I have made it clear I won't pay him for information.

The next day at 10:00 p.m., I get a notification that I have a new message. He says he took time to read through the victims' stories laid out in the legal complaints.

"I don't care about getting money anymore."

Next, he encourages me to go after the company that is literally keeping the Pornhub crime scene online and serving its content to the world—a web hosting and server company based in Massachusetts called Reflected Networks. This company has been providing hosting services to Pornhub for years despite Pornhub content violating their own acceptable use policy. Why do they do this? BBJE sends me the last year's worth of paid invoices showing MindGeek paid Reflected Networks $23,600,000.

Mike decides to depose Reflected Networks in his case, and I share the information with other law firms pursuing MindGeek, hoping they will add them as a defendant. My team and I at the Justice Defense Fund are adamant that *all enablers* of bad actors like MindGeek need to be held accountable in order to see lasting change.

48

WHO TORCHED THE
PORNHUB PALACE?

At MindGeek headquarters, things are not looking good. Sources tell me that multiple deals to sell the company have fallen through because no one wants to take on the liability of all the lawsuits and the negative media exposure. Besides this, the company structure itself is unexplainable.

Not only is MindGeek being sued by Mike Bowe, but they are also facing two class-action lawsuits in Canada on behalf of victims worldwide for $600 million apiece and two class-action lawsuits in the US on behalf of trafficked children. Nine women are suing them in South Carolina for monetizing spy camera footage of them from a school locker room, and fifty adult trafficking victims are in the process of settling a major lawsuit with them in California.

On top of all of this, they know Mike Bowe is planning to sue them again with dozens more individual lawsuits in addition to the thirty-four lawsuits he already filed. This time around he is planning to sue Mastercard as well as Visa.

According to my sources, Feras is still set on taking the advice of his lawyers and is not addressing the "scandal" with those working at the company. The MindGeek VPs, aka "the Divas," and other executives are uncomfortable about this, but Feras is digging in his heels.

But what really sets them against Feras is his musing about *shutting down Pornhub*. He is tired of all the bad press, of fighting off lawsuits and government investigations. He knows it will never end as long as Pornhub is on the internet because the site is still full of illegal content. The only way out that Feras can see is to actually shut it down.

Fearing losing their incomes, the Divas decide to turn on Feras.

The ringleader of the revolt against Feras is Alan Abou-Atme, the VP of sales, insiders tell me. Even Karim El Marazi, the chief products officer who was hired and promoted by Feras, is ready to turn on him. All of the Divas and executives reach a consensus that they must go straight to Bernd Bergmair, the majority shareholder.

Not only do they complain to Bernd that Feras wants to shut down Pornhub, but they accuse Feras and David of bleeding the company resources for their own personal gain. They tell him Feras's family is using the company cafeteria's sales to enrich themselves and are taking seven-week vacations paid for by MindGeek. They tell Bernd about the personal drivers, assistants, and property managers for Feras that are all paid by MindGeek.

After hearing all of this, Bernd is furious that they have been siphoning money from him and embarks on his own investigation with the help of MindGeek's chief financial officer Eddy Di Santo. Soon he confirms that what he was told is true and the hammer comes down hard. Bernd wants to oust Feras and David, but they resist. Instead, they let go of the employees on MindGeek's payroll who are being utilized for their personal benefit and try to address the internal strife.

———

Feras and David decide to do something they have never done as the CEO and COO of MindGeek. They are finally going to speak to the media, because their silence has been kindling anger within the company. The VPs have been frustrated and angry that Feras, at the advice of his lawyers, has refused to address the scandal publicly in the media. Part of Feras and David's rationale is that doing a story with a friendly journalist will appease the angry Divas as well as majority shareholder Bernd Bergmair.

They choose to give their story to Adam Leith Gollner, a writer for *Vanity Fair* who is from Montreal and who graduated from Concordia University at the same time they did. After initial conversations, they conclude he will be sympathetic to them and harsh to MindGeek's enemies.

When Adam reaches out to this MindGeek enemy, his approach is deceptively soft:

> Dear Laila,
>
> My name is Adam Gollner and I am a reporter working on an article about Pornhub for *Vanity Fair,* and I would like to include you and your work with Traffickinghub in the article. Please let me know if there is a time that's convenient for a phone interview next week.
>
> Thank you.

I get back to him the same day and ask what his angle is.

He tells me he is writing about Pornhub "in general" by looking at numerous obstacles the company has been facing, then adds, "I am interviewing a range of voices and am looking forward to including you as well." He signs off with a friendly "All my best."

If there is one thing I have learned, it is to be suspicious of journalists. First, no one writes about Pornhub "in general," second, when he says a "range of voices" that probably means he is planning on interviewing Pornhub shills. I had no idea those shills were Feras and David. I have a strange feeling about this, so I tell him just to send me his questions via email and I will answer them in writing. He protests but then agrees.

The questions he sends are not alarming in the least and I answer them easily.

"Thank you for participating in this important story," he concludes in a friendly tone. Then he writes back with a question that I find strange: "What did you think when you learned that Pornhub CEO Feras Antoon's house was set on fire?"

"I was relieved to learn no one was hurt, and I am sure it will be thoroughly investigated," I write back.

He thanks me and I hear nothing from him again until days before publication, when he asks me to respond to the accusation that I have personally exploited Pornhub victims. I am disturbed and offended by his question. My gut feeling about him was right.

I tell him it isn't true and if he intends to publish any other attacks against me or Traffickinghub in his piece, he must allow me the right of reply. "That's what any ethical journalist would do," I say. He is clearly bothered by my comment. He never sends another communication.

———

The *Vanity Fair* **headline** is clickbait: **XXX FILES: WHO TORCHED THE PORNHUB PALACE?** "When the CEO of Pornhub's mega-mansion mysteriously burned to the ground, there was no shortage of possible suspects. Now, for the first time, the site's shadowy founders tell their story."

"I was building the house of my dreams . . . And everything was going great," laments Feras at the opening of Adam's article. Adam paints readers a portrait of Feras, the victim.

". . . He can't help recounting how he lay in bed that night, powerless, two miles from the still-unfinished building, asleep at home with his wife and children, as the company's security officer alerted 911. By the time police showed up, the Pornhub Palace was in flames . . . Antoon finally woke up when his brother got through on the landline. Driving over, he told me, he kept hoping it would turn out to be something small—maybe just some teenagers messing around . . . Arriving at the scene, he recalled, 'I was devastated.'"

Then Adam gets to the point that he and Feras wanted to make.

"Antoon's inferno was searingly symbolic. It represented not just bad juju befalling the XXX site, but an overheated, inflammatory political climate in the ongoing war against online porn."

Adam goes on to let Feras suggest who he thinks it was that incited the attack. "I can't even count how many comments I saw from people saying to burn the company or my house down. For a while, it was easy to dismiss the tweets as just people on the internet talking. Then my house burned down."

The tweets . . . ?

Adam clarifies for the reader *exactly* whose tweets Feras is talking about. Mine.

"During the lead-up to the torching of Antoon's mansion, extremists began doxing Pornhub employees and issuing violent threats online. Shepherding this movement was an outfit called Traffickinghub . . . 'Burn them to the ground!' read a tweet shared on the Traffickinghub founder's profile four days before the arson attack."

I never uttered or wrote those words and Adam knows it. He also knows that I have often publicly condemned acts of violence and have always called for accountability within the bounds of the law. But truth doesn't seem to matter when you are a "pick me" journalist with the chance to get the CEO of MindGeek on the media record for the first time in history.

Not only does Adam regurgitate all of MindGeek's attacks against me and Traffickinghub, but he endorses Feras's claim that I am responsible for inciting criminal arson. I'm irate as I read through this trash article and immediately write to *Vanity Fair*'s editor in chief Radhika Jones demanding a retraction. Adam puts his social media accounts on private and Radhika digs in her heels and refuses to correct the false statements.

Then I get a vindicating call.

It is from a MindGeek insider so close to Feras they could be family. "Feras doesn't believe anyone related or inspired by you and Traffickinghub burned his house down. That is a made-up lie. What he told his family, and what they also believe, is that one of his Mafia-connected neighbors did it.

"It was a professional job. They hate Feras, and it has been a long time coming. They have hated him since he first bulldozed down 220 trees in the neighborhood's nature preserve without a permit to build his disgusting monstrosity. He tried to get his contractors to hide all the trees he cut down, but he couldn't cover up what he did. Then after the *New York Times* article, the neighbors found out he had also been harming children. Journalists had been swarming the neighborhood all the time, knocking on the neighbors' doors—with cameras and questions. They had had enough of Feras, so they burned it down. That is what Feras himself believes and that is what he tells those who are closest to him."

49

FERAS DETHRONED

I s she trustworthy?" I ask Mike.

Having been burned by *Vanity Fair*, I'm nervous when a journalist from *The New Yorker* named Sheelah Kolhattkar reaches out to me about MindGeek. She said she has spoken to Mike Bowe and now she wants to speak with me.

Mike assures me. "She covered my SAC Capital case—actually wrote a book about it. She is going to be fair, and she is going to be balanced. I don't think you have anything to worry about with Sheelah."

I still have reservations, but I realize the importance of keeping this story in the press and the pressure on MindGeek. "Okay, I'll talk to her." I decide to meet Sheelah for a two-hour interview over tea in an airport hotel lobby in New York. It's clear that Sheelah is an honest reporter with a genuine interest in advancing the story. We stay in touch over the next few months and I repeatedly emphasize the importance of bringing to light the fact that the credit card companies went back to Pornhub.

After several months of editing and fact-checking, *The New Yorker* publishes Sheelah's eight-thousand-word article.[1] She opens with a story about an underage victim named Nicole, whom she calls "Rachel." Nicole reached out to me not long after the Traffickinghub movement began and has been adamant about wanting me to use her real name instead of a pseudonym. She wants to show the world she isn't afraid of her abusers, and I admire her courage and conviction. By now my organization, the Justice Defense Fund, has an incredible team of highly experienced advocates providing licensed trauma therapy, social work services, legal services, and more. We have been assisting Nicole with trauma therapy support because at only twenty years old, she has gone through more heartache and trauma than anyone should handle in a lifetime. She was preyed upon by the notorious convicted serial pedophile Abdul-Hasib Elahi, who had targeted nearly two thousand victims worldwide.[2] According to the United Kingdom's National Crime Agency, some of his victims were as young as eight months old. Nicole was one of his victims.

Elahi, a stranger to fifteen-year-old Nicole, had contacted her via an unsolicited message on WhatsApp. He proceeded to blackmail and coerce her into sending him nude images and photographs. When she complied, instead of leaving her alone as promised, he blackmailed her further, threatening to send the images to her friends and family if she did not send more. He demanded eighty nude images and two videos of her penetrating herself and spitting on herself. Fearing that he would act on his threat, Nicole complied with his demands. He didn't stop there. Elahi threatened her further and demanded videos of her drinking her own urine and eating feces. It was then that Nicole cut him off and sought help. The videos and images ended up being widely distributed on Pornhub and MindGeek's other tube sites.[3]

Some of the most devastating things that Nicole shared with me are the pleading emails she sent to Pornhub again and again, begging them to remove her child abuse and challenging them on why they allow her abuse to be uploaded over and over.

"How can I somehow stop them from being uploaded?" one email asked. "I don't want to be posted anymore and I'm considering reaching out for legal advice to take action against Pornhub."

A year after she wrote to Pornhub in 2019 threatening legal action she was represented by Mike Bowe to sue them.

"You really need a better system to stop anyone being allowed to upload anything," she continued. "I tried to kill myself after finding myself reuploaded to your site after I had it removed. I don't know what else I can do."

Another email she sent to Pornhub said, "Why do videos of me from when I was 15 years old and blackmailed which is child porn continuously get uploaded without going through any type of filter or check? . . . Why is money more important than the well-being of victims constantly being uploaded . . . ?"

Seeing those emails and speaking with Nicole prompted Sheelah to open her article with Nicole's heartrending story.[4] She also shares the accounts of other victims she has spoken to while methodically explaining the business model and origins of MindGeek, and what has been done thus far to hold them accountable. Throughout the article, Sheelah speaks of my work. I am thrilled when I see how she ends the piece by highlighting how Visa and Mastercard went back to Pornhub.

"Still, Mickelwait continues to search for illegal content on Pornhub. In January, she said she received a call from a former MindGeek employee who told her that Visa and Mastercard were still processing payments from advertisers . . . Mickelwait sat down to type out a Twitter post. 'The lucrative ads on MindGeek-owned Pornhub are purchased through TrafficJunky which MindGeek also owns . . . MasterCard and Visa process the payments for the ads,' she wrote. 'Hold them accountable.'"

It is my call to action. Hold them accountable. Hold them *all* accountable.

———

Bernd Bergmair is in his hideout in Hong Kong when he gets the link to the *New Yorker* piece. It is another devastating blow for MindGeek as

Sheelah doesn't spare the appalling truth about the company. New employees that she has spoken with have made Feras, David, Corey, and Bernd look worse than ever. It seemed impossible that Pornhub's reputation could ever be rehabilitated after thousands of blows in the media, and now this seems to be the knockout punch.

Insiders tell me that Bernd has had enough. He calls Feras and gives him the ultimatum. Either he and David resign immediately, or they will both be forced out. The announcement is quickly made that they are "stepping down" from their roles. The same day that Feras and David suddenly leave the company, Bernd issues a decree to fire over two hundred MindGeek employees immediately. The layoffs are done without even a day's notice, via Zoom, in batches. One employee says "the people being laid off were forcefully muted so they couldn't speak or ask questions. The layoff was immediate, and all accounts were disabled within minutes."[5] Minutes after the mass firing, MindGeek employees wanting to out the company begin reaching out to me.

The unraveling of MindGeek continues around the globe as another wave of hundreds of media articles are written about the shocking news of Feras Antoon's "resignation."

The King of Porn is suddenly no longer on his throne.

50

BIG PLASTIC'S LIP SERVICE

The momentum of the *New Yorker* piece and the wave of press around David and Feras "resigning" means I have a great news hook for the article I wrote but couldn't get published, "Why Are Visa and Mastercard Still in Bed with Pornhub?"

I circle back to *Newsweek*, who previously turned down the article because it was too "hard-edged," and tell them, "*The New Yorker* just published a piece heavily featuring my work. It ends with the call to hold the credit card companies accountable for still doing business with Pornhub. If I toned down the language to be less hard-edged and explicit, is it something you may be interested in?"

I get a response a few minutes later: "open to reconsidering." I take that as a yes, stay up until 2 a.m. rewriting it, and then send it back to *Newsweek* before dawn. In the morning, *Newsweek* replies, "We can take it, thanks very much."

Soon the piece goes live on *Newsweek,* where I fully expose what Visa and Mastercard have done and call for them to cut off Pornhub once and for all.

. . . We need to hold Visa and Mastercard to their word. They said they were going to stop doing business with Pornhub, so they must stop doing business with Pornhub's main source of revenue. Lip service won't stop the global distribution of sex crime footage for money. It's time for Visa and Mastercard to act on their public promises.[1]

The first thing I do is send the article to Bill Ackman and then to Mastercard.

After months of silence, I finally hear back from John Verdeschi at Mastercard, who had asked for a meeting and then ghosted me when I made clear what I wanted to discuss.

> Hi Laila,
>
> Thank you for sharing your article. As you know, we treat allegations of illegal conduct very seriously . . . If you have a specific example of illegality that we can independently verify, please share.
>
> Thank you,
> John Verdeschi
> Senior Vice President
> Franchise Customer Engagement & Performance

Is he serious? Are we doing this all over again, the same dance we did for an entire year in 2020? Yes, yes, we are. Months ago, I delivered a book's worth of evidence to him, and he never wrote back.

So, I play the game and jump back on Pornhub. Again, as usual, I find illegal videos easily. I make a list of links and descriptions of some of the most egregious cases I find and send it back to John with a copy of the entire email I sent months ago to remind him that I have already sent specific examples.

Then, I wait for his response. It never comes.

I wait some more. Nothing.

Maybe the profit incentive is too powerful to pull away. The credit card companies can charge exponentially higher transaction fees for Big Porn because it's a "high-risk," poorly regulated industry. With almost five billion ad impressions sold daily on Pornhub to advertisers, cutting off TrafficJunky is a big loss.

I can't see a clear path forward right now and am so frustrated that I lose my appetite for nearly a week. After the kids go to bed each night, I spend hours thinking and desperately praying. One night in the midst of my despair, I am encouraged by a realization. When I get to my deathbed, my life won't be measured by whether I was "successful," but it *will* be measured by whether I was faithful to love and serve the people brought into my life to the *best* of my ability. Success is ultimately out of my control, but continuing this fight to bring justice to victims is absolutely in my control, and I am determined not to give up.

―――――

Even billionaires get sick sometimes. Bill Ackman has COVID and is stuck at home in isolation, spending an unusual amount of time on Twitter, where he sees my tweets about "vacuum bag torture" on Pornhub. Since Pornhub did not verify the age and consent of those featured in the videos, it's possible the women who appear to be suffocating to death *are indeed* suffocating to death.

Bill sends me a message expressing his disgust for what I shared. I respond a few minutes later and send him my *Newsweek* essay again and a link to a new tweet, "We are all still waiting for an answer to this question: Why are Visa and Mastercard still doing business with Pornhub?"

I put my phone down on the kitchen counter, as if walking away from it for a few minutes will give me some distance from this fight. When I come back and pick it up, I see that Mike Bowe called. Then I see he left a voicemail.

"Hey, it's Bowe. We just got a great decision in the case. Give me a call."

51

VISA'S MOTION TO DISMISS IS DENIED

July 29, 2022

After playing Mike's voicemail, I call him back immediately to ask what happened.

"We are reading through the whole decision right now, but it's good," Mike tells me. "Visa is being held in the case and we got jurisdictional discovery for MindGeek. I was supposed to go out to California next week to argue all this in front of the judge, but he just made an early decision. This is a very good decision for Serena."

This is Serena's big case against MindGeek and Pornhub, and I am so proud of her as I read the judge's landmark decision denying Visa's motion to dismiss the case. The words of Honorable Cormac J. Carney of the United States District Court are a scathing rebuke:[1]

If not for its drive to maximize profit, why would MindGeek allow Plaintiff's first video to be posted despite its title clearly indicating Plaintiff was well below 18 years old? Why would MindGeek stall before removing the video, which Plaintiff alleges had advertisements running alongside it? Why would MindGeek take the video and upload it to its other porn websites? And why did Plaintiff have to fight for years to have her videos removed? Plaintiff claims that MindGeek did these things for money and Visa knowingly offering up its payment network so that MindGeek could satisfy that goal.

Visa's team of high-powered lawyers tried to get the judge to dismiss Serena's case. They tried to argue that Visa had nothing to do with Mind-Geek's actions to monetize her abuse and therefore shouldn't be held responsible at all. The judge isn't having any of it. He continues,

> When MindGeek crosses the line, or at least when MindGeek is very publicly admonished for crossing the line, Visa cracks the whip and MindGeek responds vigorously. Yet, here is Visa, standing at and controlling the valve, insisting that it cannot be blamed for the water spill because someone else is wielding the hose.

He continues his takedown of Visa's defenses.

> Visa pushed the first domino when it continued to recognize Mind-Geek as a merchant with knowledge of its illicit nature. With that decision—which Visa alone controlled—in place, the means to profit from child porn was ensured . . . Visa lent to MindGeek a much-needed tool—its payment network—with the alleged knowledge that there was a wealth of monetized child porn on MindGeek's websites.

And then my favorite quote of the whole decision:

> Visa is not alleged to have simply created an incentive to commit a crime, it is alleged to have knowingly provided the tool used to complete a crime.

I get a text from another advocate who also just read the decision. "Mastercard should be shitting their pants right now."

After reading the decision, the first thing I do is send a congratulatory text to Serena for this milestone in her case, then I send a copy of the decision to Bill Ackman with a message.

"Visa just lost its motion to dismiss in Serena's case . . . Mastercard might start taking this more seriously, this is huge."

Bill responds the next morning, asking for the full set of court papers and for me to put him in touch with Mike Bowe.

"I want to do something special here and need to do a bit of work. I think we can get a lot done this week. You have done the hard part. Now I can really help."

His words intrigue me and the timing is amazing. Bill is stuck at home recovering from COVID, which means this is a once-in-a-lifetime moment where one of the busiest men in the world has time to focus his attention on this.

I immediately send all the case documents to Bill, and follow that by looping him and Mike into a group email and text message. I'm overwhelmed with excitement as I think of what Bill might be planning.

It is Saturday morning and Joel wants to take the kids for a bike ride, so I decide to go along. Joel pulls them in a little trailer that attaches to the back of his bike, and I follow behind, pedaling through the beautiful mountain scenery and obsessing over what Bill might be planning. We are making our way back home when I see Mike Bowe on my caller ID. I answer it with my Bluetooth as I am riding. Mike starts to tell me he just got off the phone with Bill when Bill's name appears on my caller ID.

I quickly hang up with Mike, pull over, drop my bike on some bushes, and answer. "Hey, Bill! How is it going? How are you feeling? I hope you are recovering quickly." Bill says he is doing much better and almost feels fully recovered. His voice is warm and slightly raspy from being sick.

We go back and forth, recounting the facts and timelines about what has transpired with Visa, Mastercard, and MindGeek since this fight began. Bill asks me to share all the communications I've had with Visa and Mastercard since I first engaged them in May 2020. I still have no idea what plans Bill is hatching in his penthouse in Manhattan, but I can't wait to find out.

As I race home on my bike to catch up with Joel and the kids, I might as well be flying because my spirit soars with hope. Sunlight peeks through the trees above and casts a glow on the path in front of me. Carrying a heart full of optimism, I realize I'm in the midst of a moment I will never forget.

An hour later I see Bill Ackman's name on my caller ID again and I immediately answer.

"Check Twitter," Bill says with an unusual tone of excitement. "I think you are going to like what I just posted."

I open Twitter and read with astonishment the thread Bill just published to the watching world.

"Yesterday, a Federal judge rendered a decision . . . that no one has likely read. You should." He links to the judge's decision.

"Visa claims it has no liability, protested that the payments industry would collapse if it did, and attempted to dismiss the suit . . . The judge in a carefully reasoned decision disagrees: 'Visa is being kept in this case because it is alleged to have continued to recognize as a merchant an immense, well known, and highly visible business that it knew used its websites to host and monetize child porn.'"

Then he goes for the jugular.

"I would recommend that Visa's board, and separately Mr. Kelly, should hire independent white collar and criminal counsel . . ."

The astonishing thread ends with one brilliant phrase:

"Et tu @Mastercard?"

Bill Ackman just told Alfred Kelly, the CEO of Visa, that he needs to hire a criminal defense attorney. Bill isn't afraid to call people out. He doesn't mince words and he is hard-hitting in his activism. To me, he feels like a kindred spirit.

I call Bill back right away to tell him how much I love what he wrote. "I have over two hundred journalists following me on Twitter and I am going to send this tweet out to each of them one by one," I tell him.

"Great. This will catch on—just give it a little time. By the end of the week, Visa and Mastercard won't be doing business with Pornhub anymore. I guarantee it."

Sunday morning I get an email from Bill telling me that he reached out to CNBC's Andrew Ross Sorkin and that Sorkin is inviting both of us onto his show *Squawk Box* on Tuesday—one of cable news' top-rated morning programs that makes news before financial markets start trading. Bill and I jump on a Zoom call with Mike on Monday afternoon to prep and as we log off, Bill and I give each other a virtual high five.

I'm excited. This is going to be good, but my nerves are on edge. Tomorrow's interview is important, and I have to bring my A game.

52

"ONE OF THE BIGGEST STORIES IN BUSINESS"

August 2, 2022

As the rest of the city sleeps, I enter my rented coworking space to prepare for my interview. The boardroom sounds echoey, so I haul a few comforters with me that I spread out all over to help with the sound. I bring in a couple of extra lights, set up my microphone, test it about ten times, and then I get on Pornhub to check the status of the site while I wait until it's finally time to log in to CNBC's *Squawk Box*. Bill is going to broadcast the implications of the judge's decision for Visa and I am going to educate viewers on Pornhub's complicity in crime. And if Visa's stock price plummets as a result, maybe it will finally do the right thing—if only to protect its bottom line.

It's awkward to do an interview by staring at a completely black screen with only your own face looking back at you from the top right corner. You are supposed to look like you can actually see the host and the other interviewees when you can only hear them. But I've done enough interviews now to make it look like this is a real face-to-face conversation.

A few seconds before we go live, I smile when I get a text from Mike.

"DON'T FUCK IT UP."

As my heart pounds and adrenaline rushes through my body, I see on the screen that I am getting red splotches all over my neck from the nerves. I close my eyes and take a few deep breaths to try to calm down enough to make the spots go away. They don't, but oh well . . .

"Welcome back to *Squawk Box* this morning," Andrew Ross Sorkin says.[1] "One of the biggest stories in the world of business, a US district court judge denying Visa's request to be removed from a lawsuit that also targets Pornhub and its owner, a company called MindGeek."

Andrew starts by asking Bill how it all began for him.

"I guess my interest comes from the fact that I have four daughters. And I read the article that Nick Kristof had written in *The Times* describing how MindGeek and Pornhub operate, and the harm it's caused, and the horror of it all. And one of the centerpieces of the article is how the business persists because the payments are funded through the Visa and Mastercard network.

"Visa is one of the most important brands in the world . . . But remarkably, the company, despite being entirely aware that there's child pornography on these sites, continued to provide payment services until the Kristof article. And then they shut down the sites overnight . . . But then within a matter of weeks, they reauthorized the merchants and they started accepting payments again. And the crime continues . . ."

Andrew directs the conversation to me.

"Laila, you have been fighting this cause for a very long time. You've been in touch with Visa. You've brought your concerns to them directly. There have been emails and other documentation about this. What has been the reaction that you've gotten from Visa?"

"Visa has known about this for a very long time," I state. "As you said, not only from my own personal communications all the way up to CEO-level executives and VPs but also through the news. They were very aware that this has been going on . . . almost every legitimate corporation has stopped doing business with MindGeek. But Visa persists. And they have persisted, and they have refused to disengage from this company . . . And it's unacceptable."

I am relieved as my words flow with ease.

"I could take my Visa card this moment and I could go purchase Pornhub ads that commercialize the torture, and the immortalization of the torture, of these victims . . ."

I imagine I am looking right into Al Kelly's eyes, rebuking the CEO of Visa personally as I look into the camera.

"And Al Kelly *needs to stop*, and he needs to disengage. Then he needs to implement policies that would prevent this from happening in the future."

Andrew, the host, jumps in again.

"Bill, you have said online, just in the past seventy-two hours effectively, that you believe that there could be huge liability for Visa as a company, for the board, and the board members individually, and for Al Kelly personally, potentially even criminally. Why do you say that?"

Bill explains how companies like Visa are obligated to have a monitoring system in place to make sure that their product or service is not causing harm. "If they don't have that system in place and are not properly monitoring that risk, they are exposed to what's called 'caremark liability.'" Bill describes a recent Supreme Court case finding boards of directors can be subject to personal liability for not having safety monitoring systems in place. He then explains that the Visa board and CEO could also have *criminal* liability.

"If they do have a system in place and they understand what's going on, then they have criminal liability for being aware of and facilitating the payments that enable child trafficking. And there is a criminal statute for this. Obviously, the government does not allow this kind of conduct and the payment rails that enable this conduct create criminal liability for the CEO."

Bill continues and I smile with gratitude as I hear his words.

"I mean, Laila, as you can tell, is a fierce advocate. She's not afraid to reach out to people in power. She shared with me emails she sent to the company, she's been dealing with the executive vice president of global brand reputation and security. I mean, you know, the highest-level people at the company who report to the CEO."

Bill and I continue to go back and forth with Sorkin and it's perfect. Bill brings his understanding of the world of finance and I bring my firsthand experience with victims and knowledge of how MindGeek works.

We are given an extraordinary seventeen minutes on the show.

After the interview the headlines start blowing up, creating a huge swell of press coverage on almost every major news outlet. *The New York Times, The LA Times, Forbes, Bloomberg, BBC, ABC, NBC, The Boston Globe, Fox, Fortune, Institutional Investor*, and so many more.

The pressure is on. How will Al Kelly respond?

53

FINALLY, A PARIAH

The answer comes quickly. Visa responds in *Fortune* with a lie. They say they are not monetizing Pornhub content.

I immediately go over to MindGeek's TrafficJunky website to take screenshots of evidence that Visa is indeed still in business with Pornhub, and I call out Visa on Twitter with the images. "Lying to the public isn't going to help your court case." Bill shares what I posted.

I decide to send an email to Al Kelly, the CEO of Visa, using his personal email address to ensure he gets my message and I copy Bill Ackman. In the email is a link to my *Newsweek* essay and the thread of communication I had with his executives in 2020 explaining, with proof, how they were involved in monetizing child abuse and trafficking on Pornhub. I emphasize to him that his company is now blatantly lying to the press.

The next morning, Bill Ackman calls me. "I have some good news, but you can't share it with anyone just yet." He sounds cheerful and excited as he speaks. This must be big news. "I promise I will keep it confidential," I reply, overwhelmed with anticipation.

"The CEO of Mastercard just called me," Bill says. "They are cutting off TrafficJunky and Pornhub completely."

I let out a shout of joy and relief. "Oh my God! Thank you, Bill! Thank you! This is incredible and it couldn't have happened without you!"

"I'm sure we will hear from Visa momentarily with the same decision," he adds.

And we do. In an unprecedented move, Al Kelly releases a *personal statement* announcing he is cutting off Pornhub. Finally.

". . . It is not customary for an executive to weigh in on legal matters in advance of a final ruling. This situation, however, is different, and as CEO—and a father and grandfather—I feel compelled to speak out . . . We will suspend TrafficJunky's Visa acceptance privileges based on the court's decision until further notice. Visa cards will not be able to be used to purchase advertising on any sites including Pornhub or other MindGeek affiliated sites."

Tears well up in my eyes as I read the statement and the headlines.

Shortly after this, Mastercard releases their statement, prompting Bill and me to now go after Discover. He tweets about them publicly while I send a strongly worded letter to the CEO, Roger C. Hochschild, using his personal email address. Discover doesn't make a public statement, but I quickly confirm with MindGeek's customer service, by posing as a prospective advertiser, that Discover has also cut off TrafficJunky.

Now finally all credit cards have cut off Pornhub completely. For real.

There is a new enormous cycle of hundreds of articles in the media about Visa and Mastercard cutting off Pornhub once again, so many I can't keep track. They are from everywhere—the US, Japan, Brazil, Ireland, Nigeria, Canada, the UK.

I think of the first call I had with Mike almost two years ago and remember the words he said: "With the filing of the cases and with each major decision there must be a media shitstorm to keep the spotlight and pressure on these companies."

Another victory arrives when Meta shuts down Pornhub's 13 million follower Instagram account.[1] The press loves it. Other advocates and I have been pressuring the decision makers at Instagram for months. I sent them the judge's scathing decision against Visa and to me it's clear they permanently cut off Pornhub because they don't want the legal liability. By the end of the year, thanks to the National Center on Sexual Exploitation, TikTok and YouTube[2] have also permanently booted Pornhub off their platforms.

At this point no legitimate company's executives in their right mind will take the risk of doing business with Pornhub. Now Visa, Mastercard, Discover, PayPal, Grant Thornton, Heinz, Unilever, Comcast, Xfinity, Roku, and so many others are refusing to do business with the site. Even Astroglide, KY Jelly, and Weedmaps have stopped advertising on Pornhub because they don't want to be associated with a "criminal enterprise."

Pornhub has officially become a pariah.

A journalist from Montreal who's been on MindGeek's trail the last two years has been watching all of this unfold and sends me a satisfying text.

"MindGeek is completely fucked."

54

THE CALL I'VE BEEN
WAITING FOR

An unknown number from New York shows up on my caller ID, and as is my habit, I don't answer. It goes to voicemail, and I hit play.

"Hi, this is Special Agent Ana," she says as I miss her last name. "I am with FBI New York. I was wondering if you could give me a call back." She leaves her number.

But it's not the local sheriff's office like last time, I reassure myself. This is the FBI; they are calling from New York and I don't live in New York. This is not about me.

Then the reality hits: The FBI is finally calling me about Pornhub.

To be on the safe side, I text Mike and Brad asking what they think of the message and they both say to call back immediately.

"Hi Ana, this is Laila Mickelwait returning your call."

She tells me they would like to meet and ask me some questions. I agree to meet and then ask if there is now an open criminal investigation into Pornhub and MindGeek. I nearly cry with relief when she confirms that, yes, there is an open investigation! This is something I have been waiting so long to hear.

But I can't do any confidential meetings out of my coworking space anymore because the last time I was doing a podcast interview in the boardroom, a guy walked in afterward, sat down, told me he overheard my conversation, that he is the owner of a major porn company and has Feras's and David's cell numbers in his phone. I almost spit out my coffee as he said it. "Really, you know Feras and David?"

"Oh yeah, we have known each other for a long time. . . . You know they aren't the real owners, right?"

"Uh yes, I do know that."

"No one knows who the real owners are. It isn't just that guy Bergmair, there are others behind him."

"Oh really?" I say, acting as if I am surprised. I ask him his name and when I look him up, he isn't lying about working with MindGeek. He is the owner of a major porn company that works with them. Small world.

Mike had already suspected there may be other hidden owners behind Bergmair. That is why he named "John Doe 1-10" in his lawsuit complaint as anonymous defendants. If they do exist, he will unmask them during the discovery process.

I am soon alerted by the sixth-floor MindGeek whistleblower that a new deal to sell the company is about to close. Fabian was unsuccessful in his bid to regain control and it's being sold to a hastily concocted private equity firm laughably called Ethical Capital Partners. The same men who were part of the previous failed deal are named partners, including criminal defense attorney Solomon Friedman, who is taking the lead as the "new owner" of Pornhub. I remember that Solomon has a history of defending pedo-criminals in court. As part of a rebrand they are going to rename MindGeek "Aylo." I am told by those close to the deal that Feras, David, and Bernd will slide into the background while still receiving payments from the "sale." The same CPO, CLO, CFO, and Divas who have been there for over a decade will continue running Pornhub's day-to-day operations.

When it is time for the meeting with the FBI, I log on to the video conference call with the FBI from a private spot, and meet two US attorneys, two FBI agents, and the two lawyers from the Federal Trade Commission I had met previously. They are difficult to read, showing no expression as I speak, just taking in information but giving nothing back. It's clear this is a one-way street.

Soon after, they reach out for a follow-up meeting, and we do another two-hour video call. I make sure they know what mental state Feras Antoon is in now that everyone at the company has turned on him, according to my sources. I tell the FBI that, in a humiliating move, Feras's access to the MindGeek office building has been revoked and he can't enter the building anymore without approval and a security escort. Feras has been betrayed by everyone at MindGeek and he has no loyalties to anyone at the company anymore. I also let them know he is considering escaping to Dubai and has even opened a company there called Red Bird so his wife can pretend she works for it in order to get a visa.

At the end of the meeting they let me know they are interested in connecting with more company insiders. I quickly reach out to Mateo from Montreal and Alex from Cyprus to ask if they would be willing to speak to the FBI. They both agree to fly to New York.

A few days later Mike texts me to call him. When we talk he tells me a high-level insider reached out with the names of two men who were involved in the transfer of MindGeek back when Fabian was involved. He was told both men are wanted by the FBI. The timing of this couldn't be better.

Mateo and I meet face-to-face across a bistro table at the Moxy hotel in New York City. As I look into his eyes, it strikes me how grateful I am for his courage to do what he is about to do.

"Thank you, Mateo."

"It is the least I can do for these victims," he replies.

The next morning, he is wearing a crisp, pressed dress shirt and tells me he was up at 4 a.m. trying to find an iron. He couldn't sleep because his nerves were on edge. We get some coffee and I call an Uber. We sit quietly in the back seat and try to make small talk, but our minds are clearly on something else. I escort him into the building where the FBI agents and government attorneys are waiting to talk to him. He opens the conversation with a nervous joke that makes them laugh and everything is smooth sailing from there as he answers every question, detailing as an eyewitness the complicity of MindGeek in profiting from mass sexual crime. I can see Mateo is relieved when it's all over.

As I exit the building, stepping into the rainy New York afternoon, I smile as I remember the words Nick Kristof said to Serena and me during the aftermath of his *New York Times* article when Serena was being attacked by MindGeek. "Someday you'll laugh and tell your grandkids about this, and they'll say, 'Really, there was a company like that?' And then you'll take them to Montreal to see the site of the former MindGeek offices where there will be a statue of Serena as a memorial."

Someday Pornhub will be a memory.

My thoughts are brought back to reality when my phone buzzes in my jacket pocket. It's a text from Mike letting me know he is going to meet with Mateo in person later. I want some fresh air and time to process, so I decide to skip the cab and walk. Looking out at the busy crowd, everyone seems to urgently be headed somewhere important. I take a deep breath, pull the hood of my black raincoat on, put my head down, blending into the sea of humanity, and begin the trek back to the hotel. As I watch the rain fall onto the wet pavement beneath my feet, one of my favorite sayings comes to mind again: dripping water hollows out stone, not through force but through persistence.

There's still work to be done.

Onward.

EPILOGUE

Lily Rose's tiny hand squeezes mine as we walk up the grassy hill to my dad's grave. I come here each year to shine the headstone that is engraved with his picture and spend time with his memory. Mario is now lying beside him. I tell Lily Rose that Papa's and Mario's bodies are in their "treasure boxes" but their spirit is in heaven, and one day she will meet her papa and see Mario again. Without prompting, she leans in and kisses her papa's picture. I ache wishing he were alive, wishing I could see her kiss his warm cheek as he hugs her tight. I still long for his presence in my life, but I take comfort in knowing he has been watching all of this unfold from his seat in heaven. Sometimes I think he has been helping all along from above.

As I look at the vase of fresh lilies I brought with me from bulbs my dad planted with his own hands, I recall the many long walks we took together when I was young. We would walk side by side, holding mugs of tea. He would often stop to pick a flower from the side of the path. We would admire the symmetry and the vibrant colors together. Then he would say to me, "Things this beautiful don't happen by accident."

My sister has found happiness and healing, and she is stronger now than she has ever been. I know my dad is most proud of her for how she has persevered in her life. Eventually Sofia reached out to say she found protection and assistance at a safe house. This story was told through my eyes and with my voice, but the real heroes are the victims—some who raised their voices to speak out, some who pursued justice in court, and most who are courageously using everything within them to make it through another day.

I have so many lingering, unanswered questions about what has transpired and what is to come, but one thing I know for certain is I won't stop fighting for a world where rape is no longer a commodity to be bought and sold on the internet for profit and for a world where children are no longer ruthlessly exploited with impunity.

I also know I'm not the same person I was before this fight began. The trauma of so many victims . . . the horrors of abuse I can't ever unsee . . . the elation of many triumphs . . . the smears and attacks . . . the applause and praise. All of it has changed me.

I have learned how to be tough in the face of criticism and that making enemies is part of creating change. I've learned there is value in being a broken record, in not faltering from one singular goal. There is something to not stopping. Not giving in, or giving up, or letting up but continuing to throw punches until ground is taken.

As much as I have learned to be tough, and persistent, I have also learned the importance of staying soft—to being open to change, to feeling deeply, and to crying for what has been broken, lost, and can never be recovered. I've learned that love and compassion will sustain a fight longer than vengeance or anger.

When all of this began so many people told me that MindGeek was too big to fall, but maybe it was too big to aim at and miss. MindGeek was a true giant, but it was arrogant, sloppy, and had blind spots. The bestselling author Malcolm Gladwell explains in his book *David and Goliath* that the same medical condition that makes giants grow so huge also makes them go nearly blind, and an average-sized person who can overcome fear and is skilled with their weapon of choice can get close enough to deal a fatal blow.

Maybe giants are not as invincible as they seem.

LETTER TO THE READER

Dear Reader,

We have come a long way since this story began. But we still have work to do. Pornhub has faced a reckoning, but at the time of this writing Pornhub is still online. We aren't giving up the fight to shut down Pornhub and I hope you will join me and so many others who are still pressing ahead—we are so close. The *full weight of justice* must be brought to bear on these corporate traffickers if we are going to truly vindicate victims and deter future abusers.

But *Pornhub is not alone.* Its competitors operate the same way. That is why the North Star in the long-term battle against online criminal sexual abuse should be the adoption of governmental and corporate policies that require user-generated porn sites (and any sites or platforms that allow user-generated porn) to have reliable, third-party, age and consent verification processes for every individual in every video. These preventative policies can and must be implemented—or sites must be forced to shut down.

Most importantly, this key policy must be implemented by credit card companies, payment processors, and financial institutions. Because when Visa and Mastercard enact this preventative policy for sites that distribute user-generated porn, as a requirement of doing business with them, the policy will take effect instantly and globally. And, as we have learned in these pages, online porn sites are *highly motivated* to comply with credit card company demands, because without the support of financial institutions, there is no profitable online business.

(As an aside, I also believe that children should be protected from being exposed to online porn, and that is why mandatory third-party age verification for users of sites that distribute porn is also important.)

But, as Martin Luther King Jr. once said, "Change does not roll in on the wheels of inevitability." These transformative changes will only happen through *intense and sustained* public pressure campaigning coupled with *strategic* civil litigation. Lawsuits must continue to be brought on behalf of courageous victims, coupled with skilled attorneys equipped with the financial resources to go toe-to-toe with these corporate bad actors to the point where they realize they must change their business model or shut down. Lawsuits must also continue to be brought against enablers like the credit card, hosting, and search engine companies until they realize that supporting and profiting from online sexual crime is a terrible business decision.

I firmly believe that the powerful combination of continued intense public pressure campaigning, coupled with strategic litigation, will finally halt this kind of criminal abuse on user-generated porn sites once and for all. As we go forward in these endeavors it is critical that survivors are well supported in their journeys toward healing and justice.

This is the work that our team of advocates, therapists, social workers, attorneys, policy specialists, PR experts, and more continue to do every single day at my nonprofit organization, the Justice Defense Fund. And we are looking for bold, big-thinking, relentless partners to join us in this fight—people who believe that the era of impunity is over and that together we can make the internet a safer place for generations to come. If you want to join me and my team in the pursuit of justice, go to justicedefensefund.org to learn more. At the JDF website you can be a part of Team Takedown and join millions of others in signing the Traffickinghub petition. It takes all of us coming together to bring down abusers this big.

If you were moved by this story, please don't hesitate to reach out to me. I want to connect with you and hear your thoughts and ideas for change. As I said at the beginning, I am here to learn from you, too.

And lastly, before we part ways, I want to encourage you to press forward to take on whatever giant you may be facing in your own life—whether it be depression, addiction, past trauma, or a human rights issue you are passionate about. Whatever it is, take courage, because the breakthrough you have been hoping for might be just around the corner.

Let's keep fighting together.

Until Justice Prevails,

Laila Mickelwait

Acknowledgments

This story would not be possible without the important contributions and participation of hundreds of organizations and survivors, and millions of individuals. Without question, the effort to hold Pornhub accountable has been an enormous group effort and I am grateful for every organization, survivor, and individual who has been involved. I want to say a special thanks to Morgan Perry, my good friend and cofounder at the Justice Defense Fund, who has played an important role in advancing this work. I am also eternally grateful for the unconditional support of my husband Joel, for my mother's encouragement along the way, and for my precious children Jed and Lily Rose, who inspire me every day to make the internet a safer place for children.

Notes

1. Pablo Palatnik, "The Top 10 Visited Websites in the U.S. in 2020," *etrend* (blog), November 2, 2020, etrend.com/the-top-10-visited-websites-in-the-u-s-in-2020.
2. Pornhub Team, "The Pornhub Tech Review," *Pornhub Insights*, April 8, 2021, pornhub.com/insights/tech-review.
3. Pornhub Team, "The 2019 Year in Review," *Pornhub Insights*, December 11, 2019, pornhub.com/insights/2019-year-in-review.
4. Matt Diggity, "The Tech Companies That Have Had the Biggest Impact on Society in the 21st Century," Diggity Marketing, accessed July 21, 2023, diggity marketing.com/most-influential-tech-companies-2020.
5. Patricia Nilsson and Alex Barker, "Inside the Secret, Often Bizarre World That Decides What Porn You See," *Financial Times*, June 23, 2022, ft.com/content/cff23e36-b507-4717-8830-8b06741c8fd5.
6. Otillia Steadman, "Pornhub Purged Almost 80% of Its Content—More Than 10 Million Videos—from Its Site," *BuzzFeed News*, December 15, 2020, buzzfeed news.com/article/otilliasteadman/pornhub-removes-videos.
7. Doe v. MindGeek Case 8:21-cv-00338-CJC-ADS Document 145-13 Filed 09/01/23 Page 2 of 16 Page ID #:9926.
8. Jazmin Goodwin, "Mastercard, Visa and Discover Cut Ties with Pornhub Following Allegations of Child Abuse," *CNN Business*, December 14, 2020, cnn.com/2020/12/14/business/mastercard-visa-discover-pornhub/index.html.

1: THE DISCOVERY

1. "Man Sentenced to 40 Years for Sexual Exploitation of a Child, Advertising Child Porn, and Distribution of Child Porn," U.S. Attorney's Office, Middle District of Alabama, May 19, 2022, justice.gov/usao-mdal/pr/man-sentenced -40-years-sexual-exploitation-child-advertising-child-porn-and.

2. *CV1 Mother et al. v. Franklin et al.* (M.D. Ala. Jul. 10, 2022), storage.courtlistener .com/recap/gov.uscourts.almd.78851/gov.uscourts.almd.78851.1.0.pdf.

3. Scott McDonald, "Florida Man Arrested after 58 Porn Videos, Photos Link Him to Missing Underage Teen Girl," *Newsweek*, October 24, 2019, newsweek .com/florida-man-arrested-after-58-porn-videos-photos-link-him-missing -underage-teen-girl-1467413.

4. Pornhub Team, "The 2019 Year in Review." See also Pornhub Team, "2018 Year in Review," *Pornhub Insights*, December 11, 2018, pornhub.com/insights/2018 -year-in-review and Pornhub Team, "2017 Year in Review," *Pornhub Insights*, January 9, 2018, pornhub.com/insights/2017-year-in-review.

5. Garret Sloan and Jack Neff, "Kraft Heinz and Unilever Vow to Steer Clear of Pornhub," *AdAge*, November 4, 2019, adage.com/article/digital/kraft-heinz-and -unilever-vow-steer-clear-pornhub/2212581.

6. Shanti Das, "Unilever and Heinz Pay for Ads on Pornhub, the World's Biggest Porn Site," *The Times*, November 3, 2019, thetimes.co.uk/article/unilever-and -heinz-pay-for-ads-on-pornhub-the-worlds-biggest-porn-site-knjzlmwzv.

7. Rachel Louise Snyder, "When Can a Woman Who Kills Her Abuser Claim Self-Defense?" *The New Yorker*, December 20, 2019, newyorker.com/news/dispatch /when-can-a-woman-who-kills-her-abuser-claim-self-defense; Nicole Addi-mando was initially sentenced to nineteen years to life in prison. Subsequently, her team of advocates and lawyers appealed, and her sentence was reduced to seven and a half years. See Nicole Fidler, Ross Kramer, "New York Appellate Court Issues Landmark Ruling on DVSJA in the Case of Nicole Addimando," July 23, 2021, sanctuaryforfamilies.org/dvsja-appeal-nicole-addimando.

8. *Jane Doe Nos. 1 through 40 v. MG Freesites, Ltd. et al.* (S.D. Cal. Dec. 15,2020), documentcloud.org/documents/20425190-mindgeekjanedoes1-40.

9. "Twenty-Year Sentence in GirlsDoPorn Sex Trafficking Conspiracy," U.S. Attorney's Office, Southern District of California, June 14, 2021, justice.gov /usao-sdca/pr/twenty-year-sentence-girlsdoporn-sex-trafficking-conspiracy.

10. Alex Riggins, "Fugitive GirlsDoPorn Boss Added to FBI's 10 Most Wanted List," *San Diego Union-Tribune*, September 7, 2022, sandiegouniontribune.com /news/courts/story/2022-09-07/fugitive-girlsdoporn-boss-added-to-fbis-10-most -wanted-list.

11. Das, "Unilever and Heinz Pay for Ads on Pornhub."

12. Das, "Unilever and Heinz Pay for Ads on Pornhub."

13. Doe v. MindGeek Case 8:21-cv-00338-CJC-ADS Document 145-13 Filed 09/01/23 Page 2 of 16 Page ID #:9926.

2: #TRAFFICKINGHUB

1. See 22 U.S. Code § 7102(11)(A). Additionally, as per 22 U.S. Code § 7102(4), the term "commercial sex act" means any sex act on account of which anything of value is given to or received by any person.

2. Michael Kan, "Pornhub Is Now Available as a TOR Site to Protect Users' Privacy," *PCMag UK*, January 23, 2020, uk.pcmag.com/news/124629/pornhub-is-now-available-as-a-tor-site-to-protect-users-privacy.

3. Laila Mickelwait, "Time to Shut Pornhub Down," *Washington Examiner*, February 9, 2020, washingtonexaminer.com/opinion/time-to-shut-pornhub-down; x.com/LailaMickelwait/status/1227003417983213568?s=20 and x.com/LailaMickelwait/status/1227009125898342401?s=20.

4. Laila Mickelwait, "Time to Shut Pornhub Down," *Washington Examiner*, February 9, 2020, washingtonexaminer.com/opinion/time-to-shut-pornhub-down.

5. Megha Mohan, "'I Was Raped at 14, and the Video Ended up on a Porn Site,'" *BBC News*, February 10, 2020, bbc.co.uk/news/stories-51391981.

3: PORNHUB'S CENSORSHIP TRICKS

1. Jonathan Chadwick and Luke Kenton, "Pornhub Removes All Unverified Videos from Its Platform," *Mail Online*, December 16, 2020, dailymail.co.uk/sciencetech/article-9054935/Pornhub-removes-unverified-videos-platform.html.

2. Joe Castaldo, "Lifting the Veil of Secrecy on MindGeek's Online Pornography Empire," *The Globe and Mail*, February 4, 2021, theglobeandmail.com/business/article-mindgeeks-business-practices-under-srutiny-as-political-pressure.

3. At that time in 2020, Pornub's Exploited Teen Asia partner channel had 446,000 subscribers and 481 million views.

4. This conclusion was confirmed by hundreds of comments throughout the site that were censored in the exact same way, as well as by MindGeek moderators who also provided verified internal documents of MindGeek's "Red Words" list that were censored throughout the site.

4: WELCOME NEW BEDFELLOWS

1. Matt Burgess, "Pornhub Accused of Illegal Data Collection," *WIRED*, June 29, 2023, wired.com/story/pornhub-tracking-cookies-gdpr-video-history/#:~:text =Complaints%20filed%20in%20the%20European,data%2Dcollection%20 policies%20under%20GDPR.&text=There%20aren%27t%20many%20websites %20bigger%20than%20Pornhub.

2. Dan Hall and Niamh Cavanagh, "Fury as Pornhub Ambassador Says She Would Rape 13-Year-Old-Boy and Blasts 'F**k the Law' in Sickening Unearthed Video," *The Sun*, August 31, 2021, thesun.co.uk/news/16013669/pornhub-host -sex-13-year-old-boy.

3. Das, "Unilever and Heinz Pay for Ads on Pornhub."

6: THE ZUCKERBERG OF PORN

1. Jon Ronson, "The Butterfly Effect," Episode 1, Audible Original, July 27, 2017.
2. Nilsson, "MindGeek: the Secretive Owner of Pornhub and RedTube."
3. Jon Ronson, "As a Bonus for Listeners to *The Butterfly Effect*, Here is Fabian's Aquarium and Diver," Twitter post, August 9, 2017, 7:49 p.m., twitter.com/jon ronson/status/895356472967561216?s=20.
4. As later confirmed by Joe Castaldo, "Lifting the Veil of Secrecy on MindGeek's Online Pornography Empire," *The Globe and Mail*, February 4, 2021.

7: A FAMILY MAN AND PORN KING

1. US District Court for the Northern District of Georgia, "United States of America v. $5,282,495.03 Seized from Fidelity Bank Account X-0691 et Al," *Justia Dockets & Filings*, December 1, 2009, dockets.justia.com/docket/georgia/gandce /1:2009cv03371/163217.

8: BLAKE THE FAKE

1. "18 U.S.C §§ 2257- 2257A Certifications," U.S. Department of Justice, last modi- fied May 28, 2020, justice.gov/criminal-ceos/18-usc-2257-2257a-certifications #:~:text=This%20means%20that%20producers%20of,the%20location%20of %20these%20records.

2. Priyam Chhetri, "Petition to Shut Down Pornhub Claims Adult Website Is a 'Hotbed' of Child Exploitation and Sex Trafficking," *MEAWW*, February 24, 2020,

meaww.com/traffickinghub-petition-pornhub-shut-down-sex-trafficking
-exploitation-aiding-profiting-from-videos.

3. Antoinette Lattouf, "The Global Push to Shut Down Pornhub Gains Traction,"
10 Daily, March 13, 2020, web.archive.org/web/20200421184445/https:/10daily
.com.au/news/world/a200227jordt/the-new-global-push-to-shut-down-pornhub
-20200313, and Naga Pramod, "Pornhub: "Less than one percent" of content
uploaded is child abuse," *Reclaim the Net*, March 20, 2020, reclaimthenet.org
/pornhub-less-than-one-percent-of-content-is-child-abuse.

11: WHEN SNAKES ARE CORNERED

1. "Ronn Torossian, 31," *Ad Age*, August 7, 2006, adage.com/article/special-report
-40-under-40/ronn-torossian-31/110905.

2. PRNEWS, "Ronn Torossian Departs as 5WPR CEO, but Remains Chairman,"
PRNEWS, March 4, 2022, prnewsonline.com/disgraced-ceo-torossian-departs
-5wpr-remains-as-chair.

3. Laila Mickelwait, "Big Porn Cashes in on Racism and Anti-Semitism," *New
York Post*, June 23, 2020, nypost.com/2020/06/23/big-porn-cashes-in-on-racism
-and-anti-semitism.

12: WHO IS @EYEDECO?

1. The organization Knockout Abuse West in Los Angeles and the campaign
Arrêter ExploitationHub in Montreal were holding ongoing weekly protests.
Protests were also held in the UK and South Africa.

2. mindgeeklitigation.com/asset/2021.06.17%20-%20Dkt.%20001%20-%20
Complaint.pdf, 134–36.

13: PORNHUB'S ADMISSIONS UNEARTHED

1. reddit.com/r/awfuleverything/comments/ful20a/comment/fmduv94/?utm
_source=share&utm_medium=web3x&utm_name=web3xcss&utm_term
=1&utm_content=share_button&rdt=60294.

2. X.com/lailamickelwait/status/1251149946645917696?s=46; x.com/lailamickelwait
/status/1280019480450486275?s=46.

3. X.com/lailamickelwait/status/1346150526967296000?s=46.

4. X.com/lailamickelwait/status/1247594436789493765?s=46.

5. X.com/lailamickelwait/status/1244040549817933824?s=46.

15: BETRAYAL FROM WITHIN

1. MindGeek, "MindGeek and INHOPE Join Forces to Protect Children Online," *PR Newswire*, June 24, 2019, prnewswire.com/news-releases/mindgeek-and-inhope-join-forces-to-protect-children-online-300873649.html.

2. Martin Patriquin, "MindGeek Donation Spurs Canadian Charity to Withdraw from Global Anti-Child-Trafficking Group," *The Logic*, November 26, 2020, thelogic.co/news/mindgeek-donation-spurs-canadian-charity-to-withdraw-from-global-anti-child-trafficking-group.

19: MEET THE MODERATOR

1. For context, Facebook and TikTok both employ 40,000 moderators and Twitter/X employs 2,300. Source: U.S. Senate Judiciary Committee hearing, "Big Tech and the Online Child Sexual Exploitation Crisis," January 31, 2024, judiciary.senate.gov/committee-activity/hearings/big-tech-and-the-online-child-sexual-exploitation-crisis.

2. Per CEO Feras Antoon, Doe v. MindGeek Case 8:21-cv-00338-CJC-ADS Document 145-9 Filed 09/01/23 Page 3 of 4 Page ID #:9909.

21: CONTENT IS KING

1. This practice was also confirmed by other MindGeek employees and examples of many such videos were pointed out by those employees and were documented.

32: A BILLIONAIRE ACTIVIST INVESTOR GETS ACTIVE

1. Svea Herbst-Bayliss and Arunima Banerjee, "Ackman Ends Public Battle with Herbalife, Takes Stake in United Technologies," Reuters, February 28, 2018, reuters.com/article/us-pershing-square-utc-stake/ackman-ends-public-battle-with-herbalife-takes-stake-in-united-technologies-idUSKCN1GC2N0.

33: THE CREDIT CARDS DROP PORNHUB

1. Hamza Shaban, "Mastercard Severs Ties with Pornhub, Citing Illegal Content," *Washington Post*, December 10, 2020, washingtonpost.com/business/2020/12/10/pornhub-mastercard-ban-mindgeek.

2. Gillian Friedman, "Visa and Mastercard Block Use on Pornhub," *The New York*

Times, December 10, 2020, nytimes.com/2020/12/10/business/visa-mastercard
-block-pornhub.html.

3. Ina Fried, "Mastercard, Visa, Discover Cut Payment Services to Pornhub,"
   Axios, December 11, 2020, axios.com/2020/12/11/pornhub-mastercard-visa
   -payments.

34: FERAS GOES FOR BROKE

1. Doe v. MindGeek Case 8:21-cv-00338-CJC-ADS Document 145-9 Filed 09/01/
   23 Page 3 of 4 Page ID #:9909.
2. Nilsson, "MindGeek: The Secretive Owner of Pornhub and RedTube."

35: FUCKING STUPID

1. Benjamin Wallace, "The Geek-Kings of Smut," *New York Magazine*, January
   18, 2011, nymag.com/news/features/70985.

36: PORNHUB ON TRIAL

1. Standing Committee on Access to Information, Privacy and Ethics, "Pro-
   tection of Privacy and Reputation on Platforms Such as Pornhub," House of
   Commons Canada, June 14, 2021, ourcommons.ca/Committees/en/ETHI
   /StudyActivity?studyActivityId=11088039.

37: FERAS AND DAVID TAKE THE STAND

1. Emails uncovered in legal discovery in Doe v. MindGeek Case 8:21-cv-00338-
   CJC-ADS demonstrate that at least on May 27, 2020, eight months before this
   hearing, Feras Antoon was personally aware of Serena's specific abuse when it
   was still live on Pornhub and clearly showed her face. The link to Serena's video
   was sent to MindGeek's executive team via Mastercard along with screenshots
   of comments on the video indicating it was abuse. The email exchanges debate
   whether the video should be kept on the site or removed and show Feras
   saying, "Can we say it slipped through the cracks?" Doe v. MindGeek Case
   8:21-cv-00338-CJC-ADS Document 145-11 Filed 09/01/23 Page 2 of 5 Page
   ID #:9915.

38: MY TURN TO TESTIFY

1. Kieran Leavitt, "Despite a 10-Year-Old Law, RCMP Says the World's Biggest Porn Website Has Never Told It about Any Suspicious Videos," *Toronto Star*, March 1, 2021, thestar.com/politics/federal/despite-a-10-year-old-law-rcmp-says-the-world-s-biggest-porn-website-has/article_284a090a-63aa-53b7-a54e-a0d529706d94.html?.

2. Christopher Reynolds, "Survivors, NGOs Call for Criminal Investigation of Porn Giant MindGeek," CBC, March 4, 2021, cbc.ca/news/politics/calls-for-criminal-investigation-mindgeek-1.5937117.

3. The Canadian Press, "More than 70 MPs, Senators Call for Criminal Investigation into Pornhub's Canadian Owners," *National Post*, March 15, 2021, nationalpost.com/news/canada/more-than-70-lawmakers-call-for-criminal-investigation-of-mindgeek.

4. Doe v. MindGeek USA Case 8:21-cv-00338-CJC-ADS Document 145-8 Filed 09/01/23 Page 3 of 16 Page ID #:9893.

5. Doe v. MindGeek USA *Case 8:21-cv-00338-CJC-ADS Document 145-7 Filed 09/01/23 Page 8 of 10 Page ID #:9888.*

6. Doe v. MindGeek USA *Case 8:21-cv-00338-CJC-ADS Document 145-7 Filed 09/01/23 Page 7 of 10 Page ID #:9887.*

39: FABIAN'S SURPRISE INTERVENTION

1. Vanmala Subramaniam and Joe Castaldo, "Chuck Rifici's Bruinen Investments in Talks to Buy MindGeek Assets, Including Pornhub, Sources Say," *The Globe and Mail*, last modified June 20, 2021, theglobeandmail.com/business/article-bruinen-investments-in-active-talks-to-buy-assets-of-mindgeek.

2. cpdonline.ca/law/child-pornography.

3. drive.google.com/file/d/1ya0t2OevDsmhCoyPRENgH_DSTr2mM-zx/view?usp=share_link; drive.google.com/file/d/1Um1BDIYzx_pIDKOn4MydKDgu5l223ghk/view?usp=share_link, sourced from twitter.com/solomonfriedman/status/388377646142205952?s=46 and twitter.com/solomonfriedman/status/388540277482586112?s=46.

4. Andrew Seymor, "Illegal Computer Search By Ottawa Police Sinks Child Porn Case: Judge Acquits Man Found with 7,730 Explicit Images on Flash Drives," *Ottawa Citizen*, October 10, 2013 web.archive.org/web/20131011054909/http://www.ottawacitizen.com/news/Illegal%2Bcomputer%2Bsearch%2BOttawa%2Bpolice%2Bsinks%2Bchild%2Bporn%2Bcase/9022212/story.html.

41: LOCATING BERNARD, ER, BERND

1. Joe Castaldo, "Lifting the Veil of Secrecy on MindGeek's Online Pornography Empire," *The Globe and Mail*, February 4, 2021, theglobeandmail.com/business /article-mindgeeks-business-practices-under-srutiny-as-political-pressure.
2. Shanti Das, "'Think of the Children,' Pleads Wife of Pornhub Tycoon Bernd Bergmair," *The Times*, May 23, 2021, thetimes.co.uk/article/think-of-the-children -pleads-wife-of-pornhub-tycoon-bernd-bergmair-b0hz9vxzq.
3. Shanti Das and Alastair Johnstone, "'Think of the Children,' Pleads Wife of Pornhub Tycoon Bernd Bergmair," *The Times*, May 23, 2021, thetimes.co.uk/article /think-of-the-children-pleads-wife-of-pornhub-tycoon-bernd-bergmair -b0hz9vxzq.
4. Alexi Mostrous, Patricia Clarke, and Xavier Greenwood, "Hunt for the Porn King," *Tortoise*, May 24, 2021, tortoisemedia.com/audio/hunt-for-the-porn-king.

42: MIKE'S "NOVEL"

1. *Fleites and Jane Doe Nos. 1 through 33 v. MindGeek S.A.R.L. et al.*, 2:21-CV-04920 (C.D. Cal. Jun. 17, 2022), mindgeeklitigation.com/asset/2021.06.17%20 -%20Dkt.%20001%20-%20Complaint.pdf.

49: FERAS DETHRONED

1. Sheelah Kolhatkar, "The Fight to Hold Pornhub Accountable," *The New Yorker*, June 13, 2022, newyorker.com/magazine/2022/06/20/the-fight-to-hold-pornhub -accountable.
2. Simon Hamalienko, "Evil Paedo Whose Youngest Victim Was 8 Months Old Sold Footage as 'Box Sets,'" *Daily Star*, December 10, 2021, dailystar.co.uk/news /latest-news/breaking-evil-paedo-whose-youngest-25656698.
3. mindgeeklitigation.com/asset/2021.06.17%20-%20Dkt.%20001%20-%20Complaint.pdf.
4. Kolhatkar, "The Fight to Hold Pornhub Accountable."
5. Martin Patriquin, "Mass Layoffs, Executive Resignations at MindGeek," *The Logic*, June 22, 2022, thelogic.co/briefing/mass-layoffs-executive-resignations -at-mindgeek.

50: BIG PLASTIC'S LIP SERVICE

1. Laila Mickelwait, "Why Are Visa and Mastercard Still Doing Business with Pornhub? | Opinion," *Newsweek*, June 28, 2022, newsweek.com/why-are-visa -mastercard-still-doing-business-pornhub-opinion-1719060.

51: VISA'S MOTION TO DISMISS IS DENIED

1. *Fleites v. MindGeek S.A.R.L.* et al., CV 21-04920-CJC(ADSx) (C.D. Cal. Jul. 29, 2022), brownrudnick.com/wp-content/uploads/2022/08/MG-Dkt-No.-166-Order -Granting-in-Part-and-Denying-in-Part-Visas-MTD367477.pdf.

52: "ONE OF THE BIGGEST STORIES IN BUSINESS"

1. Yun Li, "Bill Ackman Blasts Visa, Saying It Has the Power to Pressure Pornhub to Remove Child Pornography," CNBC, August 2, 2022, cnbc.com/2022/08/02 /bill-ackman-blasts-visa-saying-it-has-the-power-to-pressure-pornhub-to -remove-child-pornography.html.

53: FINALLY, A PARIAH

1. Vishwam Sankaran, "Pornhub Permanently Banned from Instagram," *The Independent*, September 30, 2022, independent.co.uk/tech/meta-pornhub -instagram-account-ban-b2177721.html.
2. Todd Spangler, "YouTube Removes Pornhub Channel, Citing Multiple Violations of Guidelines," *Variety*, December 16, 2022, variety.com/2022/digital /news/youtube-removes-pornhub-1235464049.

Index

Abdul-Hasib Elahi, 255
Abou-Atme, Alan, 249
Ackman, William ("Bill"), 170–74, 260
    as activist investor, 169
    Mickelwait contacted by, 240–41,
        264–66
    on *Squawk Box*, 267–70
activist investors, 169
Addimando, Nicole, 13, 288n7
ad impressions, 117
adult digital content, 41
advocacy, 19
age verification
    documents, 57–58, 83–84, 107–8
    on Pornhub, 20–21
    processes, 281–82
    for video uploading, 57–58
Akira, Asa, 33–34
Alex (whistleblower), 103–9, 276
algorithms, 27–28
Angus, Charlie, 196–97, 202–3
anti-Semitism, 77
anti-trafficking organizations, 39, 70, 92
Antoon, Feras, 49–55

emails about Serena's abuse live on
    Pornhub, 293n1
interviewed by Adam Gollner, 252–53
legal notices sent to, 176–77
mansion burns down, 211–12
MindGeek and, 45, 177–79, 249
parliament committee letter from,
    199, 202–3
resignation of, 257–58
Thylmann selling to, 48, 124–25
in virtual hearing, 189–98
Asian victims, 138–39
Aylo, 275

Banga, Ajaypal Singh, 93, 170, 173, 241,
    243–44
Bergmair, Bernd, 124, 127–28,
    249, 275
    locating, 213–17
    as MindGeek majority shareholder,
        178–79
Bergmair, Priscila, 215
Blake the fake, 56–58, 104, 189
Boko Haram, 3–4

Bowe, Mike, 38–40, 184
    credit card lawsuit plan of, 127–28
    journalist attacks and, 79
    Lilly in contact with, 133–34
    Mateo speaking to, 119
    Mickelwait's help request of, 226–27
    MindGeek lawsuits by, 41, 218–21
    MindGeek lawyers and, 187–88
    Nicole represented by, 256
    preservation letters sought by, 159
    Reflected Networks deposed by, 247
    Serena in contact with, 150
    Thylmann questions from, 123
    victims in touch with, 42–43
Brazzers (porn company), 49–50, 126
Bright Imperial, 124
business ventures, 51–53

cafeteria, of MindGeek, 52
Cammarata v. Bright Imperial, 124
Canada, 195
Canadian Centre for Child
        Protection, 204
caremark liability, 269
Carney, Cormac J., 262
Carollo, Leonard, 113
Castaldo, Joe, 213
CBS This Morning, 220
censorship, 24–31
child rape, 22–28, 109
    torture and, 43, 112, 142–43
    video takedowns on, 204–5
child sexual abuse material, 44–48, 113
    in Canada, 195
    criminal code on, 197
    Homeland Security learning about, 161
    Mastercard monetizing, 94–95
    underage abuse in, 28, 141–42
    video uploading of, 110–12
children, 89–90, 106–9, 150–52, 242
"The Children of Pornhub" (Kristof),
        163–68, 268

child sexual abuse, 3, 101, 200, 204–5
    as federal felonies, 182
    on Pornhub, 34–35, 58, 81–82,
        112–13
    preventive policies against, 282
    Serena's video of, 148–50
    sexual abuse and, 1, 97
    Visa profiting by, 91–92
Christ-like, be, 69
civil litigation, strategic, 282–83
Cleanest Porn Ever Campaign, 87
Cohen, Steve, 38–39, 221
commercial sex act, 20, 94, 200, 289n1
conference call, 39–40
Congress, sex trafficking bill in, 11
consenting adult, 5, 14, 19
copyright claim, 122
court hearing
    with Antoon and Tassillo, 189–98
    with Mickelwait, 200–204
    on Pornhub, 184–88
    with Serena, 184–85, 262–63
COVID, 57, 73, 85, 221, 260
credit card companies
    Ackman pressuring, 171–73
    anti-trafficking organizations and, 92
    Bowe's lawsuit against, 127–28
    changes made by, 145–46
    customers using, 122–23
    Pornhub and, 6–7, 126–27, 146–47,
        174–75, 236–39
    pornography monetized by, 44
    prepaid cards from, 238
    pressure put on, 40–41
    preventive policies by, 282
    profit incentives of, 260
    sex trafficking monetized by, 242–43
    Thylmann on, 122–23, 126–27
crime scenes, 82–84, 243–44, 256,
        263–66
criminal codes, 197
criminal investigation, 274–76

data, searchable, 116
David and Goliath (Gladwell), 280
Department of Justice (DOJ), 129–30, 145–46
Digital Millennium Copyright Act, 182
Di Santo, Eddy, 246, 249
Discovery, 174–75, 272
Doe v. MindGeek Case, 293n1
DOJ. *See* Department of Justice
Dong, Han, 196
drunk helpless girls, 18–19
Dyer, Wayne, 68

email exchange debate, 293n1
Erskine-Smith, Nathaniel ("Nate"), 164, 192–94
Ethical Capital Partners, 275
Exodus Cry organization, 4–5, 12, 70–72, 103
Exploited Teen Asia channel, 26, 289n3
@EyeDeco (Twitter account), 78–80, 98, 166–67

family members, sexual abuse and, 97
federal law, 57
felonies, 81–84, 88–89, 182
firings, at MindGeek, 257
Fischer, Heather, 130–32
Ford, Christine Blasey, 61
Franklin, Rocky Shay, 10
freedom of speech, 14
Friedman, Solomon, 206–7, 275

Galarza, Victor, 161
gaslighting campaign, 185–86
Gaudreau, Marie-Hélène, 195
General Data Protection Regulation, Europe (GDPR), 33
girls
  Asian, 138–39
  drunk helpless, 18–19

unconscious, 138–39
underage, 141–42
GirlsDoPorn, 13, 60, 201
Gladwell, Malcolm, 280
GoFundMe, for Serena, 166
Gollner, Adam Leith, 250–53
Google search results, 116–17
Gregoire, Thibaut, 93–95, 142–47

Hall, Tiffany, 243
Harris, Stacie, 129
hate speech, 74, 76–77
headlines, 220
Hochschild, Roger C., 93
Homeland Security, 161
homeless children, 150–52, 242
homeless community, 69–70
human trafficking, 4, 39, 70
human trafficking advisor (White House), 130–31
The Hunt for the Porn King (Mostrous), 215

illegality warnings, 141–42
illegal videos, 106–9, 259–60
INHOPE. *See* International Association of Internet Hotlines
Inspiration (Dyer), 68
Instagram account, 272–73
International Association of Internet Hotlines (INHOPE), 89–90
Internet, 46, 164
Internet Watch Foundation (IWF), 34–35, 89–90

James (pseudonym), 59–60
Jameson, Jenna, 35
Jed (son), 12, 134, 278
Johnson, Christopher, 12
Jones, Radhika, 253
journalists, 79, 101, 165

Justice Defense Fund, 4–5, 42,
        165, 244, 283
justicedefensefund.org, 283

Kasowitz Benson Torres firm, 38–39
Keezer, Matt, 49–50
Kelly, Alfred, 93, 265, 269–72
Kimmel, Jimmy, 5, 67
King, Martin Luther, Jr., 282
Kolhattkar, Sheelah, 254–55
Kristof, Nicholas, 157–60, 170–75
    "The Children of Pornhub" by,
        163–68, 268
    evidence sent to, 143
    lawsuit plans of, 165
    Mickelwait grateful for, 175
    Mickelwait in contact with, 137–38
    as New York Times journalist, 101
    Pornhub article planned by, 136–40, 162
    Serena and words from, 277

Langford, Fred, 89
lawsuits
    against Bank of America, 64
    Bowe's credit card, 127–28
    civil litigation and, 282–83
    Kristof plans for, 165
    MindGeek facing, 41, 133–34, 218–21,
        248–49
    against Pornhub, 7
    sex trafficking civil, 37–38
layoffs, at MindGeek, 257
legal notices, 176–77
Lilly (victim), 110–12, 133–35, 153
Lily Rose (daughter), 12, 134, 278
long-term battle, 281–82

Maher, Bill, 5
Mahoney, Kevin, 231
Manos, Nicole, 49
Mansef company, 50
The Man Show (television), 5, 67

mansion, burning down, 211–12
El Marazi, Karim, 176, 249
Mario (uncle), 228–29, 278
    death of, 232–33
    illness of, 222–24
Mastercard, 107
    Ackman influencing, 174
    child porn monetized by, 94–95
    communications with, 142–47, 172–73
    crime scenes monetized by,
        243–44, 256
    journalists pressuring, 165
    Mickelwait email exchanges with, 142,
        149, 171–73, 243, 259,
    Mickelwait phone call with, 94,
        142–45
    Mickelwait sends letter to, 93
    Kristof investigated by, 170–73
    Pornhub dropped by, 173, 271–72
    TrafficJunky and, 236–39, 271–72
    victim information sent to, 160–61
masturbators, chronic, 31
Mateo (whistleblower), 115–19, 276–77
Mickelwait, Laila, 158–59, 228–30, 258–60
    Ackman contacting, 240–41, 264–66
    answers sought by, 7
    Antoon and Tassillo's letter about,
        199, 202–3
    Antoon following, 54–55
    background of, 67–72
    child pornography and, 231–32
    DOJ in communication with, 129–30
    Gollner's article attacking, 250–53
    help requested by, 226–27
    human trafficking studied by, 70
    investigation of, 234–35
    Kristof in contact with, 137–38
    Mastercard's communications with,
        142–47, 172–73
    Mateo meeting with, 276–77
    nonprofit organization launched by, 42
    Sicilian blood of, 64–66

on *Squawk Box*, 267–70

Standing Committee invitation to, 198

threats to, 58, 61–64

Thylmann contacting, 119–23, 180–83

in virtual hearing, 200–204

Washington Examiner publishing
    essay by, 22

Milville-Dechêne, Julie, 78

MindGeek, 52–53, 59–60, 204–9

age verification documents and,
    57–58, 83–84, 107–8

Akira as brand ambassador for, 34

Antoon and Tassillo, 45, 177–79, 249

Bowe hearing from lawyers of, 187–88

Bowe's lawsuits against, 41, 218–21

child rape detected on, 109

company renamed to, 48

crazy American woman attacking,
    158–59

criminal investigation into, 274–76

existential-threat-level litigation
    against, 40

@EyeDeco association with, 166–67

gaslighting campaign by, 185–86

INHOPE and, 89–90

investigators knowledge of, 234–35

lawsuits faced by, 41, 133–34, 218–21,
    248–49

layoffs and firings at, 257

Mickelwait attacked by, 199–200

Mickelwait followed by employees of, 55

moderators working for, 9–10, 104–9,
    181–82, 201

money bottom line for, 43–44, 117–19

Nilsson's investigation of, 127–28

personal businesses and, 246

as Pornhub parent company, 6

privacy policy of, 32–33

problems for, 273

protestors gathering at, 78–79

Red Words list of, 289n4

safe for work website of, 87

shut it down, 35–36

TrafficJunky advertising arm of,
    118–19

victims request video takedown by,
    193–94

missing teen, on Pornhub, 12, 21

money, bottom line of, 43–44, 117–19

money laundering, 125, 130

Mostrous, Alexi, 214–17

mummification, 108

Myles, Bradley, 37, 171

National Center for Missing and
    Exploited Children (NCMEC),
    26, 96, 99, 111, 204

links sent to, 112–13, 160

MindGeek claims to be partner
    with, 190

Pornhub video takedown demand
    from, 113–14

testifies never a partner of
    MindGeek, 204

testifies never received any CSAM
    reports by MindGeek, 204

National Center on Sexual Exploitation,
    91, 273

NCMEC. *See* National Center for
    Missing and Exploited Children

Nefarious (documentary), 70

Newsweek, 244, 258, 260, *271*

The New Yorker, 254, 256

New York Times, 101, 136, 163,
    253, 277

Nicole (victim), 254–56

Nilsson, Patricia, 127–28, 178

Nolot, Benjamin ("Benji"), 71

nonprofit organization, 42

Office to Monitor and Combat
    Trafficking in Persons, 110

OnlyFans website, 225

Organized Fraud Task Force, 50

Paolucci, Paul, 94, 142–47
Patriquin, Martin, 90, 241
payment processing, 173
PayPal, 164
Perry, Morgan, 42, 227, 244
petition, 30–31, 36, 73–74, 100–102
physical attacks, 153–56
Polaris Project, 37
Pornhub, 13, 83–90, 136–40, 162. *See
    also* MindGeek
  age verification on, 20–21
  algorithm used by, 27–28
  background of, 50
  censorship by, 24–31
  child rape on, 22–28
  child sexual abuse on, 34–35, 58,
      81–82, 112–13
  chronic masturbators on, 31
  court hearing on, 184–88
  credit card companies and, 6–7,
      126–27, 146–47, 174–75, 236–39
  criminal investigation into, 274–76
  drunk helpless girls on, 18–19
  Google search results for, 116–17
  homeless teens on, 150–52
  illegal videos on, 259–60
  Instagram account closed of, 272–73
  lawsuits against, 7
  long-term battle against, 281–82
  Mastercard dropping, 173, 271–72
  MindGeek parent company to, 6
  missing teen on, 12, 21
  NCMEC takedown demand to, 113–14
  PayPal dropping, 164
  petition to shut down, 30–31, 36,
      73–74, 100–102
  popularity of, 5–6
  PR campaign by, 14–15, 74
  racism and hateful language on, 76–77
  rape videos on, 10, 22–30, 111–12
  Reflected Networks hosting, 247
  sexual crimes on, 16–17, 178

  Sofia and accountability of, 96–97
  Traffickinghub movement and, 21–22
  uploading test of, 15–17
  user-generated porn on, 6
  verification on, 20–21
  video exposing, 103–4
  video uploading on, 15–17, 105–7,
      110–12
  Visa dropping, 272
  website content removed by, 6–7, 178
  whistleblower on, 129–30
porn industry, 4, 187, 226–30
  adult digital content in, 41
  age verification processes for, 281–82
  studio-produced videos in, 26, 177
  Thylmann buying companies in, 47,
      50–51
  user-generated porn in, 6,
      117, 281–82
  Zuckerberg of, 45–48
pornography, 35, 44–48, 225
PR campaign, by Pornhub, 14–15, 74
prepaid credit cards, 238
preservation letters, 159
preventive policies, 282
privacy policy, 32–33
profit incentives, 260
protestors, of MindGeek, 78–79

Queen of Porn, 35

racism, 76–77
Ramirez (predator), 242
rape, 4, 10, 35, 138–39, 203. *See also*
    child rape
rebill shift, 238
Red Words list, 289n4
Reflected Networks, 247
Rene (whistleblower), 56–57
Reuters, 88–89
RICO cases, 39, 41, 219
Rifici, Chuck, 206

SAC Capital, 221
safe for work website, 87
safe room, 61
Saturday Night Live, 85
Scofield, Elizabeth, 91–92
searchable data, 116
search engine optimization (SEO), 115–16
search terms, on Pornhub, 13
SEO. *See* search engine optimization
Serena (victim), 166–67, 196–98, 277
   Antoon and abuse of, 293n1
   article with picture of, 163
   child sexual abuse video of, 148–50
   real name used by, 159–60
   in virtual hearing, 184–85, 262–63
sex trafficking, 4–5, 70–72, 97–99, 101, 269
   civil lawsuits for, 37–38
   congressional bill on, 11
   credit card companies monetizing, 242–43
   by GirlsDoPorn, 13
   of homeless teens, 150–52
   injustice of, 94
   underage girls in, 141–42
   victims of, 11–12, 20, 186–87
sexual abuse, 1, 97
sexual crimes, 16–17, 178
signatures, first million, 100–102
Silver, Curtis, 87
Sinclair, Grace, 98, 167
slavery, sexual, 3–4
Sofia (victim), 97–99, 154–56, 279
Sorkin, Andrew Ross, 266–70
Squawk Box (morning show), 266–70
Standing Committee on Access to Information, Privacy and Ethics, 198
Stubbs, Shannon, 190–92, 202
studio-produced videos, 26, 177
suicidal victims, 161

Tassillo, David, 50, 53–54
   on child abuse material, 200
   legal notices sent to, 176–77
   Mickelwait letter from, 199, 202–3
   MindGeek and, 45, 177–79, 249
   resignation of, 257–58
   Thylmann selling to, 48, 124–25
   in virtual hearing, 189–98
tax evasion, 47, 125, 130
Thornton, Grant, 176
Thylmann, Fabian
   Antoon and Tassillo buying out, 48, 124–25
   Bowe's questions for, 123
   credit card companies and, 122–23, 126–27
   free porn access goal of, 45–48
   Mickelwait contacted by, 119–23, 180–83
   MindGeek sale and, 207–9
   porn companies bought by, 47, 50–51
   as Zuckerberg of Porn, 45
Tortoise Media, 214
torture, 43, 108, 112, 142–43, 260
traffic bar indicator, 241
TrafficJunky service, 32
   account setup with, 241
   Mastercard dropping, 236–39, 271–72
   MindGeek advertising through, 118–19
   payment processing stopped for, 173
   Visa returning to, 236–39
Traffickinghub movement, 36, 88, 165
   Pornhub and, 21–22
   Urman using media to attack, 74–75
Trafficking Victims Protection Act, 94
trauma therapy, 255
Trudeau, Justin, 164
truth, 23
Twitter, truth campaign, 244–45
Twitter users, 19–20, 98

unconscious girls, 138–39
underage sex, 28, 141–42
United States (U.S.), 3
United States Law 18 USC 2257
        (federal law), 57
Urman, Corey, 158, 184, 189
    as Blake the fake, 56–58
    on content moderators, 201
    media attack on Traffickinghub, 74–75
U.S. See United States
user-generated porn, 6, 117, 281–82

vacuum bag torture, 108, 260
Vanity Fair, 250–54
Verdeschi, John, 94–95, 142–47, 171,
        243, 259–60
victims. See also specific victim
    Bowe in touch with, 42–43
    child trafficking stories of, 186–87
    Franklin raping boy, 10
    as heroes, 279
    Kristof in touch with, 157–59
    lawsuits from, 41
    Mastercard receiving information
        about, 160–61
    MindGeek blaming, 121–22
    online, 65
    of sex trafficking, 11–12, 20, 186–87
    suicidal, 161
    Twitter users commenting on, 19–20
    video takedown requests from, 193–94
    violent attack of, 139–40
video takedowns, 204–5
video uploading
    age verification for, 57–58
    anonymous, 25
    of child rape, 110–12
    information stripped from, 28–30
    MindGeek moderators for, 9–10,
        104–9, 181–82, 201
    no consent required for, 16
    on Pornhub, 15–17, 105–7, 110–12

Viersen, Arnold, 194–95
violent attack, 139–40
virtual attack, 88
Visa
    child sexual abuse profit by, 91–92
    crime scenes monetized by, 263–66
    illegality warnings ignored by, 141–42
    journalists pressuring, 165
    Kristof's claims investigated by,
        170–73
    Mickelwait emails CEO of, 271
    Mickelwait meets with, 91–92
    motion to dismiss denied, 262–66
    Pornhub dropped by, 272
    TrafficJunky service return of, 236–39
VPN download, 62

Washington Examiner, 22
website
    on Internet, 46, 164
    NCMEC receiving links to, 112–13
    with online victims, 65
    Pornhub's content removed from,
        6–7, 178
    Pornhub's traffic increasing on,
        85–88, 162
    safe for work, 87
    shutdown of OnlyFans, 225
    unvetted videos on, 88–90
whistleblowers, 104, 127, 129–30,
        157–59. See also specific
        whistleblower
White House (human trafficking
        advisor), 130–31
"Why Are Visa and Mastercard
        Still in Bed with Pornhub?"
        (Mickelwait), 258
Wilberforce, William, 4
Wisam (father), 1–3, 278
Wisam, Laila. See Mickelwait, Laila

Zuckerberg, of porn, 45–48